Potluck

Hope you enjoy this!.

Fondly—

Potluck

LITTLE STORIES
FROM A BIG TABLE

Paula Thomas

Bay City
PUBLISHING, LLC

Contents

Acknowledgments

The completion of this book would have been impossible without the advice and encouragement I received from my wonderful nephew, Rex Strother. For almost two years, Rex's loving support was just a phone call, text, or e-mail away. On numerous occasions, he interrupted his own projects to aid me in mine. Did I mention he's a genius? Thank you, Rex.

My sister, Kay Bernards and these other accomplished professional women must also be acknowledged: Katie Janics-Geeza, Vicki Prelesnik, Pat Melican, Lana Nicol, and Diane Remus. As the first readers of my manuscript, these ladies provided extensive notes and suggestions that helped me improve my writing and offered kind words that encouraged me to complete the project.

I also want to thank all of the helpful people who combed through photo albums and yearbooks, and scanned photos: Sean Daniels, Sharon Russell, Alice Ryan, Yvonne and Allan Ansdell, and Janice Frome. I couldn't have done it without your help.

Lastly, thank you family and friends for reading my stories through the years and saying, "Paula, you need to write a book." You folks made me believe that I had something worthy of sharing.

Why I Wrote This Book

I grew up in the early sixties, one sister in a large and slightly poor family living in a rich country. In our loud, dysfunctional, turbulent family, my sense of humor kept me sane.

All my life I have told stories and made people laugh (sometimes intentionally). My stories are about idiotic things I have done or witnessed others do, mistakes I have made, embarrassing moments I have endured, or poignant and tender realizations from seventy-four years of living.

All my life people have said, "You have got to write your stories down." After marinating these stories deliciously in my mind for more than half a century, the time has come to do just that: write them down.

Auntie Mame (the madcap, fun-loving, extravagant character created by Patrick Dennis) famously says, "Life is a banquet and most poor fools are starving to death." I think my life was a potluck. It was a veritable tasty combination of people and events, like the homespun casserole dishes I relished as a kid on Sunday evenings at the Seal Beach Methodist Church. Everyone in our life brings something to the table to feed us; sometimes what they bring wrinkles our nose, sometimes it spills over our belts, sometimes it sends us to the bathroom at 2 a.m. Not unlike some church potluck casseroles.

Some have doubted the truth of these stories but, I assure you, these events are real. Mark Twain wrote, "Truth is stranger than fiction," and I think my life and my stories can attest to that. However, if you fail to write it down quickly, any recipe you are cooking is bound to change over time. Even if the basic ingredients and the flavor remain about the same, fading memory may impact the measurements slightly.

Mark Twain wrote, "Truth is stranger than fiction" and I think my life and my stories can attest to that.

When two of my sisters were discovered on a local Los Angeles TV talent program in 1951 and later went on to become RCA recording artists and film and radio stars, the potluck was kicked up a notch and turned into dinner theater.

Our little poor-as-mice family got to rub shoulders with the likes of Bing Crosby, Bob Hope, Frank Sinatra, Esther Williams, and Conrad Hilton (meeting all the grown-up celebrities wasn't that big a deal to us kids; they were Mom and Dad's idols, but not ours). A much bigger deal to us kids was that we got to meet the *Mickey Mouse Club Mouseketeers* and the cast of *Space Patrol*, which were TV programs we actually watched!

So many people—friends, family, strangers, even critters—brought something to this potluck to be shared. I just put the hot dishes on this table and the cold dishes on that table, and humor was almost always the dessert. And the whole meal became my life.

Looking back, I see now that it was all more bountiful than a small-town girl dared dream. And having finally written it all down, I'm feeling really full.

Paula Thomas

1

~~~~~~~~~

The Beach Jacket

> ## 1951

Her Singer sewing machine was the most valuable item Mom brought along when my family moved to California from Kentucky. This move happened before I was born and right after Japan bombed Pearl Harbor. America declared war and was in desperate need of airplanes for the war effort. California needed men to build those airplanes and if the government started rationing gasoline, my parents feared they would be stuck in Ashland, Kentucky, until the war ended, whenever that would be. So it was with patriotic fervor and pioneering spirit that my parents loaded their new Chrysler to bulging with four kids and all the belongings they could heft on top and stuff inside. There was no way Mom's Singer sewing machine would be left behind.

The trip to California was not without drama. My older sister, Kay, almost died from bronchitis that developed into pneumonia. She had a high fever and a horrible cough. My parents were frantic. The local doctor came to the tiny

1945 This picture was taken before my parents bought the beach cottage at 232 5th Street in Seal Beach and before Alice was born. Left to right: Kay, Judy, Mom holding Rex, Cynthia, me, and Sharon.

motel the family bunked in because of Kay's illness, and he injected her with a drug that had just come on the market. "They say this stuff works miracles, and we need one here," the small-town doctor told my frightened parents.

That drug was Penicillin and it *was* the miracle they needed. My mom told us later, "I knew we almost lost Kay, because the doctor came to our door the following morning to follow up on Kay's condition." Evidently, that meant he was very worried.

"By God," the doctor said in delighted amazement the next morning. "That stuff *does* work miracles."

The family settled into a big old house in Pomona, not far from the hospital where I was born a few years later.

After my birth, in 1943, we moved to Seal Beach, a coastal community about thirty miles west of Pomona.

Because World War II was raging at the time, Dad worked a lot of overtime at Keiser Steel Mill and was able to save enough money to purchase a small, wood-framed beach cottage just a block and a half from the Pacific Ocean. "We wanted you kids to grow up with the freedom to run and play at the beach," Dad told us later.

Seal Beach was a very typical small town when I was growing up. It had a Main Street that ran perpendicular from Pacific Coast Highway (the major thoroughfare running north and south through California) down to the pleasure pier at the end of the beach and out into the water. Even today, Seal Beach has kept its small-town charm and is a friendly and inviting place.

My earliest memories of living in Seal Beach were of walking down to the beach and chasing the seals (for which the city was named) back into the water. The big brown sea creatures would sun themselves on the warm sand and they looked like stacks of soft brown pillows, until you got up close and smelled the salty, musty odor on their skins. The beach was crowded with the creatures, big and small, and they yapped noisily when disturbed by a bunch of boisterous kids like my brother and sisters. The town was originally called Bay City, but the seals won out.

Seal Beach Elementary, my grade school, was located just a few blocks from the beach on the corner of Twelfth Street and Pacific Coast Highway. It was the school I attended from kindergarten through the sixth grade, when the town built J. H. McGaugh, the school up on the hill (the hill was really just a gentle slope above our town).

Two milestones in my school career that I clearly remember happened in the third grade. First, third grade was the year that each student got his or her own desk. Prior to that, we had sat at long tables we shared with our fellow students. My first desk was a brown wooden desk with an attached chair and a flip-up top with an ink-well on the corner edge. (In those days, we learned cursive writing and we used pen and ink. Boy, have things changed.) The second milestone was that third-graders were allowed to attend the annual end-of-year school picnic at the beach.

Once a year, in the last week of school, the students of grades three through five would walk the four or five blocks to the beach for a picnic. It was the highlight of the school year and it was the only time, in my third-grade mind, that our teachers seemed approachable and human. At the beach picnic, they seemed to relax, and we actually saw them smile. Maybe it was because the year was ending and summer vacation was near, or, more likely, having fun together made the teachers see us as people and not just little human projects that needed to be taught, improved, and repaired.

The day before the big picnic, a bunch of us girls were gathered by the monkey bars at recess, talking about the picnic. The main topic of the conversation was beach jackets. It seemed to me that every girl in my class was getting a new beach jacket for the occasion. "I'm getting a new beach jacket too," I chimed in, proudly. "My mother is making me a beautiful beach jacket tonight." Back in those days, most mothers sewed.

Only two of my friends were actually *buying* new beach jackets. Yvonne, my best friend, and the only one in our group whose mother owned a business and worked outside the home, told us about hers without a hint of bragging. "It's red and white gingham, and has a terry cloth hood. Mom ordered it from the new Sears catalog."

Without any of Yvonne's humility, Karen, who was the wealthiest girl in our class, told us about her new jacket in a show-off and snobby way. "Mine was purchased from Lovely Little Ladies in Belmont Shore." None of my friends shopped in Belmont Shore, it was far too expensive and trendy. Then Karen added, with a smug smile, "My beach jacket was made in San Francisco, and it is china blue with small white stripes and gold buttons on the pockets." I had never heard of San Francisco, but it sounded like somewhere important and exotic. We all kept talking about the jackets and the upcoming picnic until the bell rang, and then we scampered like rabbits back to class.

I knew my beach jacket would be wonderful. I had confidence in my mother because she was a seamstress extraordinaire and a clothing designer at heart. Mom had already purchased the fabric and planned to sew it that evening. The cloth was yellow and white with an all-over pattern of sand buckets and seashells. Mom planned to line the jacket in white terry cloth, and she had large red rickrack for trim. I was sure my jacket would look just as good as Karen's, even if it was not made in that stupid San Francisco place.

After dinner and the dishes, Mom put her portable Singer sewing machine on the kitchen table. As I always did when Mom was sewing for me, I made her a cup of coffee, with sugar and lots of cream. I wasn't concerned that Mom was just starting the garment at bedtime. We had sewn Halloween costumes on many occasions and she used to say, "I do my best work under pressure." I was confident the beach jacket would be ready for the picnic the following morning.

Mom cut out the pattern carefully and pinned it for me to try on the pieces. I remember the uncomfortable feeling of the thin paper pattern on my skin and the occasional pin prick I received as she made tucks in her design. After a couple of adjustments, Mom sat down at the old Singer and started to sew the lining.

Mom threaded the bobbin and the needle, lowered the pressure foot, and started to sew. The fabric bunched up and the thread caught in a big clump under the pressure foot. "Shoot," Mom said.

It took several minutes to pull the fabric clear of the needle and cut through the mass of thread stuck to the bobbin. She did this very carefully, so as not to damage the fabric. When everything seemed to be set right, Mom started to sew again, and the same thing happened; the fabric bunched up and the thread caught under the pressure foot.

"Doggone it!" Mom said, irritated. She took the machine bobbin apart and rethreaded the entire machine. "Maybe this bobbin is faulty," she said out loud to herself.

Mom filled a new bobbin with thread and began the process again. No go. The needle stuck in the fabric just like before. Frustrated, Mom was not going to give up easily. She took out the Singer sewing machine instruction pamphlet, which had been torn and mended in several places with cellophane tape over the years. After studying the instructions for several minutes, Mom adjusted a couple of dials on the

Easter morning when I was in the third grade. Left to right: Alice, Rex, Paula, Judy, Kay, Sharon, and Cynthia.

Singer. Then she made a trial run on some different fabric. But, still no go. The machine refused to sing *or* sew. After another hour of adjusting and struggling, it was evident the Singer was broken. She turned to me.

"I'm so sorry, sweetie. The darn machine won't work. Maybe we can borrow something you can wear from one of your sisters."

A sorrowful little third grader went off to bed, because there would be no new beach jacket to wear. At the age of eight, my world was clearly ending. I had told my friends I'd have a beautiful new beach jacket for the picnic, and now I wouldn't. I was sure the news would make Karen very happy, and I felt pretty sure she would accuse me of lying. Sad and disappointed, I cried myself to sleep. Third grade, much like war, is hell. In the morning, I was in no hurry to get up and head to school. I walked slowly into the kitchen where Mom was packing lunches and fixing breakfast for the kids. To my astonishment, on a hanger next to the cupboard hung *my* beautiful new beach jacket, just like Mom had promised. It was yellow and white with an all-over pattern of sand pails and seashells, lined in white terry cloth, and decorated with big red rickrack.

"You got the sewing machine working again?" I asked my mom, happily. Mom didn't answer. She just smiled and went about her morning tasks. I tried the jacket on. I squealed and jumped around the table with tears of joy rolling down my cheeks. "Look everyone. The beach jacket fits perfectly. It's beautiful, Mom. Oh, thank you."

This was just one example of my mother's tenacity and pioneering spirit. She wasn't about to let a broken sewing machine get in the way of her child's happiness. No matter how tired or overworked this mother of seven was, she was not going to let her daughter be disappointed, even if it meant *staying up all night and sewing the jacket by hand.*

"It was a labor of love," Mom told me later. "It was a labor of love."

2

The Seal Beach
School of Dance

1951

I grew up with a best friend who was prettier than me, richer than me, and had six fewer siblings than me. So, it really wasn't surprising to me that Yvonne was going to take tap dancing lessons at the new Seal Beach School of Dance and I wasn't.

In a small town like Seal Beach, the opening of a new business was a big event. When Yvonne and I saw the sign for the Seal Beach School of Dance go up next to the drug store, we were so excited. The sign said that the teacher was from New York City and had danced on Broadway. "Just think," I told Yvonne excitedly, "a real New York dancer is going to be teaching in our town." We could hardly wait.

The sound of the old upright piano rang softly in my ears as I peered through the window of the Seal Beach School of Dance. I stood for a long time, staring as my best friend and all the other little girls lined up in a row

Me, a year or two after I started tap and ballet lessons at the Seal Beach School of Dance.

on the wooden floor. The teacher, Miss Reagan, wore shiny black tap shoes and a short, full skirt. She had bright red, curly hair pulled up with a bow on top of her head and wisps of ringlets that fell down around her pretty face, and she wore more makeup than I had ever seen. "Did you see her makeup? That's how you can tell she really danced on Broadway," I told Yvonne later.

Miss Reagan was warming up the class with shuffles, first with the left foot and then with the right. Shuffle left, shuffle right, shuffle left, shuffle right; the class danced in unison as Clara, Miss Reagan's heavyset pianist, pounded out the tunes. I slipped quietly through the door of the dance studio and took a seat next to some waiting parents, but my eyes never missed a step or beat as these luckier girls continued the warm-up routine. Down deep in my soul, I *knew* I was a dancer and I was sure I could tap dance better than any girl in that class, including my beautiful best friend.

Shuffle step, shuffle step, shuffle step; the class continued practicing in time with the music. My mind tracked, cataloged, and stored every instruction with that special memory given only to a person with the gift of dance in her feet. Long after Yvonne's class finished, I stayed behind, sitting with new parents, and watched the other lessons. The advanced group did dance routines to familiar Broadway tunes banged out by Clara on the wooden upright. Every dance step was recorded in my keen dancer's mind, and I mentally practiced each step and learned every move and intricate turn. Then, I ran out to the concrete sidewalk in front of the dance school and I practiced the steps I had seen. I boldly practiced as I peered through the window, oblivious to the looks of people passing by on the sidewalk. Shuffle step, shuffle step, shuffle step, turn, ball change.

I could hardly wait for Yvonne's next tap dance lesson. Twice a week, as soon as school was out, we hurried up Main Street together toward the studio. Again, I watched and practiced in my mind, and again I ran to the front of the building and danced on the sidewalk, practicing every step and turn Miss Reagan taught her students. When Yvonne's class ended for the

It is with your feet that you move . . . but it is with your heart that you dance.

—AALAYNAH THOMPSON

day, I danced down Central Avenue toward home. I practiced the routines of the older students as I sang the show tunes loudly. Practicing the intricate arm movements and turns and taps, I danced and danced and danced.

Oh, how I longed to take dance lessons at the Seal Beach School of Dance. I dreamed of standing with the other girls in shiny tap shoes, doing the turns I had already mastered and the tap steps I had quickly learned. But there were nine of us at home; nine people to feed and clothe and drive about. I knew my parents would be hurt if I asked for this, knowing they couldn't afford to give me dance lessons. So, I just wouldn't ask.

By the time I got to the corner of Fifth Street, where we lived, I was resolved to the fact that dancing would have to be postponed; dance lessons were not in my future. I could only observe and continue my secret dancing out in front of the school. To my surprise, Dad was walking briskly up fifth Street toward the mailbox as I rounded the corner. He had a bunch of letters in his hand, and he stopped and asked me why I was so out of breath. I told him I had been dancing and then told him about the new dance school down on Main Street. "The teacher danced on Broadway in New York City, and Yvonne is taking lessons," I blurted out enthusiastically.

I didn't ask if I could take lessons. I had trained myself not to request things I knew I couldn't have. But the words I used must have been different from the message I conveyed without words. Perhaps Dad responded to the unspoken plea he saw in my eyes. Or maybe he recognized my potential as a dancer. You know, I never asked him why. I just remember that he handed me the five dollars that was the cost for two months of lessons. Five dollars. A five-dollar bill. My heart nearly stopped beating. I stared at the five dollars as if it were a million dollars and whispered a "thank you" that was barely audible. Then I turned and ran like the wind back to the Seal Beach School of Dance.

My hand was shaking as I handed the precious five dollars to Miss Reagan. Within minutes, I was wearing a borrowed pair of shiny black tap shoes and was standing in line with a group of older girls. When the music started, my heart began racing and the teacher asked me if I'd like to watch at first. Before she could say another word, I burst into the advanced girls' dance routine. I already knew every step of their routine from start to finish.

Miss Reagan stared at me, and a knowing smile came to her face. She knew we were kindred spirits and that we shared that special gift of dance. I felt her embrace me with her eyes and accept me with her heart. Few moments in my life can compare with the glee that filled my heart that afternoon as we began to shuffle and step to the sound of Clara's piano. Shuffle step, shuffle, shuffle step, ball change. Tears filled my eyes. I felt just like Cinderella arriving at the ball. I belonged in those slippers. I was home.

What goes around comes around. That's how it works. Sooner or later the universe will serve you the revenge that you deserve.

—Jessica Brody,

The Karma Club

Miss Reagan never asked me for another five-dollar payment for as long as she taught me dance. I have no idea why. All I know is that she taught me for many years and that her generosity of spirit lives in me today. Thank you, Miss Reagan.

Our first dance recital was held a year later, at the Seal Beach City Hall, in front of town dignitaries, families, and friends. When the curtain opened and Clara started playing, I froze . . . completely froze. I never moved a muscle and I didn't dance a lick. Miss Reagan said it was stage fright. Maybe it was. I mean, I happily and successfully danced in many other recitals. But I still suspect that first recital stage fright was a toe shoe in the bottom from Karma for bragging, "I could tap dance better than any girl in that class."

3

Football

1951

I don't know how many women enjoy football, but I do; and the reason I do is because, unlike that famous old TV sports announcer, Howard Cosell, I played the game. My experience with football wasn't from school physical education or an organized city youth sports program. My football career began in a dirt lot of Fifth Street in Seal Beach, when I was just a little kid.

Our neighbors' front yard was our football field. That's me in the center of a couple of the neighborhood boys.

There were eight of us kids assembled on the playing field, which was the unmowed front lawn, with its only tree, a single palm, standing like a burned-out torch on the side of our yard. Our season coincided with the pro teams' schedule on the radio and TV and ran from October through

When it came to neighborhood sports, Judy was the boss. She was the best athlete amongst us and, in her mind's eye, the only one who understood the rules. So, Judy made the rules we played by.
Rex and Judy, the football years.

December. My tomboy sister, Judy, was the best athlete in the family and was the organizer of our games.

Judy's face was covered with freckles and she had matching braids in her red hair that hung down to the top of her football jersey, which was at least two sizes too big. She stood with her grey-blue eyes squinting against the warm California sun as she explained the rules to my brother Rex, youngest sister Alice, and a bunch of neighborhood kids who looked just like characters from the *Our Gang* movies of the 1940s.

"Each team gets four chances to make a touchdown," Judy said with authority. "Those are called downs. After four downs, if your team hasn't made a touchdown, the other team gets the ball and the other team gets four downs. It's very easy," Judy added, adjusting the worn-out ball cap which was a permanent part of her boyish wardrobe.

Judy then divided up the kids into teams. "Rex, you get Tommy Campbell, Paula, and Glenny. I'll take Alice, Clarence Bridges, and Mike."

Rex, my only brother, started howling. "No fair. That's not fair. Clarence and Mike can both catch and Paula is useless except for blocking."

Judy stood her ground. "Well, I had Paula last time and besides, I have Alice and she's too little to do anything."

Alice and I were not exactly regarded as primary team assets. But we did keep the teams even, and we added a certain amount of unpredictability to the game.

"Tommy is my only good player," Rex added with a moan. "And everybody knows Glenny is no good. He's afraid of the ball."

Judy wasn't having it, and she gathered her team up near our neighbors' fence. "Anyway," Judy added over her shoulder, as she walked away, "Mike can only stay until the 4:30 whistle blows at the power plant."

Rex knew any further argument with Judy was useless. She was the boss and she was in charge. "Okay," he yelled in defiance, "but, it still isn't fair." Rex, sporting a temporary pout, assembled his motley crew on the ground just a few yards away from Judy's team.

Rex was the only player wearing any authentic football gear, a big old beat-up football helmet he had received for Christmas last year. As the game got underway, Rex's disappointment about team selection quickly faded. His big brown eyes were glowing with quarterback enthusiasm as he scratched out a play in the grass with a broken twig. "Tommy, you hike the ball to me and then go around to the left side of the field and out for a pass. Paula, I'll fake a handoff to you and then you go up and block Judy." A fake, I had learned long ago, was the *closest* I ever got to actually touching the football, unless I picked it up during a fumble.

Rex's eyes were opened real wide, causing tiny wrinkles across his forehead, which were barely visible under his mammoth helmet. "Glenny," Rex added with authority, "you block Clarence and Mike." A tiny bead of sweat rolled down Rex's forehead and onto his tanned nose, clearing away the dirt in its path as it meandered. Rex was glowing as he spoke, unaware of the mounting fear swelling up inside Glenny, our skinny little neighbor.

"Me? You want me to block Mike and Clarence?" Glenny asked, timidly.

"Sure," Rex cajoled. "Don't be such a cry baby about a little tackle, Glenny."

The tension began to mount as our scruffy team broke huddle and lined up reluctantly against what appeared to me and Glenny as Judy's invincible warriors who, except for Alice, were twice our size. Mike and Clarence were hunched down in a proper football crouch while Glenny stood upright, looking from side to side in fear, his knees tightly held together. As the seconds began to tick away, Judy's team started pawing the ground like bulls ready to attack a matador in the ring. Hunched over in her faded blue jeans and oversized football jersey, Judy's clear eyes narrowed and glistened as she prepared for the assault.

"Two, four, six, eight . . . hike," Rex shouted, and the play was on.

Tommy hiked to Rex and then scrambled frantically to get away from Judy and Clarence, who lunged at Glenny and me with hurricane force, blowing us aside like a couple of cotton balls. Scampering proficiently out of their grasp, Rex was barely able to get a pass off to Tommy before he was crushed by an onslaught of braids, freckles, dirt, sweat, and blue jeans. Tommy caught the pass and fled dramatically toward the goal line, which was two pieces of brown paper bag held down by rocks.

The play ended in a spontaneous combustion of argument and loud accusations.

"Interference!"

"Out of bounds!"

"Foul!"

"PENALTY!"

Words filled the air like a bunch of seagulls startled by a dog on the beach. The "good players" became referees and started yelling simultaneously at the top of their lungs, each describing their version of what had happened on the play.

Not surprised by the resulting hysteria, I used the break in the game to practice my tap dance routines. Alice and Glenny likewise took a rest and dropped to their knees and began to pick the fragrant white flowers we liked to gather and tie into flower chains. Then we practiced cartwheels and somersaults together until the pandemonium ended and the game resumed, and we either made a touchdown or were forced to kick.

Our football games were always fun and full of excitement. But, without a doubt, the kickoff was by far the greatest moment in the game. Before each game, as part of her instruction, Judy would announce that *she alone* had enough coordination to actually kick the football. The rest of the players were ordered not to kick, but rather to throw the ball downfield to the opposing team.

Judy's words of instruction never seemed the slightest deterrent to Rex. When it was time for our team to kick, Rex seemed to go into a hypnotic trance. You could see his eyes glaze over, and at that moment Rex was not a ten-year-old boy playing football in his front yard. Oh no, Rex was a professional kicker for the Green Bay Packers, standing in the middle of a football arena filled with flag-waving and beer-drinking fans, all on their feet and screaming wildly because the score was tied 7 to 7 and there were only three seconds left in the game. In his mind, a nervous hush falls over the stadium as the crowd begins to focus their attention on the one lone kicker poised at the 25-yard line. The clock would start and then it would happen, Rex would hoist our only football into the air and drop kick it . . . into oblivion.

Almost every time, without fail, that ball would go careening into the street, bouncing off the tops of cars like a pinball bounces off rubber bumpers, or up onto the second-story roof of a neighbor's house, or over the fence and into the alley, disappearing into someone's trash. Or, worst of all, it would fly into and rest in the top of our beloved palm tree. The one place the ball *never* went was in the general direction of the opposing team's goal post.

Regardless of where the ball headed, Rex would gaze into the air with a look of complete satisfaction filling his face. It was obvious to me his glassy stare meant he was being hailed a hero by the adoring crowd in his fantasy, as he again made the perfect kick and the Green Bay Packers again won the game. Rex was silent and Rex was complete. Judy's reaction was instant. Her face turned angry red and it would not have surprised me to see cartoon smoke billow out her ears. But, regardless of how red Judy's face got, regardless of the billows of imaginary ear smoke, regardless of how she stamped the ground in rage, and regardless of Judy's threats to never let him play gain, as soon as he got the opportunity, Rex would go into his kicking trance and again drop kick our only football into the Twilight Zone.

That was how I learned that some things in life cannot be stopped: gravity is one and my brother's infamous drop kick was the other.

I have Judy and Rex to thank for my introduction to football. It was from them that I learned the meanings of "fake," "forward pass," and "hand-off," and gained respect for a great block and an accurate hike. I wonder how many women my age ever took part in the celebrated Statue of Liberty play?

My older sister, Sharon, once told me that if you give someone a present, you have given him a gift for a day, but if you teach a person a skill, you have given him a gift for life. That is so true. Thanks to my freckle-faced sister Judy and my fame-dazed brother Rex, I can enjoy the fabulous game of football. Thanks to them I've know the "thrill of victory and the agony of defeat." Unfortunately, there is one thing I don't think I will ever see duplicated now that I'm grown. That, of course, is my brother's unforgettable drop kick.

4

~~~~~~~

The Bell Sisters

> **1951**

W hen people say, "Only in America," they are talking about the kind of unbelievable success that
seems to happen so often in the good ole USA. You know
the story: An immigrant comes to America, unable to
speak the language, puts himself through college, and ends
up the CEO of a major US company. Or a poor country
girl from Tennessee grows up in a family of twelve kids,
sets her sights toward the Grand Ole Opry, and ends up
being a beloved cultural musical icon. Or two sisters from
a small town in California win a local talent show, and
become TV, radio, and movie stars. That last one, that's
what happened to our family.

We Strothers (my maiden name) loved to sing. It was
a bonding experience that glued our family spirit together,
and it was something we could do that didn't cost a dime.
We were musical and some of us had musical talent.
According to my dad, we came from a long line of talented women.

"When I was a young man growing up in Kentucky, the Strother women used to sing up on the hill above our cabin home after church each Sunday. They sang church hymns in five-part harmony and their exquisite voices could be heard across the valley." Dad told us that folks in the valley looked forward to their Sunday serenades and always commented on how beautifully the Strother gals sang when he saw his neighbors periodically in town.

All of my sisters had great singing voices, but not me. Compared to my sisters, my voice was marginal at best. But, looking back, no one was more enthusiastic about singing and no one in the family enjoyed it more.

My oldest sister, Cynthia, was our conductor and with her guidance, the seven kids in our family sang five-part harmony, like the Strother women before us. And like our talented predecessors, together we put out a pretty remarkable sound.

Cynthia, who was incredibly talented musically, taught herself to play the piano at age six. We lived in a wonderful old three-story house in Pomona, where I was born years later. The neighbors had a piano in their living room and let Cynthia play while they operated their upholstery business in the garage. Every day for hours, Cynthia would play, "banging away" until she taught herself to play by ear. The neighbors used to laugh and say, "Good thing our business is in the garage because we don't have to listen to you banging on that contraption."

I was about three when our family moved to Seal Beach. Anita and Brownie, the neighbors who lived behind us, gave us a crummy old upright piano they had owned for years. It took half the neighborhood to get that heavy instrument down Brownie's four-step stoop, across the alley, and into our tiny den.

"My gosh," Mom stammered worriedly, "I hope our old fossil of a floor doesn't collapse under the weight of that piano." Once there, Cynthia continued her self-taught piano lessons and learned to read music.

The Bell Sisters with Peter Potter, the host of the TV talent contest my sisters won that launched them into the music industry.

Cynthia studied music in college later, but it was Halloween night in 1951, years before college, that Cynthia (age sixteen) and my sister Kay (age eleven) won the Los Angeles TV talent program, *Peter Potter's Search for a Song*. My two sisters sang a song that Cynthia had written, with lyric help from Dad: "Bermuda," a soulful song about lost love and a drowning. Looking back, I realize that the morose theme of the song was not unlike one of the many horrible headlines Dad liked to read aloud to us kids from the newspaper during breakfast.

Anyhow, if I remember right, originally the singing act was planned as a trio featuring my three eldest sisters, Cynthia, Sharon, and Kay. The second oldest, Sharon (age fourteen), had to drop out because she had laryngitis. She was a cheerleader at Huntington Beach High School. It was thus a quirk of fate that sent Cynthia and Kay into stardom and Sharon back to high school life.

I remember watching the show with the rest of my siblings on our dinky TV, crowded, as we were always crammed, into our eight-by-ten living room. *Peter Potter's Search for a Song* was a precursor for shows that are so popular nowadays, like *America's Got Talent* or *American Idol*. Not as glitzy as today's programs, that's for sure, but just as exciting to watch from where we stood.

Only in America, I said before, because, by God, they won! We jumped around the living room and screamed like wild Indians. The Bell Sisters, the name for their act taken from my mother's maiden name, were launched into an adventure unlike any our family had ever known.

I remember so clearly the phone ringing, after they arrived home, and someone saying the phone call was from RCA Recording Artists. "Yes, uh-huh, yes, sure." Then there was more screaming and jumping for joy: because it was RCA, and it was just like in the movies. My sisters had been offered a recording contract and were off to Hollywood to cut a demo of Cynthia's song. Their subsequent rise to fame was immediate; Cynthia's song was picked up that night by a music publisher who was one of the judges of the evening's amateur compositions. ("Bermuda" was a big hit, selling over seven hundred thousand copies.)

At seven years of age, I wasn't cognizant of all the intricacies of show business, of course. I remember dad saying, "The Girls," as my dad called them, "were picked up by the William Morris Talent Agency." Then I heard conversations about lawyers, movies, Las Vegas, movie stars, and money. Most significant to me was the day I came home from school and saw the brand-spanking new Cadillac sitting in front of our somewhat dilapidated cottage. It might have even been a convertible.

My sisters were celebrities and, in our small town, that meant that we other kids were too. We got noticed and talked about everywhere we went. We got new clothes, store-bought dresses, and we actually had dinner *out* in a fancy restaurant in Hollywood with Nat King Cole and his family. (Cole was a jazz pianist known for his soft baritone voice, and he was the first African-American to host his own TV show.) I still remember what I ordered that evening: veal cutlet. I thought it was the name of a dish from a foreign country.

Seeing my sisters on the big screen in one of their movies, *Those Redheads from Seattle*, was kind of an out-of-body experience. They sang and danced like real pros and they were naturally gifted actors. It was amazing and exciting simultaneously. Sure, I was a little jealous and wished I could do something

In *Those Redheads from Seattle*, Mrs. Edmonds (Agnes Moorhead) takes her four beautiful daughters to Alaska during the 1898 Gold Rush to help their father run his newspaper. From a letter she receives, Mrs. Edmonds senses a problem and decides to leave for the Yukon immediately, not knowing her husband is already dead. You can read more about this film at IMBD.com.

Upon arrival in Skagway, Alaska, the Edmonds family is met by Yukon local, Joe Keenan (Guy Mitchell). The Bell Sisters, Kay and Cynthia, Agnes Moorhead, Teresa Brewer, and Rhonda Fleming.

Kay with Gene Barry and Cynthia.

My mom, Edith, helping my sisters practice their lines.

Despite any formal dance training, my big sister Cynthia (far left) danced as well as her costars, Rhonda Fleming and Teresa Brewer.

My sisters' movie, *Those Redheads from Seattle*, holds the distinction of being the first musical shot in 3D, having beat MGM's *Kiss Me, Kate* (1953) to the screen by just a month. In 2017, the film was masterfully restored by the 3-D Film Archive and newly released in HD and 3-D by Kino Lorber, and includes audio commentary by film historians Hillary Hess, Greg Kintz, Jack Theakston and Bob Furmanek. I was honored to attend the Turner Classic Movies (TCM) Film Festival 2017 in Hollywood with my sisters Cynthia and Kay (The Bell Sisters) and view this amazing restoration in 3-D on the big screen.

Dad always called Sharon, in the middle, "the beauty of the family." Cynthia, left pointing at my dad, Gene, Sharon and Kay. Photo was taken while The Girls were performing at the 1954 Ashland, Kentucky, Centennial Celebration.

like that. But I was also extremely proud and sincerely happy for my talented siblings.

My sister Sharon was gorgeous; Dad called her the beauty of the family. She looked like a cross between Marilyn Monroe and Elizabeth Taylor. Because she was older, she got to travel with The Girls when they headlined in Las Vegas at the Last Frontier Hotel, one of the major Vegas hotels at the time. The four littlest kids in the family, me included, were always "too little" and never got to do fun stuff like that. Anyhow, I remember Sharon telling us how she got to see Frank Sinatra live at the Sands Hotel on the Strip. I'm told it was a common practice for headliners to invite other big acts to see their shows. Frank Sinatra invited the Bell Sisters to be his guests. Like all teenage girls in the 1950s,

WHOSE THAT WITH OLD BLUE EYES? That's the Bell Sisters, Cyn-

My sisters with America's heart-throb, Frank Sinatra.

Sharon was "in love with Frank Sinatra." Of course, Frank Sinatra knew that and reached for Sharon's hand from the stage. "My knees were knocking. He held me close and sang a song looking directly into my eyes. I thought I would faint!" Even days after the event, Sharon's eyes were glowing as she retold the story. Being a Bell Sisters' sister had its perks.

When The Girls went on a USO tour of Korea during Christmas 1953, I remember missing Mom. Dad became our caretaker when The Girls traveled. It was really hard with Mom gone; Dad did his best, but he had anger issues and his behavior could be scary. We constantly had to walk on eggshells around him, never sure what would tick him off.

Formerly, Dad had been an exceptional athlete, whose high school basketball team, the Ashland Tomcats, had won the National Championship and are in the Basketball Hall of Fame.

He clearly missed his more athletic days, so during Mom's absence, Dad put us all on a health food diet. "We need to cleanse out our systems," he would say enthusiastically. Health food for Dad meant a big dollop of cottage cheese with canned mixed fruit cocktail in sugary syrup, three meals a day for a week. (I think the cleansing regime was something Dad got from Charles Atlas, "The World's

Most Perfectly Developed Man," a bodybuilding program Dad adhered to religiously . . . periodically.) None of us little kids dared question his health-food regimen. Then on Sunday, Dad would cook a roast with all the trimmings. That is probably why, even today, the mere smell of a roast in the oven makes me think of Sundays.

Singing for the troops in Korea in 1953. "It was a sea of young, handsome faces." Photo taken by a vet.

The upside of Mom's trips for us kids was the wonderful gifts and stories that the three travelers brought home, especially after their stopover in Japan. To this day, I remember Mom bringing home a Japanese doll with six wigs in a wooden box for me, and matching rabbit fur muffs and collars for my sister Judy and me. (Just recently I saw a photo of the Bell Sisters wearing those same rabbit collars and cuffs on stage in Korea.) We also got golden-colored metal bracelets and some sparkly rhinestone things. The gifts seemed so fancy and elegant, nothing like I had ever seen or worn before.

The Hollywood Press interviewed Cynthia and Kay upon their return from Asia. When they asked Kay if she had purchased anything from Japan for her siblings, in her sweet innocence she answered, "Only jewels and furs." Her remarks were the talk of the town for quite a while.

Mom brought home stories too, about The Girls' adventures in Japan and Korea. "We were the tallest people in every store that we shopped in," Mom told us with a laugh. "I never had to worry about The Girls, I could see them anywhere in the store. They were a foot taller than any man or woman in the place."

The Bell Sisters fifteen minutes of fame lasted about seven years, but their popularity with fans continued much longer. It's been quite a long while now, but on occasion and out of the blue, someone will still mention hearing the Bell Sisters sing and tell me how much they enjoyed their music. It's particularly touching when it's a soldier who had been stationed in Korea and had seen their USO tour. My sister Cynthia still receives radio royalties for "Bermuda" to this day, sixty-plus years later.

Only in America.

5

Life Magazine

> **1952**

The only magazine I had ever heard of or seen when I was young was *Life*, the major American publication that ran weekly, according to Wikipedia, from 1883 to 1972. I remember seeing the big red and white title *LIFE* on the magazine rack in Brock's Drug Store on the corner of Main Street and Central Avenue in Seal Beach. Even as a little kid, I knew that having *Life* do a story on the Bell Sisters was a very big deal indeed. I remember Mom and Dad making some minor repairs around the house and doing some painting in anticipation of the "photo shoot." But with seven kids and two adults living in a five-room bungalow, there wasn't much that could be done to make our house look fancy enough to be photographed by *Life*.

Our home was a former beach cottage, used for summer vacations and summer rentals, and located just one and a half blocks from the beach. The old bathroom had a cement shower with an uncovered small window for ventilation. There was no tub, and we had just a few

Our bedroom was tiny and held two sets of bunkbeds. Cynthia, upper left, Kay on the phone, me and Sharon sitting on the floor.

wooden shelves that held towels. A rickety wooden garage was attached to the kitchen at the rear of the house. Mom always said that the garage "was being held up by termites holding hands." The garage actually blew off one year during a storm, exposing our motley assortment of kitchen appliances. Dad covered the back of the kitchen, where the garage used to be, with a big black plastic tarp. It was a family joke to tell people, "We're remodeling." Yeah, sure we were . . . for about ten years!

Reading Bell Sister fan mail. Starting left: Alice, Sharon, Cynthia, me, and Rex.

We got some new dresses and other clothes for the big event. I remember that especially. And I distinctly remember that *Life* wanted to shoot a photo of The Girls in their bedroom, as if they were getting dressed for a singing event or a prom. But, since our bedroom was dinky and crammed with two sets of bunkbeds, the photo had to be taken at a friend's house down the street. Our friend and neighbor, Louann Livengood, had a beautiful girlie-looking bedroom and a pretty prom dress that Cynthia held up to the mirror as a prop for the shoot.

My folks wallpapered the kitchen for the Life shoot. I remember thinking it was so fancy and saying, "We have the most beautiful kitchen in the world." That's me eating at the kitchen table. Cynthia is on the left above me with her friend, Louann, and my mom is serving.

My last memory of the event was the director barking at the photographer, "Hey Jon, keep that big hole in the linoleum out of the shot." My poor mom. An only child of wealthy parents, she had grown up in Kentucky in a lovely big house across from the park. Not that she ever complained, but our home was quite a step down from her childhood abundance. And here she was with *Life*

The two most prized possessions in our living room were the TV and the record player, which had been recently purchased so we could listen to the Bell Sisters' hit song, Bermuda. Far left, I'm looking on as Kay and Cynthia discuss music with Louann Livengood, a neighborhood friend.

photographing her meager existence and sharing it with the world.

Overall, it was a very exciting day for our family. But even more exciting was seeing *LIFE* magazine on the shelf at Brock's Drug Store and opening it to find an article and photos of my famous sisters and our family.

And you know what? You couldn't see the hole in the linoleum. Good work, Jon.

6

≈≈≈≈≈≈

Fang

> ## 1963

When my husband Alan and I were in college at Cal State Long Beach, two of our best friends were Diane Thomas and Roger Porter. We knew Roger from Avalon, the "big city" on Catalina Island. Roger's parents owned most of the property on Front Street at that time, and Diane was his beautiful and talented girlfriend. Diane later authored the screenplay for the movie *Romancing the Stone*. Even though we didn't attend the same colleges as Diane and Roger, we shared many wonderful and funny adventures during our college years. However, the Fang incident was one adventure I could have done without.

Fang was an alligator that Roger Porter had ordered from a mail-order company in the Florida Everglades. In those days, you could send a reptile dealer twenty-five cents by mail, and said reptile dealer would send you a real live baby alligator in a small cardboard box. Fang became Roger's pet and lived happily for many years in Roger's backyard in Long Beach, California.

Roger's mother, Evelyn, told me, "I didn't mind Fang when he was small, but as he grew bigger, it was impossible to keep a gardener." Evelyn tried to explain to a succession of gardeners, who were mostly Japanese and spoke almost no English, that her son had a pet alligator living in the bushes near the pool, but that the alligator was harmless and wouldn't bother them.

"I tried my best; I moved my arms up and down like an alligator's jaws opening and closing. But the gardeners never understood what I was talking about." Of course, moving your arms isn't really "talking," but I wasn't about to point that out to Evelyn.

The Porter family owned a big, beautiful house in a prestigious part of Long Beach, and its architecture reminded me of a home in the Antebellum South. The inside of the house was spacious, and there was a circular stairway leading upstairs. The entire length of the stairway was bordered by windows that looked onto the backyard patio and pool.

Fang really was a pet. But he certainly wasn't what the gardener expected to see in the bushes of the Porter's Long Beach home.

Evelyn continued, "One day, from the stairs, I heard the gardener screaming in Japanese and saw his yard clippers and leaf rake go flying into the air. Next thing I knew, he fled out the back gate like a madman." Fang obviously scared the hell out of the poor gardener, despite Evelyn's reassuring pantomime, and Evelyn told me that this had happened more than once. It was becoming clear to Evelyn that Fang was *growing* into a bigger problem each day.

One Easter, when Diane and I had just started dating the fellas, the guys bought us some adorable baby ducklings. Then they invited us to Roger's house for an Easter party and swim in the pool.

"The baby ducks will have so much fun swimming in the pool," the guys said excitedly. Diane and I thought that sounded wonderful and adorable, and carried our precious ducklings in a box to the Porter's backyard pool. We planned to eventually deliver the baby ducks to the City Park in Long Beach, which had a huge lake and a large wild duck population.

Oh, and no, neither of us girls knew anything about Fang. As soon as we got to Roger's house, Diane and I got into the pool with the sweet little ducklings and watched as they peeped happily and began swimming about. Then, we heard a loud hissing in the bushes next to the pool.

"What on earth is that sound?" I asked Diane. It sounded like the sprinklers coming on, only much louder. Before she could answer, we both turned toward the sound and saw a giant armored alligator running full blast on its short scaly legs toward the water.

In seconds, this creature slid gracefully into the water and swam toward us and the innocent baby ducklings. Our personal survival instincts kicked into panic mode and the two of us came close to walking (make that running) on water to get out of the pool. Last we saw of the fluffy yellow ducklings was a bit of orange leg sticking out between the giant jagged teeth of Fang's mouth. It was horrifying, to say the least. And when I say horrifying, I mean to Diane and me. The guys thought this whole scene was absolutely hilarious.

Anywho, Fang, like any "normal" family pet, used a doggie door to access the kitchen each morning. He would waddle/run through the doggie door and then slide on the ceramic kitchen tile up to the refrigerator and wait for Evelyn to come downstairs to feed him.

Fang ate two pounds of hot dogs each morning, and that would hold him until dinner. One morning Evelyn was out of hot dogs, because her son had failed to buy them as planned. "Fang was not happy about missing breakfast and followed me right upstairs to my bedroom door," she said. "He sat there, by the door, with his mouth wide open, hissing and grunting loudly, and I had to call a neighbor over to help."

That incident was the final straw for Evelyn; something had to be done. The Porters could no longer let a six-foot-long alligator run free in their Long Beach backyard. There was only one option left for them: Roger had to find Fang a new home. Giving up a pet is never easy and Fang, although it may be hard to believe, really was a family pet to the Porters. After much discussion, Roger reluctantly agreed to find a zoo or reptile farm to take him. After making the arrangements, Roger asked Alan if he'd travel with him to deliver Fang to his new home at the San Diego Zoo.

On the morning of Fang's departure, the guys fed Fang a special last supper (well, breakfast) with extra hot dogs and a sirloin steak. Fang basically ate better than I did for the first eighteen years of my life. Then, they put this beloved crocodilian creature into the back seat of Evelyn's brown station wagon for transport to the zoo. Off Fang went, with his head out the window like a dog and his mouth open slightly in the wind.

"You can't believe the looks we got on the freeway. People did double takes at seeing the alligator, and lots of people honked," Roger told us later. "It was very sad and very funny at the same time."

Roger also said that both of the fellas were crying when they dropped Fang off at the zoo.

7

Best Boss I Ever Had

> **1965**

Iquit college in my junior year for two reasons: One, I was sick and tired of history, my major at the time. And two, my husband Alan was approaching the completion of his bachelor's degree and would be drafted into the army if he didn't stay in school. The war in Vietnam was raging at the time, and I couldn't bear the thought of my husband going to war. I left school and applied for a job at North American Aviation (NAA) in Downey, California, so that Alan could start working on his master's degree and defer enlisting.

This was actually the second time I had worked at NAA. After graduating from high school, I had taken a summer position at NAA as a clerk typist. Typing was the only marketable skill I had, and for three long months, eight hours a day, I typed my brains out. Each morning when I arrived, there was a two-foot stack on my desk of mechanical specifications to be retyped. From this summer job I learned three things: One, I could type over one hundred words a minute with pinpoint accuracy. Two, I definitely didn't want to be a clerk typist for the rest of my life. And three, I needed more marketable job skills.

Now, in my defense, my high school counselor was an idiot. He didn't see any of my natural gifts, and, you know, I thought that was kind of his job. He was supposed to look at my school records and my participation in school activities and guide me into my future.

I mean, I may have been merely a decent student, but I was an outstanding school leader. As a cheerleader, I was in charge of creating a new theme and hanging new decorations each week for school sporting events. I had to organize the students to help (have you met teenagers?) and make sure the projects got done. I planned numerous successful activities and dances and helped raise our school spirit to new heights. I was popular and friendly and could get my classmates to follow me in almost any direction.

When I sat down to speak to my school counselor about my future, he didn't see *any* of those traits as useful in life. Really? I was a born salesman and idea person, and he might have suggested a career in advertising, or marketing, or business. But, oh no, that goofball said, and I quote, "Your best bet is to go to college and find a smart man to marry." Thanks . . . thanks for nothing.

After three years of college, I still didn't have marketable skills. And nobody ever asked me questions about Abe Lincoln or the Civil War (well, nobody who wanted to hire me). But I did have a very smart husband (okay, the counselor was right about that) and I had matured somewhat. I had confidence that I could learn to be a good secretary if I could talk myself into a position. Secretarial pay was pretty good at NAA and if I mastered shorthand (it's like cursive, a forgotten art), I would make even more.

When I met Chuck Ashton, a handsome and energetic advanced senior engineer at NAA, he had just received a promotion that allowed him to hire a secretary for the first time. He had a good sense of humor and I could tell he was kind. Our interview went swimmingly and despite my lack of shorthand, he hired me on the spot. This was a good omen and I couldn't have been happier. Chuck, unlike my school counselor (grrrrr . . . okay, I really need to let that go), appreciated my assets. He could see I was positive, enthusiastic, and eager to learn. Gradually, my job at NAA became, in part, party planner and activities director for our section. I kept the office amused with my unintentional idiotic antics and my instincts for mischief. Looking back, I realize I didn't have a filter on my humor. I had no idea why people might be offended when I put up a sign at Easter, saying, "For Christ's Sake Come to the Potluck."

Our section actually became the envy of the building. Section morale was important, and I like to believe my planned (and unplanned) mishaps were an asset to Chuck's career. Every once in a while, I even typed a letter for him. But, most of the time, my typing was dedicated to my husband's assignments at school. Yeah, life was good for me at NAA.

Ordinarily, for quarterly meetings, Chuck would go up one floor to the senior manager's office; this was his boss, Mr. Henry Stein. On one occasion, Stein's office and the boardroom were both being remodeled, so Mr. Stein's secretary asked Chuck to host the meeting instead. I knew the meeting was important; Chuck was always trying to impress his boss. Mr. Stein was aloof and had his favorites on the engineering team. Chuck was not part of that inner circle, so this was a big deal, a big chance.

Knowing it could help his career if everything went well, I arrived early on the day of the meeting and polished his desk and credenza and even put a vase of homegrown roses by his phone. Then I set up the conference room with a stack of yellow pads and pens for all the participants. I even sprayed the room with a nice fragrance and sat down at my desk, looking professional and competent, as Chuck's boss and peers arrived.

Once everyone was settled, Chuck gave me a jar of quarters to buy coffee with, and I went into the office to take their orders. "Okay," I said to the gentlemen, "how would you like your coffee?" I wrote down the orders carefully: three took cream and sugar, four wanted cream only, two wanted black with sugar, and four wanted black. "Why?" I thought to myself. "The black coffee from the coffee machine is awful!" But on the outside, I just smiled. "That's thirteen coffees," I said confidently as I left the room, still smiling.

One thing I haven't mentioned about myself so far (although you might have guessed) is that I'm a bit of a scatterbrain. Because I am easily fascinated with this great big world, I get quickly sidetracked and I can't help talking to people. I *love* people and I *love* to talk. When I got to the coffee machine, the usual group of ladies was getting coffee for *their* bosses.

"Hi gals, what's happening?" I interjected happily, quickly telling them about the big meeting we were hosting. I continued to talk and listen and share as I put the quarters in the coffee machine and watched the coffee drain into the cups. I grabbed a serving tray and quickly assembled the thirteen coffees on the tray. "Gotta run, gals. I'm on an important mission," I said as I headed back to the conference room.

You may not know this, but I do now: black coffee with sugar looks just like plain black coffee. And coffee with cream and sugar looks pretty much the same as coffee with cream but no sugar. Since I had been jabbering like a magpie instead of paying complete attention to what I was doing, I didn't give any of this a thought until I returned to the meeting and stared down at the tray full of coffees, which I had assembled in no particular order. Oh yes, I had them all: three with cream and sugar, four with cream only, two black with sugar, and four black. But I had no idea which was which. No frigging idea!

In the meeting, as they started reminding me what they had ordered, I admitted my mistake by saying, "Whoops," and then I took a quick sip from each cup of coffee. I mean, seriously, what else could I do?

"Yep, this one has sugar." I said. "Nope. This one is black."

My boss looked at me and then to the others and said, "I told you she's a nut."

That was how the day began . . . but the day was not done. As Mr. Stein entered the conference room, a button popped off his jacket and landed by my desk. I quickly offered to sew it back on for him with the needle and thread I kept in my top drawer for such occasions. "I would *not* let her touch your jacket, Stein, if I were you," Chuck warned his boss.

"Oh, for goodness' sake," I stammered back at Chuck, "I think I can sew on a button."

This was my chance to redeem myself. So I got right to work and sewed the button back on Mr. Stein's suit jacket, careful to sew it in the right place. Also, I made sure not to leave a big ball of unsightly thread gnarled up on the back of the button. I was, in fact, pretty proud of my efforts, and said so softly to the secretary sitting across from me. When the button was tightly secured, I pulled the needle and thread up high for drama, leaving the coat suspended and dangling slightly in the air. And, with one swift move of the scissors, I quickly cut the thread. Oh, I cut the thread alright. Oh crap! *Really, Paula?* But, the scissors also sliced an inch below the button and left a two-inch gash in Mr. Stein's coat.

As Chuck and the others eventually exited the meeting room, I was sitting there dumbfounded. Chuck took one look at me and knew something was wrong. "Where's Stein's coat?" he asked, his boss looking over his shoulder. Weakly, I handed him the suit jacket. "Oh, my God!" Chuck blurted, when he saw what I had done. "I warned you, Stein, I tried to warn you. I told you not to let her touch your jacket."

After everyone left, I stood by Chuck's office door, and he could tell I was ready to cry. He knew I was sorry. There was nothing I could say, but Chuck was a prince. He said, "Don't give it another thought, Paula. The meeting was awful and everyone was stressing out. When you screwed up the coffees, everyone lightened up and we finally got something done."

"But what about Mr. Stein's suit jacket? I ruined it. Should I offer to pay for it or . . .?" I trailed off.

"Oh, Stein's a conceited ass. Your cutting his jacket made my day! And you're the talk of the town upstairs. Don't worry about it one bit."

It wasn't like I did stupid stuff on purpose. I just screw things up because I don't pay attention and because I like to clown around. For example, another time, Chuck asked me to cut some display boards for him. He did lots of charts and graphs, and I really never figured out what they were for. The boards were huge, over four feet square. He wanted them cut into two-foot square pieces. I watched him cut the boards all the time and I thought I could do it. "The boards are expensive," Chuck warned me, "Each one costs about twenty-five bucks." He showed me how to measure where I was going to cut, and then, like I saw him do numerous times, he cut the boards on the ground with a giant paper cutting machine.

If you don't do anything stupid when you're young, you won't remember something funny where you're old.

—UNKNOWN

As soon as Chuck left the area, I started joking around and entertaining Helen, the gal sitting across from the cutting tool. "Whoops," I said, as I screwed up the first board. Helen laughed, which only encouraged further stupidity. Boards two and three were slightly better but in no way perfect, which I knew they needed to be. Boards five and six were somehow worse and had to be thrown away. It was an exercise in futility. In a very short time I wasted (well, destroyed) six expensive display boards. I felt like an idiot. Why couldn't I cut one board straight?

I was determined to cut board number seven correctly. With all the determination I could muster, I measured the final white board. The paper cutter was huge and the display boards were thick. It took a lot of pressure to make a good, clean cut. On my last try, I laid out the board, measured it carefully, got down on my knees, and pressed the handle hard. "Look Helen. This board is perfect," I said gleefully. "Finally, I cut one right."

I stood up facing Helen and held the two cut pieces of board so she could see my achievement. There was only one small problem. When I cut the display board, I also cut my skirt in half. Right up the center, cut in two. Holy crap!

Back to my work bay I stumbled, one hand holding my skirt together and the other holding the one good display board I had managed to cut. When Chuck saw my skirt, he was horrified. "Good Lord, Paula. You've got to be more careful. That machine is sharp. You could have amputated your leg."

Then there was the time the paycheck girl was out sick and they asked me to distribute paychecks to three hundred people. Okay, how hard could that be? The guy in the accounting office told me the most important thing about the job was maintaining privacy. "Make sure you don't let anyone see another person's check. If an employee finds out a coworker is making more money than he is, it can cause quite a problem."

The checks were arranged in a giant flat box by section number and desk. All I had to do was go to Section 23 and walk by each desk and hand out the paychecks in order.

"When you get to the end of the aisle, turn around and repeat the process down the other side. But be sure you fold each check over, so no one but the recipient can see the amount on the check."

"I got it," I said confidently. "Go up and down each aisle, pass out the checks, and fold them over so the amount of the check can't be seen by anyone else." It sounded pretty simple to me.

I had to walk quite a distance to get to Section 23. Section 23 was across the facility yard, up two flights of stairs, in Building B. I passed all kinds of engineering bays and even got a glimpse of the mock-up Apollo space capsule which was under construction at the time.

Of course, when I opened the door, a blast of hot air hit me in the face. "We're having A/C problems. Sorry about the heat," a guy yelled from nearby. "The big fans are irritating, but it's better than sitting here hot, right?"

"No problem," I yelled back. "I'm the paycheck girl today. Susie is out sick."

Section 23 was straight ahead, so close. But I was hot from the walk, and so I thought I'd stop at the Coke machine for refreshment. My money was in a small coin purse, which was hanging around my neck. Naturally, I put the box with all the checks on the table next to the machine while I fumbled out some change.

That's when it happened. One of the giant fans cooling the work bay oscillated toward the Coke machine. Did I mention it was a *giant* fan? Well, the wind from the fan upended the box. And the box hit the floor. And out flew the checks, in every direction. It kind of looked like the tornado in the *Wizard of Oz*. Checks went whirling around in every direction.

"It wasn't my fault," I yelled to no one in particular. "I'm a victim of circumstance."

The checks went flying under desks, were plastered to the wall, leapt into trash cans, and rested on empty chairs. I started scrambling for the checks, grabbing them from the air and off the floor. Others saw my distress and came to help, and pretty soon Section 23 was full of people with checks in their hands, calling out the names of coworkers.

"Hey, Smith, your check is over here."

"Where does Curtis Walker sit? I have his check."

"Anybody see Frank Murphy's check?"

"Who's Mary Hamilton?"

Oh, well, so much for privacy.

When I returned to the accounting office, the clerk asked me how it went. "Oh, fine," I lied. "Everything was hunky-dory." And yet, I was never asked to pass out checks again. I wonder why?

All in all, working at North American Aviation was a great experience. I learned firsthand why government contracts are so expensive. Chuck really didn't need a secretary. He worked very hard and did all the work that needed to be done himself. My position was a status symbol. A secretary was visual proof that he had been promoted to a certain level. I didn't really have anything to do and neither did a lot of other folks in that department. In fact, there was a goofy guy who sat two aisles away from me who studied my every move. One day he stopped by and told me, "I have been watching you for a full week. I counted the hours you actually worked and it came to less than three." And that *he* had time to figure that out really proves my point. How busy was he if he had time to study *my* work habits?

Chuck knew that my husband and I didn't have much extra money, so he insisted on paying for my coffee and lunch lots of times. He'd always ask, "Do you have cash for your lunch? If not, take what you need out of the coffee jar and just leave me an IOU." When I left NAA, that jar was loaded with paper slips. I was willing to make good, but he said, "Forget it Paula. You don't owe me a dime."

Every holiday there was a small gift on my desk; but more important than all of that, than all the gifts and coffee and free lunches, Chuck treated me with respect. Before I left I asked him why on earth he had hired me. As I wrote before, he really didn't need a secretary and I couldn't do most of the stuff he needed done. He said, "The minute we met I just knew you'd be a whole lot of fun."

Best boss ever (and I've worked for my husband. Shhh, don't tell).

The Work Shirt

1966

My husband's first job out of college was in Los Angeles with Ernst & Ernst, one of the Big Eight accounting firms. His take home pay was $525 per month. Our rent took about one fourth of that, and then we had to buy gas, food, clothes, utilities, insurance, and baby necessities. Our son, Roger, was just three months old when Alan graduated with his master's degree in accounting and began working.

In addition to those expenses, we tried to save one hundred dollars a month to eventually buy a house. We didn't have a car payment, thanks to Alan's parents; they had given us his mom's Volkswagen. I picked up a few extra bucks ironing for my sister Kay and her husband and babysitting for my sister Sharon. But you get it: money was tight.

Ernst & Ernst was very conservative and had a dress code; they required all their accountants to wear white, long-sleeved, Permanent Press shirts. No colored shirts were allowed. Permanent Press shirts had just been invented and were expensive. We bought one white shirt and Phyllis, my mother-in-law, sent us another so that Alan could start work. Our laundry routine was one shirt on Alan and one shirt in the hamper. It was a plan that we could handle until our budget allowed for additional shirt purchases.

When we got married, I didn't know much about doing laundry. My mom had done three or four loads of laundry a day; she *had* to with nine people living at home. We didn't own a dryer, so I used to help her hang the clothes on the line outside and take them down when they were dry. I never saw Mom scrub a collar before washing a shirt. She did hang Dad's khaki work pants on metal frames to create a crease. Our family wash loads were big and mixed.

My mother-in-law, by contrast, was a laundering perfectionist. She was the only person I ever met who ironed her dish towels and her bedsheets. It was obvious to Phyllis that my wifely skills were lacking. To protect her son, Phyllis "kindly" gave me written instructions on how to properly launder Alan's pricey shirts. Phyllis's 12-Step Shirt Laundering System was provided to me already laminated in plastic so the instructions wouldn't get wet. All these years later, I could not forget the steps if I tried:

Step 1—Remove the collar stays and set them on the window sill.

Step 2—Turn the pockets inside out and remove any accumulated lint with a soft toothbrush.

Step 3—Take a tiny bit of liquid soap and scrub the collar with a two-inch-wide soft nylon brush to remove any sweat stains. Check and clean food spots on the front and cuffs as well.

Step 4—Button up the shirt front and sleeves. This helps the garment retain its shape.

Step 5—Add ¼ to ½ cup of bleach per load of whites, depending on the load size.

Step 6—Set the temperature of the water to cold and fill the tub.

Step 7—Add the bleach and agitate the water and bleach for several minutes.

Step 8—Add the white shirts and other white garments. *No towels. No darks. No reds.*

Step 9—During final rinse, add one large capful of fabric softener. Downey is best.

Step 10—When the wash cycle is complete, put the clean shirts in the dryer for exactly fifteen minutes. Then immediately remove the shirts and hang them up. Make sure the collar and cuffs are straight.

Step 11—Put the collar stays back in the collar.

Step 12—Even though it is Permanent Press, touch up the shirt with an iron and fabric finish as needed. (*Written ironing system to follow.*)

Ironing instructions—oh boy, I could hardly wait.

Phyllis's 12-Step Shirt Laundering System seemed like lunacy to me. My mom's "system" had only three steps. Throw the stuff in the washer, add soap, and when the wash cycle was complete, hang it all up to dry. Maybe two steps.

Alan, because he grew up with a perfectionist, was a much better launderer than I. In fact, he never let me touch his clothes after I turned his underwear pink that time (that's another story—but I bet you can work it out). He was slow to change, like his mom, and preferred to follow a careful routine. We always joked about how he grew up with a silver spoon in his mouth. The spoon I grew up with was wooden. And oversized. And a little splintered from wear. Like I've said many times, opposites *must* attract.

Since I was home all day with the baby, it was clearly silly for Alan to come home after a day of work and have to launder his own shirt. I wanted to do it for him and I asked him to please let me do it; I had the time and I wanted to do my part. Alan reluctantly agreed. I promised that since we only had two work shirts, and I knew how expensive they were, I would definitely follow Phyllis's 12-Step Shirt Laundering System exactly. And I did. Really.

I assembled everything I needed on the shelf above the washer: tooth brush, liquid soap, two-inch soft nylon collar brush, fabric softener (Downey, of course), fabric finish, and bleach. Then, like a chemist, I went about my work. When the wash cycle was finished, I threw the spotless white shirt in the dryer and set the timer for exactly fifteen minutes. I was really proud of myself. Alan's only other work shirt was looking great. Maybe my mother-in-law wasn't completely looney with her system, and maybe she was wrong about my wifely skills.

When I heard the dryer buzzer go off after fifteen minutes, I headed immediately to the laundry room at the back of the house. At the same time, out the window, I saw Alan walking toward the house from the garage, his work day finished. "Hi, honey," I yelled. "Just finishing up your work shirt."

I opened the dryer door. Oh no! The cuff of one sleeve had caught in the dryer door hinge. For fifteen minutes, the spotless shirt had gone around and around and around, twisting itself into a solid, dry ball of Permanent Press fabric. When I tried to pull the shirt ball apart, it sprang back into its new ball shape fast. That was the Permanent function at work. Alan's work shirt was now a corkscrewed, wrinkled-up mess.

Alan was now inside the house, staring at the spotless ball I was holding.

"What the hell happened to my shirt?"

I felt horrible about what happened. Really, I was very sorry and didn't mean to laugh. But it was also funny, so I did.

"I swear to God, Alan, I followed your mother's 12-Step Shirt Laundering System perfectly." It just didn't mention anything about watching out for the dryer hinge!

Not seeing the humor in my screw-up, he stormed off in a huff.

I did my best to rectify the situation. I rewashed the shirt, hoping extra softener would smooth out what I had done. And it did and it didn't. The shirt was wearable, but now Alan had his "good work shirt" and "the shirt Paula had laundered." I begged Alan not to tell his mother.

You see, I was also the one who had ruined the hand-crocheted crib blanket Phyllis had made for our baby, Roger. First, concerned about germs, I washed it in hot to kill the buggers. Then I dried it in the dryer for *way* over an hour. How was I to know the blanket she crocheted was wool? It went from crib-sized to dog-bed-sized in just one wash. All her hard work had gone for naught.

"Please," I begged him, "Don't tell your mother about the shirt."

9

My BFF

I met Yvonne De Armond in kindergarten. We were very different but we instantly connected, and for the next sixty-eight years we were like two peas in a pod. She had just one sister, Jackie, who was much older than she. I was born smack dab in the middle of six siblings. Her mother was a business woman, a Republican, and an antique dealer. My mom stayed home, was a Democrat, and, believe me, also worked. From the time we met until this very day, we have been best friends.

This is Yvonne on her scooter, just about the time we met.

As different as we were, Yvonne and I didn't argue much. But, I do remember our first argument. We were making mud pies in my back yard and got into an argument over whose turn it was to use the wooden spoon (obviously the far superior tool for mud pies). She got mad at me for

Our Brownie troop when we were in the second grade. I'm in the back row, fourth from the left, in braids and a white shirt. Yvonne is in the front row, sitting cross-legged, third person from the left.

something I did and stormed off down the alley, the much-prized wooden spoon in tow. We didn't speak for three whole days, a small eternity for kids.

Our first escapade together was back in kindergarten. For some reason, we didn't feel Mrs. Mildred, our sweet, bespectacled teacher, was giving us the attention we deserved. We hatched the following plan to get her attention: We would take turns putting our fingers in the crayon drawer and slamming it. When we cried from the pain, we were sure Mrs. Mildred would come running and we'd be smothered with kisses and kindness. (It was probably my idea that Yvonne go first.) Anyhow, Yvonne put her fingers in the drawer and, as planned, I slammed it. (Maybe a little too hard. We never really discussed *that* part of the plan.)

Yvonne let out a bloodcurdling scream that brought Mrs. Mildred, and the rest of the class, running toward us from every direction. Yvonne was crying and her fingers were turning blue. Mrs. Mildred sent her to the nurse's office with the teacher's aide. I, on the other hand, was admonished for being a cruel child and banned to the dunce stool in the corner of the room. I was not even allowed to *look* at the rest of the class for the balance of the day.

A friend is someone who knows the song in your heart and can sing it back to you when you have forgotten the words.

—Unknown

So, it kind of worked; we got attention all right. I don't think Mrs. Mildred believed my explanation of the incident, even though Yvonne backed me up on the story. I never checked my school records to see if there were any notes written there, but I do know that Mrs. Mildred seemed to keep an eye on me for the rest of the year.

Yvonne and I did everything together: dance lessons, dressing up, birthdays, Brownie meetings, trick-or-treating, and, when we got older, we took art classes together and were cheerleaders at the same time. Heck, we even dieted together. In fact, she can be seen so often in our family photos that lots of folks in town thought she was one of my sisters.

Through the years, we shared many funny events and zany experiences, not unlike Lucy Ricardo and Ethel Mertz of the *I Love Lucy* show. In our sophomore year at Huntington Beach High School, we took a class called business machines from Miss Beckman, an unmarried lady in her forties and a very *naïve* teacher. During the class, we learned how to operate a typewriter, a comptometer, and stencil duplicator.

I always thought Yvonne looked like Shirley Temple, the famous child star. She was so adorable. Yvonne is below the boy on the right, in the stripped dress.

I think most people today know what a typewriter is. It's like your computer keyboard, but "clackier" sounding. And you have to put paper in the machine to type on, instead of printing out what you've written when you are finished. Plus, you had to use your hand to make the carriage return at the end of each line. Imagine!

Comptometers, the second machine we had to learn to use, were the first commercially successful mechanical calculators. I don't remember much about operating those machines, except that they had a whole bunch of keys and that Yvonne and I had no idea how they worked. To pass the class, we had to add or subtract long columns of numbers and then turn in our calculation sheets to Miss Beckman after each period. Boring!

The final machine we had to master during the semester, or at least have some competency in, was a stencil duplicator, which was a low-cost duplicating machine. Members of the small class, mostly girls, were rotated so that each girl could learn to use the various machines. Luckily for us, and unluckily for Miss Beckman, we were the first two students assigned to learn the stencil duplicator, a.k.a. mimeo machine.

After getting the rest of the class started on the typewriters and comptometers, Miss Beckman took the two of us into the closed office that contained the mimeo machine. It was a big machine with a large drum at one end. It worked by forcing ink through a *stencil* onto sheets of paper, one after another. (Mimeo machines have since been replaced by the likes of photocopiers, scanners, and laser printers.) Anyhow, Miss Beckman showed us how to operate the mimeo machine and then pointed out a stack of bulletins and other items that needed to be duplicated. When she was confident that we understood what to do, Miss Beckman left us to it. Or rather, she left Lucy and Ethel to their mischief.

"Leave what you've copied on my desk when the bell

rings, okay, girls?" And with that, Miss Beckman left the office and headed toward the principal's office for a teachers' meeting.

We made all the copies of the first document in the pile okay. It was a simple machine to operate. Then we started goofing around. To our delight, we discovered that if we pulled the mimeo machine closer to the window and removed the storage tray, we could shoot paper out onto the heads of the football players standing below (don't know why that seemed like the thing to do). Anyhow, when the team moved out of range and onto the football field, that got boring, so we started looking through all the cupboard drawers in the office (like we did when we babysat). Lo and behold, we discovered, below the stack of items to be duplicated, the tests and the answers for the upcoming semester. Even more valuable, in another drawer were the answers to the tedious work sheets for the comptometers. Finding the answers for all the tests *and* all the comptometer work sheets was the Holy Grail of student sneakery and ensured sure-fire A grades for a couple of nitwits like ourselves.

Poor Miss Beckman. She never caught on to our theft and we became her top students, getting almost 100 percent on all of our tests and calculations. Typing was not something we could cheat on, however. A timed typing test is a timed typing test. But, oddly enough, I had no problem with typing whatsoever, and neither did Yvonne. Even with a marginal grade in typing, our nearly perfect scores on the other machines made us class stars.

One last thing: Miss Beckman, in addition to her other duties, was the student advisor to the Business Club on campus. Yvonne and I stole a bunch of little gold pins we

L. to R.: K. Olsen, P. Strother, J. Motes, Y. De Armond, S. Pearsall.

When we were cheerleaders at Huntington Beach High School, beehive hairdos were the rage. I took great pride in having the biggest beehive on campus. My BFF, back row right, came in a close second.

found in one of the drawers. These were the pins awarded to officers and members of the Business Club. When Miss Beckman noticed me wearing the secretary's pin on my cheerleading sweater a few weeks later, she said, "I didn't know you were in the Business Club!" The poor lady was clueless.

Looking back at the high school years, I probably owe Yvonne's parents about a thousand dollars. On countless occasions in the school cafeteria, I would ask Yvonne, "Can I borrow fifty cents?" or "Have you got a quarter I could borrow?" Yvonne loaned (actually, gave) me untold sums of cash through the years. I seldom had the money to pay her back. She knew it and I knew it. But Yvonne, and her mother and her father, never said a word. Perhaps that's why I feel the need to be so generous now. I was blessed with friends who helped me financially so many times. I have a big debt to society that I need to repay.

I was with Yvonne at the Rendezvous Ballroom in Balboa, a favorite dance spot for teenagers, the night she met her future husband, Allan Ansdell. We were not only in each other's weddings, Yvonne let me borrow *her* beautiful wedding dress for *my* wedding (she married an Allan and I married an Alan . . . hmmmm). We had our children just a few years apart, and for several years our homes in Seal Beach were separated only by a back fence.

Our Lucy and Ethel antics continued well after high school. One incident I remember clearly involved fudge. I make really delicious peanut butter fudge (thanks, Mom) and Yvonne's husband loved it. On his birthday, I made a big, tasty batch and climbed over the fence to deliver it to Yvonne. She called her husband at work and told him I had made fudge for his birthday.

"Oh, I can't wait," he said earnestly. "I'll be home in a few hours."

His words made me smile, and I was glad I had made the candy because I really liked Yvonne's husband. While we were waiting for his arrival, Yvonne made us lunch and we had one small piece of the fudge for dessert. Then, because it was so incredibly delicious, we had a second piece.

"These are just little pieces," I said reassuringly. "There is still plenty of fudge for Allan."

Yvonne is not a sugar addict like I am, so she stopped after the second piece of fudge. Plus, she didn't want to eat any more of her husband's birthday present.

Not me.

Driven by my sugar high and needing yet another fix, I snuck a third piece out from under the aluminum foil that covered the plate. When Yvonne wasn't looking, I devoured a fourth piece, then a fifth, and in no time the aluminum foil covered nothing but an empty plate full of sugary crumbs and bits of peanuts.

When I heard the sound of Allan Ansdell's car pulling into the driveway, I ran out the back door and headed for the fence, like a thief running from the cops.

"What's up? Where ya going?" Yvonne asked, as the door slammed behind me with a bang.

When she lifted the wrinkled aluminum, she knew why I had fled.

"I'm so sorry! I'm such an idiot!" I yelled back over my shoulder, laughing.

With that, I jumped down to the ground and sprinted toward the safety of my kitchen door.

Later, I asked Yvonne, "So . . . what did your husband say?"

"He said, 'I knew I should have gotten home sooner. I know how Paula is around fudge.'"

BFFs, best friends forever, that's what we are. Yvonne and I have shared the ups and downs, ins and outs, successes and failures of living as friends for over sixty-eight years. Business careers and marriages don't last that long. Heck, some lives don't last that long.

Like I've said so often, it doesn't matter if we haven't seen each other or talked together in months. One call, one text, one email, and we are as close as ever. From Yvonne, I always got answers not tainted by jealousy or envy. Yvonne saw more in me than I ever saw in myself. Once during a high school car wash, the driver of a gorgeous new Cadillac said, "Go ahead young lady, drive the car over to the area so it can be washed." I was amazed at his trust and a little afraid too.

Afterward, my BFF said, "You shouldn't have been afraid. You looked like you *belonged* in that car, Paula."

That comment meant so much to me that I still remember it fifty-plus years later. In my family, money was always in short supply. As a kid, I sensed we were poor, and that lack left a negative mark on my persona; I never felt quite as good as my friends. Yvonne's simple comment made me see myself as something bigger than what I felt inside.

Yvonne has given me equally wise counsel on so many occasions. I remember calling her when I was thinking of moving from California, my birth state and where most of my family lives, to relocate to Florida.

Alan and I, on the left, with my BFF and her wonderful husband, Allan Ansdell. We've had so much fun together and we're still close friends after all these years.

Yvonne's advice? "There is a great big world out there, Paula. What's the worry? You can always move back if you hate it." Of course! Of course I could move back. I wasn't going to the moon!

Yvonne's answers are so pragmatic and rooted in the real world. She said once, "You're such a sentimental sap." She's right, I am, and sometimes that gets in the way. I think God knew I would need a little (okay, a lot of) extra help, and that's why he shared Yvonne with me.

Someone said, "There comes a point in your life when you realize who really matters, who never did, and who always will." I've come to that point. That's why Yvonne is my BFF.

10

Dr. Spock and Parenting

1969

It was our son Roger's fourth birthday and I wanted to plan something very special for the occasion. After all, Roger had a three-month-old baby sister and because I was so busy with her care, I was sure Roger felt a little left out and jealous. Plus, all the books on raising kids said that the fourth year was a pivotal point in a child's development.

Even after almost four years of parenting, I felt deficient and unsure of my parenting skills. All my girlfriends and siblings seemed like such competent mothers. We discussed babies and kids whenever we got together, and, from what they said during those meetings, they appeared to have the mothering thing down pat.

Not me. I was constantly searching for and reading anything I could find on child-rearing. I read Dr. Benjamin Spock's book, *Baby and Child*, like some folks read the Bible, evidenced by the numerous underlines, stars, and notes that I had scribbled in the margins. Also, my older sister Sharon, who was a well-respected nursery school teacher in our town and an amazing mom, constantly talked about age-appropriate crafts for the little ones: puzzles they should be doing at this age and books we should read to our kids. Plus, she agreed with Dr. Spock that the fourth year was a tipping point in a child's life. In my mind's eye, if I screwed up Roger's fourth birthday party, it was all over. He would surely turn into a mass murderer, or something worse, if there is such a thing.

There are only two things a child will share willingly: communicable diseases and its mother's age.

—DR. BENJAMIN SPOCK

Roger liked robots, so that was the party theme. I stayed up half the night, maybe even all night, making and then stuffing twenty or so party bags with hand-painted robots on the front for the little kids attending his party, which was being held in a small city park about fifteen minutes from our home in Seal Beach.

Tired, but bolstered by a few cups of java, I got the children dressed for the event. Roger looked adorable in new blue jeans and an "It's My Birthday" shirt I had purchased for the occasion. (I couldn't find a robot shirt anywhere. Believe me, I tried!) Natalie, our three-month-old, was dressed up in a frilly pink party dress and was sitting happily in her infant seat, which was a plastic padded shell with a carrying handle that I used to tote her around in. This was before car seats were required for infants. I was hoping she'd fall asleep and take her morning nap during the trip to the park and then be awake for the festivities.

Some of the kids and their moms were planning to meet us at the park, and I was transporting a couple of kids as well. Before my extra passengers arrived, I loaded the car with the cake, party bags, drinks, paper products, stroller, and the games and prizes for the "Robot Birthday Party Extravaganza." No kid of mine was going to be a mass murderer.

Soon the house was filled with moms dropping off their kids. Laughter and noise filled the place, and excited children were running up and down the stairs. I was feeling excited and fatigued, and a bit groggy as well. I was also suffering from new-baby sleep deprivation, on top of my party-decoration sleep deprivation. Why hadn't I just bought some party bags? What an idiot!

Anyhow, after I got all the kids seat-belted into the car and wished the moms farewell, I went back into the house and brought Natalie out. I locked the house, fired-up the "party car," and headed for the park.

Reminding myself to drive carefully, I tried to ignore the excited sounds coming from the back seats. The kids were already in a party mood, talking loudly and screaming on occasion. I had to remind them several times, "Please children, use your *inside* voices." I had learned that phrase from my sister Sharon. Before she taught me that, I probably would have yelled what my dad yelled: "Shut up, kids. I'm driving."

We arrived at the park, and everyone scrambled out of the car. Because I was early and no one else who was meeting us had arrived yet, I unloaded all the junk by myself, except the balls and toys the kids grabbed to play with. I was thinking, "Really, Paula, was all of this stuff necessary? Why do you always over-do?"

Then it happened. I looked all around and inside the car. Where the hell was Natalie? "Roger," I called frantically, "where is your sister?" With a shrug, I saw his answer; he didn't know. Holy mother of God . . . where was my baby?

"Think, Paula!" I screamed to myself. "Where did you have her last?" Then I remembered: I had left my precious little angel sitting helplessly by our front door in her infant seat.

I screamed loudly at the kids, "All of you, get back in the car, NOW!!!" When they dawdled, I screamed loudly again. "HURRY! I left the baby at home! (So much for good parenting.) Leaving party junk strewn all about the city park, I drove like a controlled maniac back toward Seal Beach. I was in breathless shock, panic-stricken and terrified all at once, not even able to wave to one of the mothers arriving in her car.

"My God," I was thinking, "the baby could be kidnapped or carried off by a coyote." (If car- or cell-phones had been invented, I could have called my neighbor.)

After what seemed like an eternity, I turned onto our street, Crescent Avenue. Ahead, in the distance, I could just make out the shape of the abandoned infant seat and its precious frilly pink contents, sitting by the door.

"Thank God!" I screamed into the air. Sound asleep, contented, little Natalie had probably slept through the entire harrowing event. I leapt from the car, broke out crying, and sobbed like a baby. What kind of mother was I? I have never felt so totally inadequate in my entire life.

When I got back into the car, Roger and his friends were just sitting there, speechless.

"Is everything okay, Mom?" the birthday boy asked sweetly.

"She's just fine," I answered, as I wiped off the black mascara-carrying tears that were running down my cheeks. "I'm so sorry if I scared you kids."

And then we drove back to the park and, despite it all, I recovered and the robot party turned out great.

I don't remember what my sister Sharon said later when I told her the story (I'm nothing if not honest about my foul-ups). I'm sure what she said was more "nuanced" than what she actually thought of my mothering skills.

Still—the emotionally pivotal fourth birthday party came off without a hitch except for the eensy-teensy, insane, screaming drive to pick up an abandoned baby.

Hmmm, I wonder if there's still time for Roger to be a mass murderer after all. Oh dear, what if he's a late bloomer!

11

The Tube Top

1972

Like most young wives, one of my desires was to stay trendy, glamorous, and attractive for my husband. What better way to achieve this than to purchase the latest fashion items? At this particular point in time, those were tube tops. Tube tops, in case you don't know, are thick elastic bands of fabric that go around your midriff, from your waist to just above the top of your breasts. You don't wear a bra with a tube top. In essence, the tube top is your bra. *In essence.*

In keeping with my goal of staying fashionable, I purchased a lovely floral dress with a tube top attached at the waist. The dress portion was long, to the floor, and I really liked how I looked in it. My husband said it looked "sexy," so that's what I chose to wear on our dinner date one Friday in late summer.

We were on a tight budget, like most young families, so going to the Fish House on the water in Long Beach was a big event. You had to make reservations a week in advance because the place was always packed. Even with reservations, you had to stand on the landing for at least fifteen minutes before they called your name. Then you'd walk down a small flight of stairs to the main dining room, where the tables overlooked the water and the bay.

It was close to sunset, and music was playing as we entered the restaurant. We waited on the landing with a small group of fellow "reservationists" in anticipation of what was sure to be a delicious and romantic meal. Alan ordered us a glass of wine from the bar, and we chatted quietly to each other, looking about at the other couples, while we waited our turn to be seated. At last, we heard, "Thomas, party of two."

I was so excited, all made up and feeling sexy in my stylish tube top dress. For a few hours, I wasn't some-body's mom, picking up toys or doing laundry; I was a grown woman out with the man I loved.

When our name was called, I went bouncing down the stairs into the dining room, sure that everyone noticed how pretty I looked. One, two, three, four, five steps down and I was standing on the main floor. There was only one small problem.

Alan had been standing on the back of my dress at the top of the landing. Before I knew it, the tube-top portion gave way and was pulled down to my waist, exposing my breasts for the entire room to see. My scream, of course, did not help the situation, discretion-wise, and pulling the top quickly up *over* my head did not help the situation either. I know I turned bright red. People were laughing and I feared Alan might actually faint.

He didn't faint. We recovered the best we could and slunk to our table like a couple of wet cats. I couldn't order another drink fast enough. "Make it a double and make it quick!"

Now, you would think that little adventure would have cured me from ever wearing a tube top again. But, oh no, I had to wear it just one more time. This time, I was just taking my son and his friend to pick up a pizza. Again, it was a Friday evening, and the local pizzeria was crammed with dads stopping for take-out pizza on their way home. I was up at the front counter paying the bill, with at least fifteen men towering behind me.

That's when my son decided to put ice down my top. And he didn't put it down the back; oh no, he grabbed the front, pulled it straight out and chucked a handful of ice cubes between my boobs, giving all the men behind me quite a show.

I let out a scream, which only caused everyone who missed the action to turn my way. I know I turned as red as marinara, because my son asked, "Why are you so red, Mom?" I grabbed his hand, and our pizza, and fled to the safety of the car.

That was it. The tube top was immediately donated. I guess the truth is that not every fashion trend fits into every lifestyle. I don't have a tattoo. I don't have a nose ring. And I sure as heck won't ever own a tube top again.

In fact, I think they should come with a warning sign: "BEWARE OF EXPOSURE—WEAR AT YOUR OWN RISK!"

12

Serendipity

I am a natural-born salesman. I love people; I love talking; and since I love houses and decorating, selling real estate was the perfect job for me. Also, I had specialized sales training. Every summer through my college years, I had worked as a waitress on Catalina Island. If you want to make great tips as a waitress, you learn how to size up people fast and meet their needs. You need those same skills to sell real estate.

Money was the driving force behind my interest in real estate. When my husband and I sold our first house, the six percent commission (the going rate at that time) seemed like a whole lot of "lost" money to me, since that commission is paid out by the sellers.

I quickly learned that all I needed to sell real estate in California was a license that, if I worked hard, could be obtained in less than three months. Is there any other business in the world that gives you millions of dollars in inventory to sell for a measly fee of $150 and a three-month education?

My only concern when I considered a career selling houses was the math involved. My brain does not have a math gene, or whatever makes a person good at math. I mean, I knew my times tables. I could add and subtract. But anything above simple division was a mystery. And I knew as much about an adding machine (we didn't have calculators yet) as I did an abacus.

Still, since we needed more money than my hard-working husband could make as a junior accountant, and since my kids were no longer in cribs, I started taking real estate classes. The weekly classes were excellent and really prepared and encouraged students to succeed. At the conclusion of each class, a test was administered. There were multiple tests for each class, and I took every test for every class over and over until I got one hundred percent on every class.

As I anticipated, the classes and tests that required math were difficult for me. But I plugged along and with tutoring from my math-genius husband, I was eventually prepared for the state exam which was held in Los Angeles and took five hours on a Saturday.

The good news about the state exam was that it included many of the same questions that had been on the practice exams. Anthony Schools, the company that offered the real estate course I had taken, had employees waiting outside the building after each state exam. They questioned us about the exam and took notes about any questions that had stumped us. With that kind of attention to detail, students like me were well prepared.

My hard work paid off and I got a ninety percent on the state exam. I was a licensed sales associate and hung my license with our realtor, Reva Olsen. I felt honored that Reva had taken me in. "In my thirty years of real estate, you're the first sales associate I've ever hired."

The day I got my license, I got a call from my dad. My folks owned a triplex in our town, and one of Dad's renters had mentioned that he and his wife were now looking for a house. I had just returned from a garage sale when I got the call. I had stopped at this garage sale because the guy holding the sale in his driveway also had a "For Sale by Owner" sign on his lawn (we call those FSBOs.) After my dad's call, I drove back to the FSBO and asked the owner for a "one-party show." That's a listing that creates a fiduciary relationship between an agent and a seller for just one client (the one party being shown the property). If my client didn't buy his house, our relationship ended.

Miraculously, I got the one-party show on the FSBO and, double miraculously, I sold it to my dad's tenant. "Holy mackerel," I thought to myself when I figured out my commission. "This is fun and it's easy."

When I called Reva, my broker, and told her I had gotten a listing, she was flabbergasted. "That's great," she said, and I could hear the smile in her voice. "Meet me at my house and I'll show you how to put it on the Multiple Listing Sheet," she added.

When I told her I didn't need to actually list the house, because I had already sold the house, she let out a gasp. "You what?"

Now, at this point, I panicked. I was so naïve and unsure of what I was doing that I thought maybe there was some rule that you had to keep a listing for twenty-four hours or get it approved or something. So I answered, "I'm sorry. Wasn't I supposed to sell it?"

Reva laughed out loud.

Serendipity, that's what it was. And, for some reason—luck, the grace of God, whatever—that's how my real estate career progressed most of the time. It had to be serendipity, because I was flying by the seat of my pants. In fact, I used to think, "Someday, someone is going to find out I don't know what the heck I'm doing, and come and ask for all this money back."

Vital lives are about action. You can't feel warmth unless you create it, can't feel delight until you play, can't know serendipity unless you risk.

—JOAN ERICKSON

Still, I don't want you to think all my deals were simple. Oh, heavens no. I had my share of disasters. One time, a seller threw my briefcase and all my papers right out his front door, yelling that he was "insulted" by the low offer I had just delivered. I guess no one told him that agents are required by law to present *all* offers.

Another time, an Asian couple accused me of prejudice because the house they were bidding on was sold to a Caucasian couple instead. I had told the hopeful buyers that this house was in a bidding war, so that the couple who offered the most money would get the place. My buyers weren't listening and thought it was all just a ploy to make more commission. They wouldn't increase their offer, so another party got the house, and I got the blame.

And, I'll never forget the time I presented a full-price, all-cash offer to a couple, and their realtor, who was also their uncle, was so drunk that he had to keep rereading the papers to make sure I wasn't "trying to screw his niece on the deal." That offer should have taken thirty minutes to present. Because he was drunk, we were there until after midnight.

I firmly believe that God puts the people in your life that you need. Two people I needed were Reva Olsen, my experienced and savvy broker, and a knowledgeable and kind escrow officer named Gertrude Campbell. Those two gals made my success possible. They never laughed at my stupid questions (and there were many), and they were exceedingly generous with their time and expertise. As my mentors, I couldn't have done it without their help.

Houses were my specialty. All you have to do is find the right house for the right price in the right location, and the property sells itself. You don't have to be slick or trick anyone into anything. All you have to do is listen to what the buyers want and then go find it. You can't stop a person from buying the house of her dreams if it fits in her budget.

Now, house commissions were nice, but the big bucks were in selling multiple units. So when a listing for ten units came into our office, I really wanted to make that sale. Serendipitously, I was on the "up-desk" when a man called and wanted to see "the units down by the beach." This was my big chance, but there was just one problem: How the heck was I going to explain to him all the tax advantages, depreciation, capital gains, and all that stuff—all that stuff that requires more than basic math?

My husband and I sat down after the kids were in bed, and he tutored me on how to justify the sale price of the units, based on their potential rental income and how property depreciation and expenses would impact the client's taxes. It was, to me, a lot of math, and my brain doesn't do math. We worked at it for hours. When I went to bed, I was still *not* confident in the least that I could explain this stuff to the client. So we got up early and went all over it again.

At 9:30 a.m., I was as prepared as I was going to be and went out to my car. The battery was dead. "Damn!" I had to call the guy and ask if he would mind picking me up; not a great way to start a difficult showing. To make matters even worse, the guy shows up in a sports car and turns out to be drop-dead gorgeous. He was a dark-skinned, blue-eyed Adonis. When he tilted up his glasses to say hello, he flashed a smile that almost brought me to my knees.

Okay, I don't do well with math and my brain just turns to mush when I'm around a guy who makes me drool. I got into the car, babbling like an idiot about my dead battery, hoping he wouldn't notice that I was blushing like a schoolgirl at the mere sight of him. My hands were shaking as I fumbled with the listing sheet.

He was very nice and things would have been fine if he hadn't asked, "Is the property north or south of Ocean Boulevard?" Okay, to recap: I don't do math; my brain turns to mush around handsome men; and, did I mention, I also don't do north or south? You'd think a person in real estate would understand how to give directions. This was way before cell phones and Google Maps. "I'm left handed," I said, kind of jokingly. "I only talk in left and right." The look on his face when I told him this was not one of admiration.

Serendipity, where are you?

After what seemed like an eternity, we arrived at the units. Thank God, the listing agent was there. Maybe he could explain all those income tax definitions and math stuff to Adonis here.

The listing agent, my client, and I entered the first apartment like a small parade, the agent pointing out the remodeled kitchen and condition of the carpet as we wandered through the unit. Then, we paraded into apartments two, three, and four. So far so good, I'm thinking. We entered apartment number five.

My mind was churning. Depreciation is how much for how many years? How do you figure capital gains? What can he write off? What's the return on investment? Does he get passive losses and if so, how much? I marched on with my pencil in my mouth, listening intently as the listing agent answered questions about the units. I wanted that pencil handy to jot down any ideas I had from what came up in the conversation.

When the two guys exited the master bath, I popped in to check my hair and makeup. And I silently screamed. That wasn't a pencil in my mouth. It was the open end of a black Magic Marker. My mouth was covered with black ink and it was in between my teeth and running across the top of my gums and tongue. I looked like a horror story.

"Paula, are you coming?" I could hear from the door.

Desperate situations call for desperate actions. And I sure as hell was desperate. I had no other choice: I pulled open drawers until I found a toothbrush and started brushing my teeth like a madman.

To my dying day, I will never forget the look on those men's faces as they peeked into the bath to see what was holding up the parade. There I was, with a stranger's toothbrush in hand, and a thick ooze of gray toothpaste running down my chin.

"What the hell are you doing?" Adonis asked in shocked amazement. I tried to explain, feebly. But the explanation did not come out—the slobber in my mouth came out instead.

Needless to say, I did not sell the units. I returned home, a humbled and broken woman. There was not enough vodka in the house to erase my embarrassment and shame (as is evidenced by the fact that I still remember it vividly enough to write it down today, decades later).

I had made a total idiot of myself.

And I had learned a valuable lesson: Stick to what you know.

13

It's in the Eye of the Beholder

> **1973**

When Ellen Smith's husband died, she called and told me she wanted to sell her house. It was a lovely custom home and I was sure I could sell it fast and get top dollar. The market was hot, and few homes were as nice as Ellen's.

Just as I thought, within a week of listing the property, I had a buyer under contract. The buyers, an older couple, had sold their condo on the beach and wanted to move into a house with a yard. They wanted a forty-five-day escrow, which was perfect for Ellen. I was thrilled that I had found a qualified buyer so quickly and even happier that I had doubled-ended the deal (I would get the commission for the seller and the buyer). I went home singing, "We're in the money," and when my husband, Alan, heard the song, he knew instantly that I had made a deal.

A few days later, my buyer called and he was furious. "What are you trying to do, Paula?" he yelled into the receiver. "Are you trying to pull a fast one on me?" I had no idea what he was talking about. I am honest to a fault. If I had done something wrong, it was because I'm stupid. I wouldn't even know how to pull a fast one. I could barely pull a slow one. It's not in my makeup.

I questioned him and quickly discovered that he was unaware there would be a fee for getting the loan on the new house he was buying. The fee, one point plus one hundred dollars, came to nine hundred bucks, and he "had no intention of paying such a fee." I hadn't told him about the fee because, honestly, I had forgotten and I thought, at his age, he'd surely know that banks charge a fee for making a loan. My assumption was incorrect: He had always paid cash in the past and had never worked with a lender. I quickly apologized and told him I would gladly pay the nine-hundred-dollar fee on his behalf. I considered it paying tuition for making an incorrect assumption. I further explained to him that the bank fee in no way feathered my nest. It was a bank charge and had nothing to do with me.

Not having heard about the loan fee from me now made the buyer distrust me. I was determined to correct that situation, because my perceived integrity was on the line. I would make darn sure the rest of the deal went as smoothly as a hot knife through butter.

The forty-five-day escrow passed quickly and the buyer got his loan. It was time for the final walk-through, which was set for the day after the seller, Ellen, vacated her old house. The walk-through is the final step before a buyer takes his certified funds to escrow. It's the last step before the closing.

I spoke with Ellen the day she moved, and I could tell her mood was melancholy. "I'm out of my lovely home, Paula. We're packed and ready to leave. The place is spic and span and ready to show." I wished her luck on her move and the next stage of her life, and thanked her for trusting me with the sale.

After that loan fee fiasco, I wanted to be sure the walk-through went well. I didn't want anything stupid to squirrel the deal. So the morning of the walk-through, I arrived bright and early at the house.

Ellen was a good person. I know she had said (and probably thought) the house was spic and span, but one lesson you learn early in real estate is that cleanliness, like beauty, is in the eye of the beholder.

Well, the kitchen was dirty. There was food left in the refrigerator. The closets had debris, plastic bags, and hangers strewn about, and the bathrooms needed cleaning as well. In addition, there were two major problems to sort: there was a dark oil stain the size of a big bucket lid on the paved brick driveway, and there was a two-by-six-foot section of carpet missing in the living room where the upright piano used to be. Evidently, they had carpeted *up* to the piano, not *under* the piano. I was flabbergasted. Who does that?

I drove home like a madwoman. I knew my husband would help clean up the place if he were home, but he was enjoying a long weekend off work and had taken the kids to the beach. My folks were too old to ask for help, so I called the only person I knew who didn't work a regular job: my sister, Judy. She lived in the trailer park in another part of town. I was thrilled when she answered her phone.

I quickly explained my problem and told her I'd give her one hundred dollars (which was a lot of money then) if she'd come immediately and help me clean this vacant house. "Yes, please bring your boyfriend, he can clean the pavers," I pleaded.

She agreed to stop by the hardware store and get something to clean up the driveway oil. I gathered up my house-cleaning supplies and my vacuum, threw an old shirt over my business clothes, and headed back to Ellen's house. With all the work we had to do, I wasn't going to have time to change before the buyers arrived.

My sister Judy is basically a good and decent person but, back then, she drank on occasion, and this was one of those occasions. When Judy drank, she got very hostile, loud, and belligerent. I was already a nervous wreck. Judy's arriving drunk was not what I needed.

"Judy," I pleaded in a sisterly tone, "please just do as I ask. This is a big deal to me. I really need your help. I'm paying you triple what it's worth. Please, Judy, just do it!" Well, she helped, but she seemed determined to make me squirm over every request. Everywhere she looked, she'd exclaim, "This isn't that dirty. What are you worried about? These people must be spoiled rich creeps if a little food in the refrigerator puts a wad up their asses." Oh boy. Just what I needed, a belligerent, semi-employed drunk lecturing me about how to run my business or deal with my clients.

Out in the front, Judy's boyfriend (let's be honest, drugged-up boyfriend) was cleaning the pavers. He was doing a pretty good job until Judy stumbled outside and started yelling his way, "The people who bought this house must be stinking rich if a little oil on the ground freaks them out! They should be proud to be working stiffs." Oh, boy, my blood pressure was rising at an alarming rate. "Judy," I screamed in desperation, "I'll pay you double if you can finish cleaning this place and get out of here in thirty minutes." I sure as heck didn't want those two around when my clients showed up.

Surprisingly, that did the trick. Judy and her boy-friend went into overdrive, and she and what's-his-name left about five minutes before my clients parked their new Mercedes in the driveway. The man got out and noticed the pavers were wet. He let out a grunt as he helped his wife up the steps toward the door.

My plan for the walk-through was to escort the buyers through the entire house before I showed them the living room. If everything else looked really good, maybe the missing patch of carpet wouldn't be such a big deal. I was praying to myself as we walked, and I was nervously chit-chatting like a gregarious parrot.

When I had first noticed the missing carpet, I was worried but not totally panicked. I figured my carpet guru (as a realtor, you accumulate repair gurus the way you accumulate yard signs!) could replace a piece that size with carpet from inside a closet and nobody would be the wiser. Of course, I would tell the buyers about the repair, but if it looked good, it probably wouldn't matter.

To my chagrin, the closets didn't have carpet; they had linoleum. Also, the upstairs carpet was not the same color as the living room. If the carpet had to be replaced,

I was sure the cost would come from my commission. My seller was a basket case, so I couldn't put the cost to her. She'd lost her husband and was in the throes of moving her family to another house in another town. I felt sorry for her, and I didn't think she could take any more stress. This was getting stressful enough for me.

It didn't help that the buyers had specifically mentioned how the living room and dining room carpet looked new. They were right. Like many families, the sellers had used the formal living room and dining room only for special occasions. The family room was where they had spent most of their time, so the carpeted living room saw little traffic.

From their comments, it sounded like the buyers especially liked the carpet and would want to keep it. Well, that beloved carpet ran from the living room through the dining room and up to the kitchen door, and because it was high-end carpet, replacing it could cost a bundle. It was stressing me out more and more just thinking about it. And the stress was all my own fault. A more experienced realtor would have known to ask if there was carpet under the piano. It looked like I was due to pay some more "tuition."

When we got to the living room, the husband and wife just stared at the place where the upright piano used to be. My heart dropped down into my stomach, my stomach jumped up into my throat, and I was sweating like a pig. (Side note: I don't know where that expression comes from. I have since owned a pig. Pigs don't sweat.) My clients just kept staring at the gaping hole in the carpet for what seemed like an hour (probably a few seconds). Then they looked at each other and over to me, and the husband said, "No big deal there. We're going to rip this out and put in Spanish tile anyway."

Relief swept over me like a tidal wave over the beach.

After answering a few more questions, I escorted my clients out to their car. There was only one more obstacle: the remnants of the giant oil stain on the driveway. The husband looked down and took notice of the wet driveway again. Before I could explain or apologize, he said gruffly, "I see you cleaned up that oil spill. Thanks for doing that." I guess he and his wife had driven by the house after Ellen moved out and already knew about the stain.

I drove home in an exhausted fog. Alan had returned from the beach and was in a wonderful mood. "How'd the walk-through go? Is it all done? Wow! What an easy deal. Listed and closed in only forty-five days, and you got both ends of it. Good for you, Paula."

Yes, I double-ended the deal and made a nice bit of money, but, I would *never* have called it easy. "Do we have any vodka?" I replied.

Real estate sales look easy, but the truth is that realtors earn every dime they make. As I got older and more experienced, I learned to avoid problems and prepare for the inevitable dirty houses and messy deals. I took additional real estate courses and learned to separate my issues from those of my clients. It definitely got easier as I got smarter and more experienced. But, for a long time, I really thought that real estate courses should include information on the benefits and appropriate use of vodka.

14

Our Christmas Tree

> **1973**

My father worked swing shift at the Richfield Oil Refinery as an electrician. Whenever he was home in the morning, he would read the newspapers aloud to us kids as we ate breakfast. He would read the headlines first. "Man Kills Child in Driveway." Dad would read every gruesome story he could find. His heart was in the right place, he was trying to warn us about things that were dangerous. He thought the stories would be safety lessons. It was his way of trying to keep us safe.

I remember one time he read how a girl was on the back of a tractor with her dad. Somehow, her long ponytail got caught up in the machine and she was scalped.

He'd read stories about car wrecks, kidnappings, kids falling down wells, kids drowning because they went swimming alone, and people getting fish hooks caught in their eyes. The warning was in the headline. "Man Smoking in Bed Burns Down House." On those mornings, I left for school thinking the world was a dangerous place.

Dad's heart was in the right place, like I said, but his head wasn't. He scared the bejeezus out of me, and I grew up afraid of doing all sorts of things. Maybe that's why I married an adventurous man. Alan was fearless; he'd try anything and he rarely saw the danger in his actions. Later Alan told me, "I married you because I thought you'd help control my impulses." They say, "Opposites attract." Obviously, they do.

On our first trip to Cozumel, Mexico, we wanted to take the kids fishing on the pier. We bought small fishing poles and tackle boxes with fish hooks and bobbers inside. The kids were little, both under eight years of age. When we went out on the pier, fear took over my senses. I started picturing Roger with a fish hook caught in his eye. I imagined him blind and screaming. I was turning into an emotional wreck. My heart wanted the kids to experience fishing, but my head was shouting, "It's too dangerous. Stop! We don't want to be a headline!"

I kept badgering Alan about the hooks, "Be careful. Watch out. Please, don't let the kids cast." I was sure the line would fly back and lodge the dreaded hook in one of their faces. My mind was churning and Alan could see panic in my eyes. Also, I was passing on my fear to the kids. Suddenly, he grabbed my face between his hands. "Paula, listen to me. There is no way in hell the kids can fish without hooks!"

I stood there in a daze. Of course, he was right. By recognizing my fear and acknowledging it, Alan helped me deal with it. I made a concerted effort to calm myself down and everything was fine. The kids fished, and no one lost an eye.

I remember Dr. Hoffman, our therapist, telling me once. "That's what good couples do: they help each other stay on the right path." He was right. You are blessed if you find someone in life who helps you confront the person you are so you can look at her and decide if that is the person you want to be. Dr. Hoffman was such a wise man.

Over time, as I experienced more things in life, I began to ignore some safety warnings. I started to head in the opposite direction. I began to think everything Dad had read about was dumb. When bad things didn't happen, I saw my dad's warnings as ridiculous and overblown. Seriously, what were the chances I'd be scalped while driving a tractor? I lived in Southern California, near the *beach*. In effect, reading those stories every morning made me less safe. Let me give you an example.

A couple of weeks after Christmas, it was time to take down the tree. The tree was dried out, despite my careful watering, and the floor was covered with pine needles. It was beginning to be a fire hazard. Alan and I agreed that it was time to take it down.

Our home was built around a center patio and, for the first time in our married life, we had a fireplace, which we had not used since Christmas day. Rather than dragging the big, dry, dirty, pine tree all through the house to the garage, I decided I would burn it in the fireplace. Now, I had heard warnings not to do that, but I wasn't planning to burn the whole tree at once. My plan was to cut and burn just one piece of the tree at a time. Obviously, I'd be careful.

I removed all the decorations and lights and put them away in the garage. Then I removed the tree from the stand and laid it on its side. I pulled the tree up to the edge of the fireplace. My plan was to put the top of the tree inside and cut it off with the yard clippers. Then I'd pull the rest of the tree back, light the first piece, and watch it burn.

That's not what happened. As soon as the tree top hit the already hot embers (which I had thought for sure were out), the tree lit up like a torch. Whoosh, the tree exploded. Flames and smoke filled the house. I could hear the tree crackling and burning as flames shot out the sides. It looked like a wildfire.

I screamed for the kids to run out into the backyard.

"Don't you mean out the front?" my son said.

"Yes! Yes! Run outside the front!" I grabbed the water hose in the center patio and started spraying the flaming tree with water. Thank God, the hose was close by. It saved our house and maybe even my life.

The neighbors called the fire department when they saw black smoke billowing from the garage. But by the time the giant red truck arrived, the fire I had started was out. "Didn't anyone ever tell you it was dangerous to burn your Christmas tree in the fireplace?" the fireman asked, as he helped me clean up the wet mess. "Of course," I said, "I'm just stupid." I really felt like a dunce.

Randy, our next-door neighbor, called over to Alan as he was getting out of his car from work. "Wait until you hear what Paula did today," Randy said playfully. "She almost burned down your house." I was the joke of the neighborhood for weeks. (And, if you can believe this, one "super-mom" neighbor reprimanded me for not calling her so that her son could meet a fireman. Yeah . . . first thing I should have done!)

One step through the door and Alan knew what Randy was talking about. The ceiling was black, the room smelled like soot, and our upholstered furniture was sopping wet.

"Tell me you didn't put the tree in the fireplace?" Alan asked.

"I swear, Alan. I thought the embers were out." Alan just shook his head in disbelief.

That was the first time I came close to being one of those headlines my dad liked to read. "Woman Burns House Down with Christmas Tree." My dad would have rolled over in his grave if he knew what I had done. God knows he tried to warn me about such things.

One thorn of experience is worth a whole wilderness of warning.

—James Russell Lowell

15

Bertha

I got a call from Quincy, our next-door neighbor, inviting us to a surprise birthday party for her husband, Randy. He was turning fifty and the theme of the party was "Western," in keeping with the art they collected. Their home was stunningly decorated with Western paintings from artists they had met through the years. "Of course," I answered, "we'll be there." I knew the party would be fun. Randy's brother, Robert, and his wife were handling the food and inviting all the guests. They didn't want anything to happen that might make Randy suspicious and spoil the surprise.

When the evening of the party arrived, we joined about fifty other guests and crowded into Randy and Quincy's home. All the cars that guests had driven were parked a block away.

"He has no idea what's coming," Randy's brother shared happily. "Okay, here he comes. Be quiet everyone." Randy walked in, and the room full of guests exploded, yelling, "Surprise!" Randy stood there speechless. He *really* was surprised.

The party was in full swing. People were drinking, eating, and telling stories. Every chair and couch was covered to capacity, and there were people sitting in a circle on the floor. The patio doors were open and people were wandering about outside as well.

When we had first arrived that night, we had been introduced to Bertha, a very large lady in a white cowgirl outfit with a very short skirt, western shirt, and sleeveless vest. To complete her costume, Bertha wore white boots and a matching cowgirl hat. At over three hundred pounds, the outfit seemed just a tad inappropriate for a lady her size. Bertha, we were told, was a friend of a friend from Arizona; probably a friend of one of the artists Randy often talked about and whose art he collected.

Bertha asked us and others standing nearby to please keep an eye out for the earring she had lost. "It's a silver boot, like this one," she said, pointing to the one ear still adorned with an earring.

We got some food and joined Bertha and a bunch of the other guests sitting in a circle on the carpeted living room floor. The food was great and the atmosphere was lively. Everybody seemed to be having a good time.

Suddenly, Bertha yelled, "There it is! There's my earring!" She screamed so loudly that all the guests looked in her direction. Then, Bertha started crawling slowly, on all fours, across the floor to the far side of the room.

"Oh, my God," I whispered to Alan. "Bertha is not wearing underpants under her skirt." I quickly followed this with a second whisper, "Holy mackerel, Bertha is wearing a thong." With her more than ample buttocks, the thong was barely visible under her cow skirt. Even worse, Bertha had pimples on her butt.

Everyone was watching Bertha as she crawled across the floor. Some people started laughing quietly and others just sat there stunned. Bertha was a spectacle that could not be ignored.

When she arrived at the spot where she said her earring was, Bertha bent down to get an even closer look at the floor. Her bare butt extended skyward like a small pimply mountain in the middle of the room. The kids watching from the stairwell squealed like piglets and fled screaming out of sight.

Then, with an unexpected confidence, Bertha lowered her bountiful bottom slowly toward the floor and stood up facing in Randy's direction. From a cassette boombox, stripper music started playing loudly, filling the room. With her hips shaking seductively to the music, Bertha approached the birthday boy and pinned him in his chair. Then she started stripping, beginning with her vest. By the time she started her lap dance, Bertha's bra was on the floor. The audience looked on in embarrassed laughter, now realizing that the earring crawl was part of the hired stripper's ploy.

I had seen strippers before, but I had never seen anyone like Bertha. Her size and shape were so much more fun than just watching some sexy little gal strutting around. She was a real pro. She wiggled and wriggled and flirted with Randy until I thought all of us would die of embarrassment. Bertha's striptease fluctuated between absolutely hilarious and ridiculously absurd. Randy loved it.

Bertha's breasts were enormous. They were shaped like pendulous melons dropping almost to her waist. Every few seconds, she'd heft one up, swing it around, and flop it on Randy's face. The poor guy absorbed the breast beating, as tears of laughter rolled down his cheeks. Then Bertha bent over and gave Randy a full view of her bulbous behind. Pulsating to the music, she gyrated her big butt back and forth. You have to admire a woman who has the confidence to do something like that with pimples on her butt. At that point, I was praying fervently that Big Bertha wouldn't remove her thong. And I can tell you, friend, that God does answer prayers.

"She's famous in Las Vegas," Robert yelled out proudly from across the room.

Randy's buddies had all chipped in and had Bertha flown in for the birthday celebration. Having her at the party was evidently quite a coup. "It's Big Bertha, Randy. It's Big Bertha from Vegas," one of the guys shouted over the music, to make sure Randy knew the famous stripper's name. "She's the best and biggest stripper on the Strip."

Bertha certainly was the biggest stripper I had ever seen, and from the reaction of the guys at the party, I guess she was the best too.

When the striptease was over, Bertha put on her clothes and went back for second helpings at the buffet. The fact that she could do that amazed me. I was still recovering from her act. But it was clearly no big deal for the best and biggest stripper on the Strip. Bertha was all business and totally comfortable with herself. It was . . . inspirational.

16

The Fat Farm

As it was for many Southern Californian wives, staying fit and trim was an obsession among the ladies in the Seal Beach Junior Women's Club. So when my best friend, Yvonne Ansdell, suggested we spend a week at a "fat farm" in Palm Springs, I was totally in. A week away from real estate sounded heavenly, even if it meant aerobic classes and diet food. Some of the other gals in the club were going, so I was sure it would be fun.

Yvonne Ansdell and I have been friends since kindergarten. She is beautiful, both inside and out. We have shared the ups and downs of living for seventy-plus years. Like I said before, even today, if we haven't seen each other for ages, the minute we start talking it's as if we have never been apart. We are soul mates. I feel honored to call her friend.

We arrived at the fat farm after lunch on a Friday. It was a famous place run by a lady considered a guru in the field. The attendant met us at the desk, and we were quickly handed a tall, cool glass of water with sliced cucumber floating inside (trust me, that's so fat farm). Then we were escorted to our rooms, which were simply appointed. Everything was white. The goal for the week was simplicity of living. I was beginning to feel like a monk. Or a nun, as in "You ain't eatin' nun of that."

After our initial weigh in, we attended an aerobics class, stretch workout, and some kind of special meditative yoga class, which put me quickly to sleep. Then, we went back to our rooms to rest and dress for dinner. I was already faltering. "I'd give anything for a glass of wine and some Fritos," I told Yvonne, half-heartedly, as we showered and dressed. "Be positive, Paula. We're lucky to be here," Yvonne said, "It's only a week." She was right, of course. We were blessed.

I knew from the brochure that our chef would be preparing a "healthy and delicious trio of natural treats" for dinner: salt free, sugar free, fat free. This was going to be one healthy bundle of fun.

First stop: "An Appetizer and Spritzer Mixer in the Garden Room." This affair was a meet and greet for all the victims, I mean guests, who were starting the week-long program. The spritzers were served in bowl-shaped crystal glasses and were a delicate combination of lime and water with "just a smidgen of imported paprika." I couldn't wait to get at those appetizers. I was starving.

The appetizers were thin slices of veggies with some kind of white dip loaded with fresh herbs. They would have been delicious, I'm sure, with just a "smidgen" of salt and pepper, which were not offered. But I was famished and quickly ate more than my share.

Our hostess gave a little talk, "The Delights of Detoxing." She explained, "The first three days here are all about detoxing. Detox smoothies, detox salads, and, yes, even detox stews. It's all about the healthy cleanse."

I looked at Yvonne. "How do they know we have stuff inside us that needs detoxing?"

It was a good thing that we slept like babies that night—no TV to clutter the mind—because we were dressed and ready to roll (oh man, I'd love a sweet roll) at 5:30 the next morning. We met the other gals at the coffee shack for coffee, decaf of course. I don't use sugar, but I do like cream. They had a white substance that they called "cream," but it never changed the color of the coffee no matter how much I used. I tried. Then, at 6:00 a.m. sharp, bolstered by water and lemon, we were off for a brisk three-mile hike in the dessert. I mean "desert," but my mind was really on food!

I have to exercise in the morning before my brain figures out what I'm doing.

—UNKNOWN

"Do you know which part of a cactus is edible?" I asked Yvonne as we marched on.

The hike was actually fun, and the surroundings were beautiful. Then it was back for a stretch class and yoga before lunch.

None of the classes they offered were mandatory. You could do as much or as little as you wanted each day. But Yvonne and I wanted to lose some weight and the place was expensive, so we took as many classes as our bodies could handle, which was way too many on day two.

At lunch, I chose the "cleansing cabbage creation." Every dish they offered had a clever name. And the "creation" was a pretty tasty salad. It had nuts, thin apple slices, and mounds of red and green cabbage. There was not much dressing, of course, but I didn't care. All that exercise had made me hungry, and I ate everything on my plate.

Appetizers and spritzers were offered each evening, followed by dinner and an informative speaker. Then, for those who had signed up in advance, there were massages and facials and other body treatments. I could hardly wait for my massage.

I really like massages, and since I was sore from all this exercise my body was not used to, I was looking forward to hearing my name called. When my turn finally came, I slipped out of my chair and followed the attendant into the quiet, dark room. Soft white sheeting was laying on the massage table and the room smelled like lilacs. It was really inviting.

I got naked quickly and lay down on the super-soft massage table and covered myself with the super-soft sheeting provided. Face up, I stared at the glistening twinkle lights draped around the room. Then, I heard a gentle knock on the door and I told the person to come on in.

I had asked for a masseuse but the person who entered my room was a masseur, a man. I told him that I had requested a woman, and he apologized, telling me that the masseuse had taken ill. Because he was an older gentleman, not some handsome jock, I felt pretty safe, and because I was sore from head to toe, I agreed to have him give me my massage.

Frank had been a masseur for almost twenty years. He explained that his expertise was in sports therapy. He asked me to turn over and rest my face in the donut-shaped pillow at the end of the table. In no time, I was convinced that God had delivered me just the right person for the job. He started at my feet with his powerful hands, and by the time he got to my calves, I was murmuring like a baby. "That hurts so good I can hardly stand it," I cooed to Frank.

Then it started. My stomach started to gurgle. Oh no, not now. My intestinal tract was detoxing in an uproar. That cleansing cabbage creation was creating a boatload of gas in my gut, and I was sure I was going to fart.

Frank couldn't hear my stomach gurgling over the sound of the music filling the room. Plus, he was old. But I could hear it and I got tense.

"Try to relax, Mrs. Thomas," Frank said kindly. "This is supposed to be relaxing. It shouldn't make you tense."

He was right. I was tense all over, trying to hold my body tight so that the gas would stay put. Over my thighs and onto my backside Frank's hands pressed on, firmly. "Mrs. Thomas, relax. Your buttocks are tight as a drum." It was a drum all right and Frank was about to play it.

When I could stand it no longer, I had to confess. "Frank, I had the cabbage cleansing creation for lunch."

"Say no more," he answered, and stepped out of the room. Just in time.

I don't know how I recovered. I was so embarrassed and red-faced when Frank re-entered the room. But he was terrific. "It happens all the time," he said kindly. "It happens all the time."

Our week at the fat farm eventually ended. We enjoyed "The Appetizer and Spritzer Farewell Mixer in the Garden

Room," and packed up our gear. It had been lots of fun. We all lost weight and, God knows, I was cleansed from top to bottom, literally.

As we were walking to our car, we invited some of the other gals to join us for burgers and fries at Carl's Jr. on the way out of town, but they declined. "Aren't you starving for some salt and fat?" we asked jokingly.

That's when they confessed their dirty little secret. Some of the ladies had *not* been sticking to the fat-farm protocols. They had been supplementing their natural, healthy, cleansing meals with "real" food and wine. Only a few monks ("nones"), like ourselves, had been sticking to the program.

"That's it: I'm having a chocolate chip malt too!" I said defiantly. And did.

So I guess it's true, "At the end of every diet, the path curves back to the trough (Mason Cooley)".

17

The Best Christmas I Ever Had

1975

When I was a little girl, I had lots of wonderful Christmases. I had Christmas mornings filled with the kind of wonder and excitement that only a child can experience. But this is not a story of a child's Christmas. This is a story of the best Christmas I ever had as an adult.

In order for you to understand the best Christmas I ever had, you must first hear about the worst Christmas I ever had. It was Christmas day 1965, and the first Christmas I celebrated as a married woman. Alan and I were in college and some of my sisters and their husbands or boyfriends were spending the day at my oldest sister and her husband's home. The smell of turkey and pine filled the air, and Christmas carols were playing in the background as we sat down to open our gifts.

Mom opened her gift first. Just like always, Dad had somehow gathered together enough money to buy Mom something truly special. Mom's gift was a bracelet with gold letters separated by pearls that spelled I LOVE YOU. Everyone *ooohed* and *aaahed* approvingly as Mom put on her bracelet and Dad beamed with pride.

Then came my oldest sister Cynthia's turn. Despite the limited budget of a growing family, Seth had purchased my sister the most beautiful beige lace nighty and robe set I had ever seen. It was such a romantic gift. They exchanged tender glances as the nightgown was carefully refolded and put away.

Sharon's gift was two crisply folded one-hundred-dollar bills placed in a card which read, "To the one I love," on the outside. That was more money than Alan and I made in three months working at the college library. Everyone in the room let out a squeal at such luxury.

Kay was the next sister to open her gifts. She was going with a couple of different guys at the time, if I remember right. One gave her a gold wristwatch and the other gave her a beautiful Geistex sweater. Geistex sweaters were very expensive and really "in" in 1965.

All of my sisters were so beautiful and I always felt inferior by comparison. It seemed to me that their gifts were befitting them. I dreaded the fact that I was to open my gifts next.

Before I tell you what I received, I have to give you some facts. Alan was raised to believe that Christmas was basically for little children, that gifts weren't terribly important to adults. In fact, sometime between October and December, Alan's mom would announce that she had purchased a "so-and-so," and that this item was her Christmas gift from Alan's dad. In other words, older members of their family usually exchanged permission to purchase something at a later date. Also, because Alan's siblings received lavish gifts during the year, another nice present was just not that big of a deal.

I came from a different background. As long as I could remember, I thought of Christmas as a time to splurge. Christmas was when you showed the ones you love that "price was no object." And it wasn't just the money; it was an attitude about Christmas. Christmastime was when you showed the other people in your life how much they meant to you. They were so important that you saved up all year to buy them "things they had always wanted," or presents that "you shouldn't have." Christmas was the time you made dreams come true.

As all the eyes in the room turned toward me, I felt a disaster in the making. "Oh, please God," I prayed to myself, "make the small package something sweet and personal, a necklace or a locket." As I opened my gifts, a lump formed in my throat. Alan had gotten me a ball point pen and a pair of heavy duty slippers. Tears welled up in my eyes. Wasn't I more important and more beautiful than a ball point pen and unisex slippers that could be worn by either a man or a woman? Was that all I meant to Alan?

I prayed for a diversion. Maybe the tree would catch on fire (I knew from experience how to make that happen) or a bomb would hit the garage. I felt so embarrassed that I wanted to die.

That particular Christmas taught me two things: One, never open my presents in front of my beautiful sisters, and two, never look forward to Christmas ever, ever again.

There were many differences in Alan's and my backgrounds, so it wasn't surprising that we ended up in marriage counseling years later. It happened to be Christmastime when we started therapy.

Dr. Hoffman started off the session by asking me what problems would arise during the holiday season. That was easy for me to answer: "Disappointment and depression." So Dr. Hoffman came up with this wonderfully simple idea; make Alan a shopping list.

"What?" I protested. "You mean that it still *counts* if the gift is requested?"

I believed what I had seen in the movies. Alan was somehow supposed to magically know the deepest desires of my heart. "You mean I could write him out a list and if he gave me an item on the list, it would show that he loved me, even if he hadn't thought of it himself? Amazing," I muttered to myself.

"You mean the longing looks as I passed the crystal department and the quiet glances toward the jewelry counter weren't enough? Are you telling me, Dr. Hoffman, that the man doesn't know what I want by magic?

"Okay!" I said defiantly, "I'll make the man a list."

I will never forget the serious way I approached my list writing. Poised with a hot cup of coffee and a sharp pencil, I proceeded. First, I thought, I should probably put down something he wants also. That way I am more likely to get the gift. I honestly felt *that* unworthy inside. So a color TV headed up the list, followed by the microwave oven. He'd benefit from that as well. Then I became more daring and I asked for a crystal decanter. No, what the heck, I reckoned, I wrote down, "a Fostoria crystal decanter."

If this was a test for Alan, I was going to make it a good one. I threw myself into the task with reckless abandon and filled two full pages. I wanted to make sure that there could be no excuse that the stores "were out of it."

When Dr. Hoffman asked for my list, he questioned me to make sure that the items listed were my most secret desires. I concurred that if I received any one of these items on the list, I would be happy. I thought to myself as I drove home, good Lord, I'd be happy for life.

On December 23rd, I opened the front door to a TV service man. He said, "Where do you want the TV, lady?" My heart jumped as I screamed to the children, "Kids, Daddy bought us a color TV."

Then, on Christmas Eve, a microwave oven arrived. My heart was pounding as I opened the package. It was just like I'd seen in the movies, wrapped in gold with a big red bow. "Thank you, Dr. Hoffman." I shouted into the air. He was right. It did feel just as good if you spoke up and let the other person know what you wanted.

On Christmas morning, I was totally content. I eyed the color TV in the living room. It was just the model I wanted. As I happily heated rolls in my new microwave oven, I thought of different ways to tell my sisters about the gifts.

As I wandered back into the living room with a tray of hot chocolate for the kids, I heard these startling, amazing words: "Mom, there are some other presents for you under the tree."

I thought these were probably some sweet handmade treasures made by our children, Roger and Natalie. But when I sat down, I saw a gift clearly from Bullocks, a high-end department store in Long Beach. I squealed as I opened the Fostoria decanter. My neighbors told me later they could hear me screaming. Next I opened an incredibly beautiful pink nighty with matching robe and "super feminine" slippers from Robinsons (no man would wear *those* slippers.) What would my sisters say when they saw the crystal sugar and creamer to match the decanter, a real leather handbag with a matching wallet and key holder, and a gold locket with "Love, Alan" engraved on the back? To top it all off, there was a gold watch in a black velvet case. My God, Alan had purchased everything on my list and he'd thrown in the watch for good measure.

I don't remember what Santa brought the children that year, I'm sorry to say. I was too busy screaming and jumping up and down and crying myself. When I finally calmed down, I looked over at Alan and saw he had tears in his eyes. He was in shock and his face held an expression of sheer amazement.

He choked up as he said, "I never knew it would make you so happy or I would have done it years before."

I realized several things that Christmas. I realized that I was a worthy person, but that I had to declare that fact myself before others would. Whether I received the gifts or not was not important. What was important was that I had written the list. The list was my declaration of worthiness. Alan's purchasing the gifts was a confirmation of that declaration. I learned from that declaration that I can't depend on others to affirm my worthiness. I have to do that myself, and I do it a lot now. In fact, this IBM Selectric typewriter was a gift to myself so that I might write this story.

Alan learned a few things that Christmas too. He learned how much fun it is to find something special for the ones you love. He now looks for things I want and he listens carefully to find out what special secrets are in my heart. Best of all, he learned that he could help me most by encouraging me to fulfill my own dreams for myself. And he does that.

I think back on that Christmas occasionally and I believe Natalie summed it up best when she said that morning, "This is so much fun. Let's do it again next year."

18

Dr. Hoffman

1975

Surprisingly, I am not sure when or how I first met Dr. Hoffman, the wonderful psychologist who saved my marriage and improved my life so dramatically. I suspect we were introduced during a holiday gathering at my sister's home, because Cynthia babysat Dr. Hoffman's daughter. However it happened, meeting Dr. Hoffman and attending therapy was one of the best decisions my husband and I ever made.

Dr. Hoffman's office was in North Long Beach, about forty minutes from our home in Seal Beach. Unassuming and sparsely decorated, his office was on the second floor of a modern building and was furnished with Swedish modern furniture and high-end paintings he collected from local artists. Dr. Hoffman and his wife were collectors, they frequented the local art scene and eventually opened a small art gallery.

Because he was easy to talk to and incredibly smart, out first visit to Dr. Hoffman went so well that in no time

Alan and I scheduled ourselves for weekly visits. These visits continued, off and on, for over ten years. (Actor and director Woody Allen is the only person I have ever heard of who went to therapy longer than we did; not sure exactly how I feel about this.) Whenever I got impatient about how long the process was taking, Dr. Hoffman would say, reassuringly, "It took years to get screwed up, and it's going to take years to undo the mess."

"It took years to get screwed up, and it's going to take years to undo the mess."

—DR. HOFFMAN

I liked Dr. Hoffman's no-nonsense and up-front approach to therapy. He was kind, patient, and brutally honest. His comments often made me laugh and frequently made me cry. Our weekly sessions were not always pleasant, and I threatened to flee from his office on many occasions. But, because I could see we were making progress, I continued the grind. Anyone lucky enough to have really engaged in therapy will tell you that it's hard work and it's not for sissies; it takes grit and perseverance to clear the muck out of your mind. Old habits are hard to break and self-examination is uncomfortable. Nobody likes to admit his known or suspected shortcomings to another person. Starting and sticking to therapy is something I am proud of.

Of course, like many spouses who begin therapy, I thought I was perfectly fine and it was my husband who needed the help.

Wrong.

"I hate to tell you, Paula, but healthy people don't marry sick people. Sick people marry sick people." That zinger of a comment really hit me hard. I was happy as a clam when I thought our therapy sessions were going to be all about "fixing" my husband. I wasn't quite as excited when I discovered I had my own stuff to work on.

"Are you saying Alan's *not* the sick one in this relationship?" (I kind of emphasized the "not" here.)

Dr. Hoffman was quick to answer, "I'm saying you both have issues."

Crap.

It took years of weekly sessions to learn how to be the person I wanted to be, instead of the person I had become. And it took a long while to realize that changing myself was the only way to change my marriage. Dr. Hoffman gave me new life skills that, when applied, made my life more manageable. As I began to react differently to life's situations, my life began to change for the better and I began to enjoy life more fully. As my husband also began to change, our marriage greatly improved.

Prior to therapy, I had feared our family might split apart and become just another all-too-common divorce statistic. I could just imagine how the demise of our family unit would be noted in the newspaper: "Popular Local Realtor Divorces; Family Home Already Listed." Thanks to Dr. Hoffman, years of hard work, and pure luck, that didn't happen. (Alan and I have sold some houses, but we've always moved together.)

Dr. Hoffman was also a snappy dresser. He wore comfortable, dark, wide-cuffed trousers, long-sleeved pastel shirts, and brightly colored ties. He looked Italian and wore his long black hair slicked straight back off his forehead, held in place with an oily paste our son liked to make fun of (Roger also visited our mental mechanic on occasion).

In a famous prophetic aside, Roger once said, "Dr. Hoffman had better not get near an open flame with all that oil in his hair, or he's likely to have a grease fire."

Turns out, while on a ski trip with his family, Dr. Hoffman's car battery went dead and he had to attach jumper cables to another vehicle. Unfortunately, the spark from the jump caught his hair and clothes on fire. We saw the headline, "Noted Psychologist Burned When Hair and Clothes Catch Fire."

Roger said, "I told you so."

I'm very happy to report that the good doctor fully recovered and returned to his practice to bless others in our society with his knowledge and expertise. Thanks for everything, Dr. Hoffman, wherever you are.

19

The Nash Rambler

1977

The only car we owned after college was the vintage Volkswagen Alan's parents generously had given us. It wasn't particularly pretty, but it was cheap to drive and it was paid for. The car had just one drawback: The heater was stuck in the "on" position and, even though we stuffed the heater vents with rags, the inside of the car stayed miserably hot. Poor Alan had to drive that car to work in Los Angeles every day for two years until our budget allowed us to purchase another.

Our best friends, Allan and Yvonne Ansdell, lived in the house behind us in Seal Beach, California. They owned their own business and were doing a lot better financially than we were. They owned a Nash Rambler, "America's first compact car." It wasn't new, but it wasn't old enough to be called vintage either. In any event, it was decidedly better looking than our heat-producing old Volkswagen. But the Rambler was imperfect too. The Ansdells' Nash

Rambler wouldn't go in reverse. At all. "I've mastered driving it," Yvonne's husband told us proudly. "I just don't get myself in a situation where I need to back up."

One Valentine's Day, the four of us made plans to enjoy a double-date dinner in Beverly Hills at Lawry's Prime Rib. The place was very popular, and we had to make reservations weeks in advance. It was an extravagant

evening for the four of us. We got one babysitter to share for our four combined kids, and I think I even borrowed a dress to wear from my sister Kay.

Obviously, we'd take the Nash Rambler.

Lawry's Prime Rib was a splashy joint in the heart of Beverly Hills. We could see the restaurant's neon sign flashing as we passed the trendy shops on La Cienega Boulevard.

"This is going to be so much fun," Yvonne said excitedly.

"And, delicious," I chimed in.

Arriving at the front of the restaurant, we followed the long procession of cars up the wide, winding drive to the entrance. The Rambler was behind a sleek black Jaguar, which was following a big white Cadillac DeVille and some other very exotic car. Alan thought it was an Aston Martin, the British touring car associated with the fictional character James Bond.

The Ansdells owned a 1968 Nash Rambler station wagon that they had won on *Let's Make a Deal*, when the Seal Beach Junior Women's Club (of which were members) went en masse for a filming of the TV show in Hollywood. Yvonne told me, "I went right down to the dealership in Long Beach after the show aired and told the owner I wanted the same color as the car on the show. He drove one up, handed me the keys, and told me to make sure I got gas before I drove home. Crazy!"

"Your Nash Rambler fits in perfectly," I joked and everybody chuckled.

We inched along the driveway, stopping periodically so that people in front of us could get out of their cars. Finally, it was our turn and Allan Ansdell pulled the car forward and set the brake. Dressed in black slacks, crisp white shirts, and black bow ties, the handsome valets greeted us quickly and efficiently as they opened the car doors and helped Yvonne and me out of the Rambler. Yvonne's husband handed the valet the keys, and off we went into the "One and Only Lawry's Prime Rib."

The place was packed on a Saturday night, with lots of elegantly attired couples milling about, and a few movie star wannabees sitting at the bar and hoping to be discovered. Lawry's describes itself as a "legendary dining experience" and, from the looks of things and the smells wafting from the kitchen, I felt sure this was going to be a memorable Valentine's evening.

The restaurant was large and lively. People were laughing and drinking, and above it all, the sound of Frank Sinatra's singing could be heard. A loudspeaker would occasionally break in over the music and call the name of the next party to be seated. Eventually that loudspeaker crackled and we heard, "Will the owners of the Nash Rambler, *please* come out to the valet?"

Ansdell looked at all of us and said, "Quick! Mingle." With that, we four headed into a crowd of "beautiful people" standing near the bar. Our goal was to hide, not to be discovered by a movie producer. We ordered wine and mingled nervously until our reservation was called. Just as we headed for our table, the dreaded loudspeaker interrupted again.

"Will the owners of the Nash Rambler, *please* return *immediately* to the valet?" All we could do was laugh.

After we were seated in the main dining room, a waiter approached our table. "I see you have refreshments. Does anyone need a refill?" he asked.

As the music played softly above us, the waiter handed us menus and we attempted to settle in. Occasionally the music was interrupted with an announcement that some-one's table was ready and, yes, the dreaded repeat pleading of, "Will the owners of the Nash Rambler please come out *immediately* to the valet?" Each time the announce-ment came over the speaker, we four would laugh. And with each announcement, the voice over the loudspeaker became noticeably more irritated.

"There's no way I'm going out there," Ansdell said defiantly. "They can just deal with it."

As we were making our entrée choices, the determined valet even peeked inside the restaurant and looked franti-cally from left to right, clearly on the hunt. Yvonne saw him as he entered and said, "Quick, hide," and lifted her menu up high enough to cover her face. We all followed suit and broke into laughter at the absurdity of the situ-ation. I peeked around the side of my menu and saw the valet talking to the head waiter. After a minute or so, he threw up his hands in disgust and was gone, followed by more laughter from the four diners who appeared to be intensely scrutinizing their menus. Thankfully, as the eve-ning progressed, the attempts to locate us diminished and we began to relax.

"I feel like a fugitive," I said laughing. "Every time the speaker crackles, I flinch."

...

After our legendary dining experience, we exited the restaurant, smiling. Stuffed, relaxed, and happy, we had finally forgotten all about the car. Suddenly, we were face to face with our nemesis, the irritated valet.

"Why didn't you come out? I've been calling you guys all night!" he said in obvious frustration. "I've been on that loudspeaker a dozen times. Why didn't you come out?"

Our friends for over fifty years, Yvonne and Allan Ansdell.

"What's the problem?" Ansdell asked, with an innocent look.

"Something is wrong with your car," the valet answered. "It won't go into reverse. It took four of my guys to push it out of the way. You backed up the restaurant entrance for over an hour. Why didn't you come out?" he demanded again.

The valet was really, really mad, so Allan Ansdell had to lie. "Gee, I'm really sorry about that. It was so loud inside, I guess we didn't hear you."

The Nash Rambler had been pushed by the valet staff into a parking spot facing a big red sports car. One of the valets was just beginning to back that sports car out of its stall. Ansdell grabbed the keys from the valet and thanked him quickly.

"Hurry, you guys. Jump in the car! We've got to pull forward as that sports car is leaving!"

If we didn't pull forward, we'd have to back up, and we all knew that was *not* going to happen. "It's our only hope to get out of this place without going in reverse," Yvonne's husband pleaded.

Like little kids playing "ding, dong, ditch 'em," we ran to the car, laughing hysterically. With lightning reflexes, Ansdell jumped into the driver's seat, started the car with a sure turn of the key, and pulled the Rambler into the empty stall before another auto could park there. Then he turned right and drove madly between two giant prickly bushes that were part of a hedge ringing the parking lot. We could hear the bushes scrape both sides of the car as we flew over the curb and turned quickly onto a side street behind Lawry's. Someone started honking and we heard a car's brakes squeal as the Nash Rambler rambled on home.

It is one of the blessings of old friends that you can afford to be stupid with them.

—Ralph Waldo Emerson

How embarrassing could it get?

As I look back on that evening, I realize that it wasn't the One and Only prime rib house that made the evening special. It wasn't dressing up or being among the beautiful people that made it fun. It was being with our friends in a ridiculous situation.

Like Ralph Waldo Emerson said, "It is one of the blessings of old friends that you can afford to be stupid with them."

20

Catalina Adventures

1955–1980

My husband grew up on Santa Catalina Island, a small and beautiful island about twenty-six miles off the coast of Southern California. Avalon is the only incorporated city on the island and is a charming and delightful spot. There are gorgeous, expensive houses nestled in the hills that circle the city, and small cozy cottages on the flats. Avalon's main street runs along the water, an incredible, pristine bay with crystal blue water and bobbing yachts. Catalina Island was once owned by the Wrigley family, of chewing gum fame. William Wrigley bought the Island in 1919 and invested millions in needed infrastructure and attractions for the island, including the construction of the Catalina Casino, which remains the crown jewel of the beloved city of Avalon.

My husband grew up wild and free on Catalina Island. He had an adventurous spirit that, despite their best efforts, his adoptive parents just couldn't control. When I met Alan in Avalon on my eighteenth birthday, he was wearing red

Avalon Harbor on Catalina Island, with the iconic Catalina Casino in the background.

long-john underwear and drinking outside a bar, despite the fact he was under age at the time. Later, we met again in college, and have now been married for over fifty years.

Alan and I worked every summer vacation in Avalon during our college years. Alan drove a cab and I waitressed. Our apartment was a small room on the street level of his parents' lovely hillside home. Even though we worked very hard, we were newlyweds and it was fun. We saved all our wages and tips and at the end of the summer had enough money to pay our rent, college fees, and other expenses for the rest of the year. Avalon will always have a special spot in our hearts.

Later in life, we bought a fast-running Scarab boat and a mooring in Avalon Bay. We'd go back and forth each weekend to Catalina on our boat. It filled Alan's need for adventure and our family's need for fun. Because I get seasick, sleeping on the boat was impossible, even though the Scarab had a small cabin below. Staying in hotels on the weekend was getting more and more expensive each year. We finally worked out that it would be more cost effective to rent one of the little cottages on the flats year-round.

Golf carts are the primary mode of transportation in Avalon. Here is our golf cart decked out for the annual Fourth of July parade. The kids carried signs that read, "Change the name from Catalina to Dogalina." (Get it?) We came in first place for most original. Our grandson Thomas and I with the inspirations for our theme, Lucky and Shadow.

Avalon is a dinky town. When we were young, only about 1,500 people were year-round residents. Everybody knows everybody . . . and everybody's business. Many of the locals have families that go back for generations, and many folks have never moved back to the mainland. In the summer, tourists will flock to Avalon and it swells into the tens of thousands. But, even today, very few make Avalon their year-round home.

One permanent resident was Lois Wellcamp, the best known and oldest realtor in Avalon. Alan suggested I call her and see what she had for rent. He knew Lois would know every cottage on the flats, who was living there, for how long, and what they were paying for rent.

He added cautiously, "Don't give Lois my name."

"Why not?" I asked.

"Because she remembers the shenanigans I pulled. I have a horrible reputation in Avalon. She would *never* rent to me. Trust me on this. Don't give her my name."

Alan was right about the realtor's being savvy. Lois knew immediately that there was a cottage on the flats that would fit our needs to a tee. It even turned out Alan knew the owner of the cottage because they had been classmates in school. Like I said, Avalon is a very small town.

Anyhow, we agreed to meet Lois, and she showed us through the rental. Alan stayed out of sight as much as possible and avoided making eye contact with Lois. We agreed on the terms, I cut her a check, and we signed the lease agreement. Lois insisted on taking us out to the Buffalo Nickle Restaurant in her golf cart, which is how everyone in town got around, for a Buffalo Burger to celebrate the deal. That's the kind of place Avalon is. I got in the front of the golf cart with Lois. Alan sat on the back bench, facing the rear. Lois started asking questions as she drove through town. Stuff like: "How old are your kids? What kind of boat do you have? How long have you been coming to Avalon?" As we putted along I could hear people call out to Alan from the narrow streets.

"Hey, Alan. How's it going?" yelled a fella who also knew Lois and called out her name.

"Can you play golf later?" Jose yelled from the side of the pier.

"Hi, Paula. Hi, Alan. How long you going to be in town?"

Lois began to realize we weren't newcomers to Avalon. She asked, "How come you know so many people?"

I casually answered, "Alan grew up here." Oops.

With that, Lois Wellcamp slammed on her brakes, turned around and looked Alan squarely in the eyes. "Wait just a doggone minute here. Are you *the* Alan Thomas? Are you Phyllis and Tommie's son?"

"Yep, that's me," Alan answered mischievously.

Lois turned back and continued driving to the Buffalo. "Well, you're lucky you sent this nice little lady in to meet me. I would have *never* rented to you in a million years."

Over lunch, Lois told us how worried Alan's mom, Phyllis, used to be about him as a kid. The gals played bridge together weekly, and I guess Alan was often the topic of conversation. Lois was amazed he had turned out all right. "I thought for sure you'd go to jail," she offered honestly. "I can't believe you graduated from college and got your master's degree."

I was beginning to realize that the stories Alan had told me about his youthful antics weren't made up. Another time, I learned further details of Alan's less-than-sterling reputation as we stood in line to buy candy at the show. The theater is inside the beautiful eighty-seven-year-old Catalina Casino. It is Avalon's Art Deco icon and the first thing you notice when you come into town. Anyhow, Alan and I were waiting our turn at the counter, trying to decide what to buy. All of a sudden, a large grey-haired lady reached across the counter and grabbed my husband by the ear.

"Darn you, Alan Thomas. I remember you always sneaking in the show," Sally Clemmons said, as she dragged Alan down the counter, bumping him into other moviegoers as she hauled him toward the door. "You never paid for a ticket, and your dad was the projectionist! You were a terrible little bugger," Sally went on rather loudly.

I began to laugh and Alan started to turn bright red. Alan told me that he always had the twenty-five cents for the movie! That wasn't the point. He loved the challenge of sneaking in. He'd knock on emergency exits until some kid would open up the emergency door. Then he'd sneak in and find himself a seat. The theater was enormous, but with so few full-time city residents, the place was almost empty and Sally knew every kid inside. When Alan exited through the main lobby after the movie ended, Sally would spot him and knew he had snuck in . . . again. It was a game Alan loved and Sally hated.

"You made my life a living hell," Sally screamed at Alan, still holding onto his ear.

By way of another example of the long island memory of Alan's childhood antics, our son, Roger, was up on the gas dock waiting his turn to fill up the boat. The gas dock is about ten to fifteen feet off the water, depending on the tide. Roger had taken the Scarab to the island with his

We have a long history with Catalina Island. Besides my husband growing up in Avalon, we met there on my 18th birthday and spent our college summers working on the island. Alan drove cab and I was a waitress at the Surf Restaurant on Crescent Street. Our son, Roger, married his lovely wife Teri, at the Catalina Island Country Club and, years after renting that first little cottage on the flats, we built our own little cottage in the same vicinity. Everybody in the family loved Avalon and visited quite often. Here we are on the back of Jim and Kathy Laurin's boat, "Seas the Day," enjoying a swim and barbeque in Avalon Bay.

friends, and he was standing and chatting with some girls who were in the boat next in line for gas. Suddenly, a guy my husband's age ran up to Roger and pushed him off the gas dock and into the water.

To a *very* surprised Roger, he shouted, "Tell your Dad that's for pushing me off the pier when we were kids." The fellow laughed at Roger's startled expression. "Your dad will know who it is." When Roger later told us this story, Alan remembered instantly; that fellow was Tim Evans and Alan laughingly confessed to the watery deed that Roger paid for.

In the old days, Avalon was famous for Buccaneer Ball, a raucous affair held annually over a long summer weekend. Thousands would flock to Avalon for the event. The harbor would fill with yachts, and the Catalina Island Steamer would pull in and out of the bay all day long, packed with incoming tourists. There were movie stars, music, drinking, and dancing. There were games for the kids and a marlin fishing derby for dads. Everyone in town dressed up like pirates, and there was even a parade. It brought in huge revenue for the shop owners, the hotels, and the city generally. But there were also bar fights and lots of rabble-rousing. Eventually, despite the income it produced, Buccaneer Ball got too wild and out of control, and it had to be cancelled.

The highlight for the kids during Buccaneer Ball was the treasure hunt. The city fathers would wait until the wee hours of the morning, when the whole town was asleep, and hide little golden treasure boxes in the sand on one of the beaches that flanked each side of the pier. Each little box contained a coin with the number of a corresponding prize. Treasure boxes were highly coveted because the city gave away fabulous prizes. You could win an expensive rod and reel, some scuba diving equipment, tickets for tours, free restaurant meals, and even clothing. On Saturday, the day of the treasure hunt, hundreds of kids would line up along the beaches, waiting for the bell that signaled the hunt was on.

Like all of the kids, Alan and his best buddy, Rod Wilcox, wanted to find those golden boxes. They hatched a plan to make it happen. On the eve of the hunt, just after dark, while the town was still bustling with activity, Alan and Rod went down to the beach and snuck under the pier between the two beaches. They used shovels and dug a giant hole to hide in at the base of the pier, up close to the breakwater wall. It took them hours. They were wet and tired when they finished. Of course, it was also exciting, scary, and fun. Late in the night, as the tide began to recede, the men in charge of the hunt appeared on the beach. They looked up and down the coastline, to make sure the beach was empty.

"We could hear the men talking, then someone yelled, 'Make sure you look under the pier.'" But Alan and his buddy were well hidden. Covered with a dark blanket and wet sand, like pirates of old, they hid.

"We held our breath and didn't move a muscle as one of the guys looked around near where we were hiding."

At last, the boys heard, "All clear," and the men started burying the treasure chests on one side of the beach.

Alan and Rod watched, careful not to be seen or heard, as the coveted treasure chests were buried. All in all, the men buried about fifty little treasure chests. The two boys could see where the chests were buried by the mounds of disturbed sand left behind.

"We were so excited. Our hearts were pounding so fast we could hardly stand it."

As soon as the men left, Alan and Rod snuck onto the beach and dug up about half of the treasure chests. They threw them into a pillow case and ran like marauding buccaneers through the deserted streets toward home. The tide came back in and covered the remaining mounds of sand, as well as the holes the boys had dug. No one was the wiser. No one knew what the local pesky pirates had done. At noon on Saturday morning, the town began to fill with excited children and anxious parents. Alan and Rod returned and sat on the low wall that separates the shops from the beach. They wanted to see who found the remaining treasure chests.

Someone asked, "Aren't you boys going to look for treasure?"

"Ah, that's for little kids," they replied.

That night was the Buccaneer Ball at the Catalina Casino, and this was when the kids would exchange the found coins for the actual prizes they had won. As coin numbers were announced, Alan and Rod went forward to redeem the prizes. One number after another, they walked up to the stage, and collected prize after prize. It soon became obvious that Rod and Alan had "found" more booty, by far, than any of the other little pirates in town.

The local townsfolk were furious. "I don't know how you did it, Alan," yelled one father, "but I know darn well you and Rod cheated!"

The boys tried to look innocent, but with more prizes than they could carry, everybody knew. Rod and Alan actually stole the treasure chests two years in a row. Alan's reputation as a hooligan was already growing. The theft of the treasure chests added more fuel to the fire.

There are few places on earth like Avalon. Every school day, at lunch, Alan rode his bike to town with his buddies and headed for the pier. Tourists arriving on the noon steamer would throw coins into the water. Alan and his friends would dive for the coins until they had enough money for lunch. In those days, it was just thirty-eight cents. Then they would buy a hamburger and malt at the Busy Bee on the pier. They could do all that and still be back on campus before the end-of-lunch bell rang.

"Didn't you shower off? Weren't you all salty?" I asked, years later, like a typical mother.

"Sure. But it wasn't a problem. We had gym class right after lunch," he explained.

The older Alan got, the more his rambunctious reputation grew. One time he shaved a guy's eyebrows off while the guy was passed out from drinking. Another time, when he was playing golf, he put a kingsnake, which looks a *lot* like a rattlesnake, in the golf bag of his buddy, Ronnie Youngkers. He knew the guy would reach into the ball pocket soon, because Ronnie had just hit his ball out of bounds. When Ronnie felt that snake and saw its head, he thought it was a rattler. He knew immediately whom to blame and chased Alan all the way home with his putter flailing in the air.

Alan's parents were always working and left Alan and his little brother unsupervised to run free. Because Alan was such a wild kid, he took chances that often put him in physical danger. One time he went camping with his younger brother on the back side of the island for a week.

Alan was eleven and his brother, Kent, was ten. Without adult supervision and guidance, they cooked on the beach. Not knowing any better, Alan put sealed cans of beans in the hot fire. Soon enough, the cans exploded and scalding beans went in every direction, leaving little burns on their bare skin. If that wasn't bad enough, after days playing in the hot sun, Alan got such severe sunstroke that his face swelled unrecognizably. The boys didn't have adequate fresh water with them camping, and he could have died.

Another time, Alan and his friend, Tay Taylor, decided to bridle up a couple of the stable horses that were put out to pasture when summer ended and the horseback riding stable had closed. Like cowboys they had seen in the movies, they mounted the horses bareback and prepared to hunt game. When Alan saw a big goat feeding in the nearby brush, he shot his .22 rifle right next to the horse's ear. The horse bolted, terrified by the frightening sound, and fled into the fig orchards, throwing Alan off and breaking his arm.

"What the hell are you doing? Are you nuts?" Tay yelled at Alan. "You're supposed to get off the horse before you shoot."

Alan had figured it was okay because he had seen the Lone Ranger do it all the time. Two summers in a row the boys saddled up the horses, and Alan spent two summers in a row with a broken arm. Another time, Alan and his younger brother took their fourteen-foot dinghy with a five-horsepower Evinrude motor to San Clemente Island, thirty-three miles west of Santa Catalina Island. They were going lobster fishing. On the way back, the clouds got dark and the weather changed. The ocean got rough and the swells were huge. Each time the small boat went

Alan's graduation photo. "I was such a rotten kid. I'm sure the teachers were happy to see me go!"

from the crest into the bottom of a wave, the pair lost sight of Catalina Island. It was getting dark, and the tiny boat started taking on water. Alan was bailing water as fast as he could. They didn't have life jackets and should have never been out in that weather.

Alan said later, "I never went out in that boat again without life jackets." It scared the boys to death.

Diving from the boat was fun for Alan, but it was not without its problems. Alan lost hearing in one ear from diving too deeply, and he suffered excruciating earaches growing up.

"I could have drowned numerous times by swimming under the Catalina steamer from one side to another."

His mom told me, "I tried to stop him, but there was nothing I could do."

Despite it all, Alan was popular in school. In fact, he was voted the student body president. The principal of Avalon High School was notoriously tardy for Friday afternoon assemblies. He'd make the kids wait fifteen minutes or more. They couldn't leave for the weekend until the assembly was over. Alan thought it was rude and didn't like it one bit. Plus, he didn't respect the principal generally. So, one Friday, with his overblown authority as student body president, and the principal's being late once again, Alan dismissed all the kids.

"If you can get out of here before Mr. Ellis arrives, you're dismissed." The room emptied in a flash.

When Mr. Ellis finally showed up and found the auditorium empty, he knew immediately that Alan was the culprit, and Mr. Ellis was furious. But, Mr. Ellis was never late for assembly again. Hmmm.

Another one of Alan's most memorable adventures had to do with his car. Alan's mom gave him her 1949 Studebaker. It was the kind of car with a pointed nose on the front and on the back. The Studebaker was old but it was in perfect condition. Alan's mother was a perfectionist, which meant that the car didn't have a spot on it inside or out. When Phyllis passed the Studebaker on to him, she made Alan promise to roll the windows up each night.

"The salt air is hard on car interiors. There is always a lot of moisture in the air, so I'll give you the car under one condition: you must promise to roll the windows up at night."

Alan promised he would do as she asked. "I promise I will never leave the windows down at night. I promise to roll them up." With that, Alan became the proud owner of a 1949 Studebaker.

Two things are funny about this car. First, Avalon has only one gas station in town, and, as I said earlier, the town is dinky. So, the guy who pumps gas knows everyone who has a car and every car in town. Alan had the money for gas, but he liked the challenge of stealing gas out of the station after the attendant had gone home. The city maintenance trucks would park in front of the gas station each night, and it was easy to sneak behind the trucks and siphon gas into a container without being seen. It was the thrill of sneaking around that Alan enjoyed.

Alan owned the Studebaker for over two years and, on one occasion, had to actually purchase gas while his dad was in the car. When he drove into the station, the guy said, "How long have you been driving this car, Alan? I've never filled up your tank before."

He couldn't say he'd just gotten it, because his dad was sitting right next to him. Alan had to say, "Two or three years."

"Well, how come I've never seen you before?" Alan's dad stared at Alan, waiting for the answer.

"You must have been off work the day I came in," Alan said half-heartedly.

The gas attendant started shaking his head, not believing a word of it, as he went about checking the oil. Alan's dad knew what had happened, but, like he did so often, Alan's dad never said a word. No wonder Lois Wellcamp thought Alan might one day go to jail.

The second funny thing about the Studebaker was this: Alan got a harebrained idea one day and decided what he really needed in Avalon was a convertible. He and his buddies took the old Studebaker to school and used a blowtorch to cut off the top when the shop teacher was absent. When he got home that night, his mom asked, as she did each evening, "Did you roll up the windows, like you promised?"

Unlike the 1949 Studebaker in this photo, the car Alan received from his mother was spotlessly clean inside and out. "The old Studebaker was funny looking because it had a pointed nose on the front and a similar design on the back. People couldn't tell if I was coming or going."

"Yes, I did Mom. Yes, I did."

When Alan's mom went to check, there sat the old Studebaker with all the windows rolled up . . . and the top gone. Alan was out of control.

Because of his bad reputation, Alan refused to go to his high school reunions. He was embarrassed, he told me, about all the horrible things he had done. One day, one of his classmates cornered him on the pier and asked why he had, *once again*, missed the reunion. Alan was honest and told the guy he felt like an idiot for all the stupid stunts he had pulled.

"Don't be embarrassed, Alan," his friend told him. "All the guys envied your life. You did all the stuff we wanted to do but never had the nerve to do. You were our idol."

Catalina Island was the perfect place for a kid who was full of adventure and out of control. The police were forgiving and there were hills to climb, caves to explore, and fish to catch. In another environment, Alan's life might not have been so wonderful. He was a free spirit and Avalon let his spirit fly. I just thank God he lived to tell about it.

Alan had so many close calls when he was a kid that it's not hard to imagine his life ending up as a newspaper headline, "Catalina Youth with Heat Stroke Falls Off Stolen Horse, Drowns."

21

Estero Beach, Mexico

> **1977**

One Easter vacation we decided to rent a big motorhome and take a vacation with the Fees family to Mexico. In those days, Mexico was a safe destination. We rented a thirty-one-foot Winnebago for the trip. It had two bedrooms, a full-size kitchen, and plenty of bunk space for the kids. Bob and Donna had a boy and girl about the same ages as our children, Roger and Natalie, and they also had two preteen sons, Bobby Jr. and Jeff. Our goal was to find a beachside resort in Ensenada, Mexico. Estero Beach was a place the kids could fish at night, and we could swim and relax during the day. Everyone was excited about the trip.

None of us knew much about motorhomes, so it wasn't a total surprise that we emptied the refrigerator all over the floor the first time we made a wide turn. We hadn't secured the door, *duh!*

We had left Anaheim, California, way before dawn. Alan and Bob took turns driving. Again, we were new to motorhomes, so there were lots of near misses just getting the enormous motorhome out of town.

Several hours later, we passed across the Mexican border. Because the motorhome was self-contained, with a kitchen and bathroom, we didn't have to stop for anything but gas. One gas stop we made was at a quaint Mexican village with only the gas station and a few small houses sprinkled about. Everyone got out of the motorhome to look around and stretch their legs, while Bob added gas to our tank. The kids went to buy Cokes from a young man selling drinks from a rickety wooden cart. He was standing roadside with his little dog. When Natalie approached, the dog bit her on the leg.

The bite wasn't serious and the dog looked healthy, but few Mexican families could afford vaccinations. After discussing the bite with a local doctor at a small clinic, we decided we should keep the dog with us until we got back to the US and could test it for rabies. The mother of the boy who owned the dog was afraid she would be in trouble because of the dog bite, but I tried to reassure her in my broken Spanish that we just didn't want to take a chance on rabies. We gave her twenty dollars, which was a small fortune then, and she tied a rope around its neck and the dog was ours. That poor little dog; we had to quarantine him in the bathroom in the Winnebago. Later, when we parked somewhere, we tied him up outside in the shade. Pretty soon, the dog was family. We petted him and fed him like a king. He was a sweet little creature. Natalie had just startled him and he bit her.

Finally, midday, we arrived at the lovely Estero Beach Resort in Ensenada, Mexico, where our giant Winnebago fit right in. The place was full of American tourists, and there was every shape and size of travel trailer and mobile home known to man.

The designated rental spots were spacious. Each had a fire pit and picnic table with benches. Alan backed the giant motorhome, with Bob's guidance, between two Winnebagos that could have been sisters to our motorhome. The guys attached all the fittings: electricity, water, and sewer. We tied the little dog under the shady front of the Winnebago, with fresh water and a few snacks. Then Donna and I started making lunch. The kids ran off to explore the long white beach. Mexico was pristine then. The water was turquoise blue and crystal clear. The view from our motorhome window was incredibly inviting.

Estero Beach was a lively spot and, as noted, popular with Americans. There were lots of families like ours, and lots of young couples visiting with their friends. In fact, on our left, there was a group of four couples sharing one Winnebago. During the week we became friends.

"We're here to fish and drink," said Freddie, one of our new friends. "And some are here mostly to drink," he added with a mischievous smile.

By evening, we were exhausted; it had been quite a drive and quite a day. We ate dinner on the picnic table outside, next to a fire blazing with firewood the kids had gathered. We had barbequed steaks, fried potatoes, and fresh salad. Donna made brownies for dessert. Like it always does when you're camping, everything tasted *so* good.

After a few glasses of wine, Alan and I decided it was time for bed. Donna and Bob generously gave us the bedroom in the back of the motorhome. Our kids had bunks in the front. Bob had promised he'd take his older boys night fishing off the beach.

"We'll probably be in late," Bob said, "We don't want to wake you two up." So, the back bedroom was ours. Off we went, tired and happy. Boy, that bed felt good, clean sheets and everything.

Our friends in the neighboring Winnebago were still going strong as we undressed. They had music playing, and we could hear them laughing and telling stories, but that didn't bother us one bit. We had gotten up so early that morning that we were spent. As we lay there, the sounds next door began to fade away and we began to trail off to sleep.

Suddenly, I heard Donna's voice coming from her bedroom. "Stop that. Go away, you idiot."

I assumed Bob and Donna were just kidding around.

"Alan, come in here and help me," Donna called in a quiet, controlled tone, obviously trying not to wake the younger kids.

"Stop messing around, Donna," Alan answered. "I'm tired. Go to sleep."

Donna's protests continued: "Get out of here. I'm serious. Get out of my bed."

I finally realized Donna might not be joking around. I woke Alan, who can fall asleep in two minutes, even with a band playing right in front of him.

"Alan, I think someone is in Donna's room."

Alan didn't believe me. He was sure Donna was just screwing around. Because I was insistent, Alan got up to check and prove me wrong. Only I wasn't wrong. There was Donna, with Freddie, the neighbor fellow, passed out cold on top of her. She was holding on to the top of the sheets for dear life.

"Get him off me," she stammered. "He's drunk as a skunk and passed out."

Since Freddie was a big guy, I went next door and told his roommates we needed help.

"Freddie has passed out on Donna and is smashing her like a bug!" We figured Freddie had gotten confused in his inebriation and thought he was in his own Winnebago with his own wife.

The guys rushed over and started pulling on Freddie's legs. But he had a death grip on Donna's sheets and no matter how hard we tried to pry up his fingers, in his drunken state, Freddie was not letting go. And neither was Donna. She was naked under the covers and she was not giving up that blanket, not with three strange men and Alan in the room. The guys kept pulling Freddie's legs and Donna kept scrunching down each time Freddie moved a few inches.

"It's a Mexican standoff," Alan said laughing, "literally."

The further down the bed Freddie slipped, the more Donna had to scrunch. About then, Bob returned from fishing with his boys. He took one look at the four guys and Donna.

"What the hell are you doing, Donna?" he demanded, as if Donna were at fault. Bob was sure Donna had done something stupid. In all fairness, Donna was famous for pulling many a stupid stunt.

I told Bob, "Freddie passed out on Donna because he got mixed up and went into the wrong Winnebago. Honest Bob, it's not her fault."

When Bob saw how tightly she was gripping the top sheet, he yelled, "Donna, quit messing around and just let go of the sheets!" He didn't realize she was naked beneath.

Finally, Alan threw ice on Freddie's back. The ice shocked his senses enough that he let go of the sheet and slid off the bed hitting his chin on the ground with a thump. Drunk and disoriented, the huge guy was stuffed through our motorhome door, followed by his laughing friends. He landed face first in the sand and lay there like a dead seal until his buddies could haul him away.

The next morning, Freddie returned and apologized profusely.

"I'm so sorry, Donna. I hope I didn't hurt you. Honest to God, I thought that was our motorhome and you were my wife." Being the sport she is, Donna just laughed.

Later that day, he brought us a bottle of tequila as a peace offering. "I think I've had enough!" he joked.

On the following Sunday, after an amazing and restful week, we disconnected the Winnebago and started home. Our plan was to stop in Tijuana and watch the bullfight, if we could find a parking spot near Plaza Monumental de Playas de Tijuana, commonly known as the Bullring by the Sea to us English speakers. Luckily, we pulled the Winnebago right up along the edge of the bullring and parked. We climbed up on top of the motorhome to watch the wild event. Being animal lovers, none of us liked it when the matadors killed the bulls, but we tried to remember this was a foreign cultural event. It was certainly one we never forgot.

To beat the Sunday traffic, which was bad even without a bullfight going on, we left before the last bull entered the ring. We were almost to the border before we realized some guy had attached himself to the back of the motorhome and was hanging from the ladder. Alan got out and yelled at him to let go.

"I just need a ride to the border. I'm an American and I'm out of money."

Alan told us later he didn't trust the guy's looks. "There was no way I was letting him come inside." A few blocks more and our visitor was gone.

We decided not to mention the dog until we had passed over the border and were on American soil. When we pulled into customs, we presented the sweet little hound to the customs agent.

"You can't bring that dog across the border," she stammered. "We'll have to quarantine him now."

That, of course, was exactly what we wanted.

On the way home to Anaheim, we heard the kids talking very quietly. We knew by their demeanor that something sneaky was going on.

"What's up, you guys? Why are all of you whispering?" I asked.

Jeff proudly held up his portable radio. He pulled off the back of the radio dramatically, to reveal a pack of firecrackers hidden inside. The little kids were smiling gleefully and you could see they were totally impressed. Mexican fireworks are illegal in the US, and Jeff had smuggled them in with this little trick. Bob deflated Jeff's ego with just one sentence.

"If the customs agent had come inside the motorhome, that's the first place she would have looked!"

Really Bob? Way to spoil a boy's fun! Jeez.

As a sad side note, we got a notice in the mail a few weeks later that the dog was rabies-free, but had been euthanized. I said a prayer for the innocent animal. He was a victim of our vacation. To this day, his unintended death makes me sad. If I could go back in time, I would have insisted we keep the sweet creature, despite the fact that we already owned two dogs.

22

The Seal Beach Pet Shop

1978

One year, my youngest sister, Alice, and I bought the Seal Beach Pet Shop. We both lived in town and, since our kids were in grade school most of the day, we thought it might be fun to own a business together. The owner had been grooming our poodle, Apple, for years. When she mentioned, during a grooming visit, that she wanted to sell the place, I called Alice and we bought it. Owning that pet shop turned out to be one of the craziest experiences of my life.

The Seal Beach Pet Shop was on the last block of Main Street, between Seal Beach Drug and the Bay Theater. It was a typical small town store, with a pair of big bay windows on each side of the entrance door. Our dad helped us paint it and put down a new linoleum floor. We cleaned the shop from top to bottom and were open for business.

The pet shop offered the usual array of small animals for sale. We sold a variety of birds, rats, mice, guinea pigs, hamsters, rabbits, lizards, snakes, and tropical fish.

Plus, we offered pet grooming, which turned out to be an important part of our business.

My husband tried to warn me about owning a retail business. "It's not like real estate, Paula, where you can work at your own schedule. With retail, someone has to be there every day." It didn't take long to realize he was absolutely right. I worked much harder and made far less money in the Pet Shop than I made selling houses. But, looking back, I wouldn't change a thing.

One day, a local man came in an offered to give us his six-foot python.

"It's gotten too big for our apartment. I thought it might be a great animal for you to sell, and it's a good way to attract customers." Exotic animals do attract people.

"Sure, if it's free." How could we resist?

We had to have a large, glass-fronted cage built to house the python. Monty, of course, was his name. The cage was ten feet long, about three feet deep, and three feet high. It took up one whole section in the back of our store. Inside was a huge water container for the snake to lie in and drink from. When the owner returned with the snake he was giving us, he was happy to see that Monty had such a nice new home. We asked the owner about Monty's feeding regimen. We knew, of course, that snakes are carnivores—they eat meat and only meat.

"I feed him twice a week. He likes adult rats. But he's getting so big it won't be long until he can be fed rabbits."

Yikes, that sounded kind of creepy. I was wondering if maybe taking Monty had been a mistake. The previous owner was right about one thing: Monty Python was a major attraction. We put a sign in the front window that

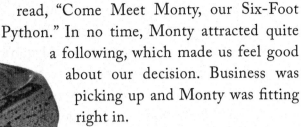

read, "Come Meet Monty, our Six-Foot Python." In no time, Monty attracted quite a following, which made us feel good about our decision. Business was picking up and Monty was fitting right in.

Every Tuesday morning, at store opening time, the Leisure World bus would drop off senior citizens in Seal Beach to shop, and the local bus stop was close to our Pet Shop. We had lots of Leisure World customers who would stop by for pet supplies and new dog and cat toys. Bird supplies were popular too.

When Monty became a member of the pet shop family, we found out quickly that lots of folks hate snakes.

Two sisters in their eighties, Minnie and Mary, came by the pet shop every couple of weeks to get parakeet supplies. They bought mirrors and ladders and our special blend parakeet food that Alice stored in small brown bags on wooden shelves in back.

"Those two little parakeets are eating us out of house and home," the grey-haired grannies joked. Alice and I really looked forward to their visits. It was people like Minnie and Mary who made owning the pet shop fun. Minnie and Mary didn't pay much attention to the other animals in the shop, but they noticed Monty Python.

"I don't like snakes. Never have, never will," Mary told us with an irritated tone in her voice. "They give me the creeps."

I assured her that the large python was safely contained and she had nothing to worry about.

"All right, if you say so. But I still don't like seeing him in the shop." That conversation was repeated at each visit, with Mary's voicing her concern and my reassuring her that Monty was not going anywhere and she was perfectly safe while she shopped. Since the Leisure World Bus always arrived as we were opening, Minnie and Mary were usually our first customers of the day.

"Good morning, ladies," I said as they entered the shop smiling. "How was your trip today?"

"Just fine," Minnie answered. "We have a new driver named Fred. I hope he's not as grumpy as the last one." This slight change in the ladies' weekly routine was stimulating for them; a new driver was something different to talk about. "I hope he's not a fussbudget like Billy. Don't you agree, Mary? Billy was such a fussbudget." Mary concurred with a nod.

After the usual pleasantries, Minnie and Mary made their way back to the rear of the store, where the bird supplies were kept. Alice's special blend parakeet food was stacked on shelves across from Monty's glass-fronted pen. The ladies started looking at the bird supplies and talking about whether they should invest in a new mirror for the birds.

"I think a second mirror would be nice for Blue Boy. You know how Sweetie Pie hogs the one near the water."

Suddenly, Alice started pointing toward the ladies and whispered something I couldn't hear.

"What's the problem?" I asked her quietly, putting my hands up in the air.

She kept up the pantomime, pointing back at the ladies as her eyes widened in fear. Her hands were shaking back and forth. Obviously, something was terribly amiss.

"What? What's the matter?" I asked, getting irritated that I couldn't figure out what she was trying to say. She pointed toward the python's cage and *then* I saw it. The glass was broken and Monty, the six-foot serpent, was not inside. Oh, my God. Where the heck was Monty Python?

Alice and I started looking around frantically for the snake. We did it in a frantically casual manner, so as not to alarm Minnie and Mary. We slyly looked on the floor under all the cages, and on the shelves by the exit, but the large python was nowhere in sight. Then, I spied him. Monty was stretched out across the top of the shelves where the special blend parakeet seed was stacked. The python's large head was hanging over the edge, comfortably rocking back and forth, about two feet from Minnie and Mary's heads.

"Do something Paula!" Alice cried, in a panicked whisper. "Do something before Monty moves!"

I knew Alice was right. If Monty started moving, and the ladies saw him dangling near their heads, one of them might have a heart attack. It was scaring *me* half to death, and I still had a young heart!

"Ladies, are you about done there?" I asked, trying to edge them away from the python and more toward the front door.

"No, I'm still looking," Mary said in earnest. "I see you have new ladders. Which do you think the birds would like, the red one or the green one with the bell?"

"Oh, my God," I kept thinking, "If those sweet little ladies look up and see that giant python, they might die of fright!"

"Let me treat you to both," I said, grabbing one of each. "Now come on up front, I have something special to show you."

"I'm not done yet. Don't rush me," Mary barked. She was in no mood to be hurried; this was her big outing, and she wanted to take her time.

"Please ladies, come this way. I have to show you Rachel, our new momma rat."

Minnie and Mary weren't budging one bit. No matter what I said to entice them, they kept looking at the bird supplies and discussing all their options. Monty was staying put as well. His large smooth neck was moving in a quiet, rhythmic motion back and forth above their heads, with his tongue flickering with each move. Snakes have long tongues and use them to smell and see.

After what seemed like an eternity, the ladies handed me a few items and said they were done. I got behind Minnie and Mary and grabbed their elbows lightly. "Here, let me help you," I said, pushing them gently but firmly toward the checkout stand and front door.

As they started walking slowly forward, I looked back. Monty was on the move. He was sliding down the wooden shelves in a smooth, fluid manner toward the linoleum floor. Within seconds, his body was fully extended, and I was reminded how really long he was. Holy Mary, mother of God, I was frantic. Alice grabbed a giant towel from the grooming table and quickly threw it over Monty's head. The owner had told us to do that before we dropped his dinner, an adult rat, into his cage.

"It will calm him, and it's safer for you. That's what I do if Monty has to be moved."

Thank God, Alice had remembered that. I was in full panic mode and wasn't thinking of anything but how I would single-handedly unwrap a python from an eighty-year-old customer being constricted to death.

The towel did the trick and the python stopped moving as soon as his eyes were covered. He lay still on the floor and I let out a big deep sigh of relief. For the moment, I felt safe. I wanted to get Minnie and Mary out of the pet shop quickly.

"Now, where's this rat you were telling us we *just had* to see?" asked the ladies.

Trying to act genuinely excited, I took the ladies to the front window to see Rachel, our momma rat, who had just given birth to twenty pink babies. Alice had fixed up her glass-fronted aquarium with pink gauzy fabric draped to resemble a canopy bed, and it really was adorable.

"Isn't that just darling?" I stammered enthusiastically. Nope, Minnie and Mary were not impressed.

Alice bagged up the ladies' purchases, and we helped Minnie and Mary to the door.

"I still don't like that big snake you have," said Minnie. "I'll be happy when he's gone."

"So will I," Mary added. "So will I."

They had no idea.

The ladies left and we quickly locked the door.

We called Monty's owner and he hurried down to the Pet Shop. He slid Monty into the giant bag he used for transport. "I'll take him home until you can get his cage fixed."

Before he left, Monty's owner worked out how the python had broken the glass. He figured out that the snake had just been trying to get under the water box and had forced it into the glass, breaking it. He suggested we redesign the enclosure so that the water container couldn't be moved. We did make this fix and Monty Python never escaped again. Later, we sold Monty to a collector. We were kind of happy to have him gone.

When you own the local pet shop, you inadvertently become the recipient of every baby bird that falls out of a tree and every litter of kittens abandoned by their mother or by that mother's owners. It's the nature of the beast. No pun intended. When people can't afford a veterinarian, they head to the local pet shop.

On one occasion, we received a litter of baby kittens that had been abandoned under a car.

"I think the mother got run over," said the gal who had found them.

They were very young and still had their eyes closed. We took the litter in and hand-fed the kittens until they grew big enough to sell. We were happy we could save their lives. Soon all of the kittens but one were placed in good homes. We named the last kitten Binky, and he was a kitten who absolutely could *not* stand to be caged. Some animals are like that. No matter what we did, Binky would cry and cry and cry until we let him out. He got to be a teenager and still no one wanted Binky. He roamed loose in the pet shop and became a sort of mascot for the place.

Finally, Alice and I decided we had to find Binky a home. He was beginning to pester the smaller animals. He was particularly interested in the baby rats.

We found him clinging to a cage on the floor one morning. He was always attacking the parakeet cages and making the macaws scream. Binky really needed a home.

We put up a sign, "Free Teenage Cat." We included his vaccinations, a collar, license, and food. Anyone looking for a cat would surely find Binky a deal too good to be true.

The bell on the front door of the pet shop signaled that someone had just come in. I was cleaning up a shelf of dog supplies that Binky had knocked over, so my back was to the door. Alice was in the back, on the phone. I heard a voice shout from behind me.

"I'll take that free teenage cat."

"Great. He's all yours," I said over my shoulder before turning around.

Binky could not tolerate being caged. (Some animals are just like that.) He roamed free in the shop, but his prowling became a problem when he started pestering the birds. Binky needed a home.

Alice came out of the backroom just as I turned. There was Binky, our mischievous little mascot, in the arms of a guy who looked just like Charles Manson, the wild-eyed American criminal who had led his "family" to commit mass murder in the late 1960s. This guy was scary looking and he was a dead ringer for the jailed criminal. He was short, like Manson was, and his hair, like Manson's, was greyish-black and flew wildly to his shoulders, accentuating his crazy-eyed stare. And he was with a couple of scantily clad girls. It was obvious that he and his girls were trying to emulate Manson and his family. He had me convinced, that's for sure. Within seconds, this Manson look-alike had grabbed the bag of free cat supplies we had promised and was heading toward the door. Alice and I looked at each other, unsure what could be done. We had said the cat was free and I had told the guy, "He's yours," but this guy looked like Charles Manson, whom we considered the epitome of insanity and violence.

After he left, Alice and I stared at each other in shock. "You've got to do something, Paula. We can't let that monster have Binky."

See, I was the older sister. Somehow things like this were my job to fix. And I was thinking as fast as I could. What could I do to retrieve Binky? What could I possible say?

I ran out the door and down the street toward the family, who were headed for the bus stop. I caught them just as the bus arrived. "Wait. Wait. Please wait!" I called to Manson. He turned, facing me, with Binky in his hands held against his chest. He was petting Binky as he listened. I quickly started spitting out a story about how Binky's owner had just called and desperately wanted him back. She'd been sick before, but now she was well and could care for Binky. I was not making a lot of sense, but it was the best I could do in the situation. Suddenly, Manson held the cat more tightly to his chest in a very kind and protective manner.

"You can't have him back. You people should be more careful. Some crazy person could come by and take this precious animal. No. He's mine. I'm not giving him back."

With that, Manson got on the bus and Binky was gone.

Alice met me at the door. "Where's Binky?" she asked, with tears in her eyes. "It's ok, Alice. Binky is gone, but I'm convinced he is safe." When I told her what I'd seen, Alice agreed that maybe Manson was more than just his looks.

When you handle animals, you have much more responsibility than when you sell other products. These are living, breathing, feeling creatures. You have a moral responsibility to make sure that they have safe and happy homes. We never knew where Binky landed but, in my heart of hearts, I feel confident he was okay.

The pet shop was sure a lot of work. Every day there were cages to clean, animals to feed, and shelves to fill. Most of the jobs were very dirty: hair, urine, feces. You get the idea. Dog grooming was a big part of our business. The hair we cut and trimmed from the dogs required constant sweeping and vacuuming. Everything had to be sanitized several times a day to keep the odors under control. We never got to just sit around.

Saturday was our biggest grooming day. On a good day, we probably groomed twenty dogs. Because each dog also got washed and dried after the trim, we always had to go to the laundromat before we closed with all the towels we had used. Those towels were covered in hair. I mean *covered*. Also, we used towels to clean up pet urine and other stinky muck throughout the pet shop. The towels were so filthy, there was no way we'd launder them at home.

The laundromat was just down the street and because we went late in the day, we were usually able to get four machines in a row. We washed the towels in hot water, of course, and we used bleach. Even after all that, the pet shop towels were totally disgusting. They smelled like wet dog no matter what we did, and they always remained embedded with fur.

One Saturday, the towels were especially dirty. A Great Dane had diarrhea and it had taken several just to clean up the big dog's big mess. This happens sometimes during grooming if a dog gets nervous or scared. Anyhow, we stuffed the filthy towels in a couple of big laundry baskets and I took them to be washed. When the washing cycle was finished, I threw the towels into a couple of giant dryers and put in enough coins for sixty minutes. We planned to pick up the dry towels on our way home. After the pet shop was cleaned up, we drove back to the laundromat to retrieve our towels. Well, I'll be damned; some laundry thief had stolen them. It was irritating, but it was also very funny. If the thieves knew where those towels had been, they would *never* have taken them home. It was poetic justice for sure. I love karma.

One of the perks of owning the pet shop was having animals to take to the science room at our children's school. The science room was an invention of our sister Sharon. She organized mothers with kids in the school to teach science lessons to the children. Sharon wanted to supplement the kids' education with additional classes in science. Her son and our four kids attended the same school. It was easy for us to take in an animal to share. The kids loved hearing about the animals. The science room was a big hit with the kids, and I think it was very educational.

One day we decided to take two giant macaws into the science room for the children to observe. The macaws were in the pet shop on consignment. They had been raised from babies and were very friendly. One was a blue-and-gold macaw, and the other was a scarlet. Macaws are larger than parrots, with proportionately larger beaks and longer tails. The owner hated to give up his birds, but he had a new job which involved international travel.

"I am not going to be home to give the macaws the attention they need. I want you to find them a good home."

The seller only wanted $175 from any sale of the pair. Anything else we could get would be profit for the pet shop. We figured we could sell them for $400 easily, which was a significant sum of money back then.

Macaws are excellent fliers, but the two we had on consignment had their wings clipped so we weren't concerned about taking them to the school. On Science Room Day, we loaded our featured feathered friends into my van and made the short trip to the campus. The birds sat on their open perch in the back of the van. They seemed relaxed and comfortable during the trip. My sister Alice was the best at handling the macaws because she had a quiet, gentle manner. Whenever anyone came into the pet shop and showed interest in the two birds, Alice would immediately put her hand beneath the chest of one of the macaws and hold it for the customer to see. The key to selling the macaws was demonstrating that they were easy to handle and friendly.

One time Alice had the blue-and-gold macaw on her hand and decided to put it on her shoulder. We had a special shoulder apron that protected your clothes in case the bird pooped. Alice was standing at the checkout stand with the macaw perched happily on her left shoulder, when suddenly I heard her say, "Paula. Would you come here? Please?"

The pair of Macaws we took in on consignment was a nice addition to our bird section and we were sure they would be easy to sell.

The minute she spoke, I knew something was wrong. Alice was not normally so formal. One look clarified the problem. The macaw had his enormous beak through her gold hoop pierced earring and was pulling it away from her ear. Each time the bird pulled Alice's earring, her head followed. He was having fun playing with the sparkly object, but I could see Alice was in pain.

"Grab a peanut and see if you can distract him," she pleaded quickly. I grabbed a peanut and tapped the macaw's beak several times. "Here, boy. Here, boy. Want a peanut?"

It took a few tries but eventually the bird got interested in the peanut and he let Alice's earring go. Alice never put a bird on her shoulder again.

The science room was down on lower campus in one of the temporary buildings. We parked our car along the fence by the school and started walking to the side gate. Alice had one bird on her hand, and I had control of the other. The macaws seemed to be enjoying the ocean breeze and the warm outdoor sun on their backs as we walked. They were attentive, looking from side to side. All of a sudden, without warning, the blue-and-gold macaw took off flying, with the scarlet macaw right on his tail.

"I thought their wings were clipped!" I screamed at Alice, as four hundred dollars worth of birds went flying down the street. We started running after them as fast as we could, but it was futile. The wind had lifted what was left of their clipped wings and they were picking up speed. With a few frantic flaps, the macaws went gliding into the top branches of a palm tree at the end of the street.

"He said their wings were clipped. I thought they couldn't fly," I yelled again, dumbfounded. Obviously, the owner had been wrong.

One of the teachers had seen what happened and called out to us, "I'll call the fire department. Maybe they can help."

That's the great thing about a small town: within minutes the fire department was there. We told them what had happened and pleaded with them to try and rescue our birds. They extended their longest ladder toward the palm, and I was relieved to see it could reach the top.

I explained to the fireman how to put his hand under the macaw's chest. "Just rest your hand on his chest. I'm sure he'll walk right onto your hand."

I also suggested the fireman wear one of the leather gloves.

"I got it, Mrs. Thomas. I own a cockatiel. I'm sure I can get your bird without the glove."

The fireman scaled up the ladder toward the birds, and I was praying they wouldn't freak out and fly away. Up, up he went, until he was standing just across from the two macaws. The fireman put his hand out slowly as I had told him, but the macaw didn't climb onto his hand. Instead, he tried to bite the fireman's hand. I'm sure the bird was upset. After all, the macaws had probably not taken flight in years.

"I think I'll use that glove after all," the fireman called, as he descended the ladder. Alice and I looked at each other and smiled.

Thank God for the Seal Beach Fire Department. Thanks to them, we retrieved our valuable macaws. Yes, losing the macaws would have been costly, but, more importantly, was the fact that someone had loved those birds very much. We were responsible for their safekeeping. Our actions had put those birds at risk.

If you have a deep-seated need to be loved and admired every day, you shouldn't be in politics. You should go work at a pet store.

—MICHAEL NUTTER

When we told the birds' owner what happened, he just laughed. "I used to take them out in the yard to sun all the time. I'm shocked they never flew away!"

Like people, every animal has his or her own temperament and personality. And they have instincts, an inherent inclination toward a particular complex *behavior*, that humans may or may not understand. No matter how much you know about a species, you never know everything an individual animal will do. Also, you're dealing with the people who love them, and you really never know what people will do. That combination makes owning a pet shop an adventure, to say the least.

23

Donna, Donna, Donna

1978–2006

My husband and I have known Bob and Donna Fees since our college days. The guys were in accounting classes together at Cal State Long Beach and graduated about the same time. They started a CPA firm in Tustin, California, and have been business partners ever since. Donna and I became fast friends during that period. I think the reason we are so close has to do with our mutual love of crafts and the fact that, like me, Donna has a reputation as a bit of a wingnut. We've now been friends for over fifty years.

The trials and tribulations of living with Donna are legendary. What follows are just a few of the most memorable events.

The Silver Teardrop Trailer

Donna and Bob have relatives in the state of Washington. Several times a year, Bob and Donna would make the twenty-hour trip by car to see them. On one occasion, they

Bob and Donna Fees, our business partners and friends since college, celebrating sixty years of marital bliss. Well, *almost* marital bliss!

pulled a small silver trailer shaped like a teardrop. It contained their camping gear and all the stuff a family of six needed for vacation.

Bob would always drive. He didn't like Donna to drive because, as he said on this occasion, "You drive too darn fast."

But it was drawing late into the trip, and Bob was getting very tired. "I've got to stop and sleep for a while," he told her.

Donna said that wasn't necessary because she could drive and he could sleep. "The kids are sound asleep. If we stop, it could wake the baby. Come on, Bob. Let me drive."

Bob refused. On he drove for another fifty miles. After an hour, the conversation was repeated, with Donna offering to drive and Bob adamantly saying no. "No, Donna. You drive too darn fast."

As the hours and miles wore on, Bob's resolve began to weaken. Finally, he agreed to let his wife take the wheel.

"Don't drive a mile over forty-five. Got it? You promise? The trailer is unstable, and if you drive fast we're likely to crash."

"Yes," promised Donna. "I'll drive like an old lady and keep it under forty-five. Relax, Bob. I promise I won't drive over forty-five miles per hour!"

Relieved of the wheel, Bob quickly dropped off to sleep. He was exhausted. The next thing Bob says that he remembers was waking up to Donna's scream. The car was weaving back and forth violently, and the teardrop trailer was passing Bob's window on the right. Off it went over a ditch into the trees, like a little silver rocket into space.

In shock, he turned toward Donna. Her eyes were wide in fear and she was teary-eyed. "I may have been going just a little too fast!" Donna stammered.

"No shit. Really, Donna? You? *You* were going too fast?"

Snowball

Another time, Donna insisted that they leave the den window slider open just six inches so their cat, Snowball, would have a place to sleep while they were out of town. Bob didn't like the idea. "The cat will be fine. The pet sitter is going to feed her outside and she sleeps outside all the time. Don't leave the slider open. *Please.*"

Donna agreed reluctantly, but after Bob was in the car, she slipped back into the house and left the slider open for Snowball (which is so Donna). What could it hurt? Donna figured. She'd rush into the house first when they got home and close the slider. Bob would never know the difference. Snowball was, after all, her baby and needed a warm place to sleep.

When Bob and Donna returned after the weekend, Bob said he could hear high-pitched squealing and wailing sounds coming from the house. "It was like something you'd hear in a horror movie. Howling and screeching, it freaked me out."

The noises were coming from the den. When they opened the den door, there was Snowball, obviously in heat, with at least twenty screaming male cats sitting on their chairs and sofa, waiting for their turn to mate. The room smelled putrid, of cat spray and urine. Feces were everywhere. It was a godawful, disgusting mess.

Bob jerked his head around and glared at Donna who stood surveying the filthy room in silence. Then she whimpered meekly, "I didn't want Snowball to get cold while we were gone."

The den had to be gutted. They threw out everything: carpet, couch, chairs, pictures, and all. The walls had to be scrubbed with vinegar to get the smell out; not once, but twice. Then the whole room had to be painted from top to bottom and re-carpeted as well.

A few weeks later, we four went out to dinner. Donna was all excited because "Snowball is about to pop." She turned toward Bob and asked enthusiastically, "Can we keep one of Snowball's kittens?"

Bob didn't answer immediately. He just stared at her in silence for a long time and then said coldly, "What do you think?"

Raccoons

When Bob and Donna moved up to Anaheim Hills, Donna began to feed the raccoons that came down the tree in the patio located in the center of their house. Bob didn't like this one bit. He feared the raccoons might get rabies one day and then bite and infect their dog. Donna promised she would stop feeding them, but, of course, she never did.

"The raccoons are getting so friendly," she told me, brightly. "They eat right out of my hands."

When Bob and Donna left for vacation, Donna made sure the patio sliding doors were closed. She had learned her lesson with Snowball and didn't want raccoons in the house. But raccoons are clever little critters and quickly discovered that, although closed, one of the doors wasn't locked. When Donna and Bob returned from vacation, the house looked like one of those Disney movies where a bear gets into the kitchen. Every kitchen cupboard was open. Flour, sugar, wheat, and other food stuffs were scattered all over the floor. The refrigerator had been opened and emptied, and it was pretty obvious the little creatures had been sleeping on the living room couch.

Once the two startled homeowners finished surveying the mess, Donna tried to take an optimistic tone and said, "Well, at least they didn't get into the bedrooms. We can be happy about that. Right, Bob?"

Bob gave Donna a steely-eyed stare. The raccoon fiasco was the final straw.

"If you *ever* feed those damn animals again, we are through!" And I think he meant it.

The Sub-Zero

Donna grew up in a big family like I did, and neither family was rich. That's probably why Donna and I are kindred spirits about shopping. When our husbands were in college, we used to go to Pic-N-Save (now called Big Lots) together, and fill up our carts with all kinds of goodies. We'd pretend we were buying stuff to decorate our houses. It was only therapy for us, because we didn't have the money to really shop. When the carts were full and our shopping fantasy was finished, we would leave the loaded carts by the front door of the store and head home.

I remember telling Donna once, "My goal in life is to someday have the money to buy everything I put in my cart." Eventually, I did.

When we got older, even though money was no longer an issue, Donna and I never quite recovered from our pasts of being poor. We both still love a bargain and always look for ways to save and scrimp. It's in our DNA. Over time, I learned that going cheap and saving a few bucks can be a big mistake. It took Donna a little longer to learn this lesson; let me give you an example.

Bob and Donna had a beautiful house on the beach in Oceanside, California. They could watch the whales during migration, enjoy majestic sunsets, and observe the handsome young surfers on the waves. It was a lovely spot and home, and the four of us spent many a wonderful afternoon lying on the warm sand and drinking margaritas.

Donna decided the house needed remodeling from top to bottom. Bob, being a sweetheart (and he was, as long as it didn't pertain to feeding wild animals), said, "Whatever makes you happy, dear."

With approval from Bob, Donna got right to work. She had fabulous new flooring installed throughout the space and retiled the baths and kitchen. She and I spent days picking out fabrics to reupholster their furniture. Eventually the granite was installed in the kitchen and it was time to have the new kitchen appliances delivered.

Since Donna loves to cook and entertain, she spared no expense on the kitchen appliances.

Everything was in except the Sub-Zero refrigerator/freezer. I know that it was expensive. Very expensive. I think it cost close to five thousand dollars. Because she had spent so much on the kitchen and remodeling, Donna was feeling guilty; which I recognized as a holdover from growing up poor. She started looking for ways to save.

Donna called me one day, furious. The appliance dealer wanted $250 to deliver the new Sub-Zero. "That's ridiculous! I'm not giving those people $250 to deliver a refrigerator. I'm going to have Jeff and Bobby do it." Jeff and Bobby are Donna and Bob's sons.

I asked Donna why the dealer was charging so much. She said the fee was high because the refrigerator had to be delivered down two flights of narrow stairs at the house. The delivery company had already installed the stove and dishwasher. They knew the stairs were tricky. It wasn't a straight shot to the bottom; the stairs went down fifteen steps to a small landing, then turned sharply down another fifteen steps to the bottom landing by their front door. Plus, the stairs were narrow and the handrails were high. So, there was an upcharge.

"What does Bob think about it? Does he want Jeff and Bobby to be responsible for a five-thousand-dollar refrigerator?" I asked apprehensively.

"Oh, Bob told me to pay for the delivery, but it's a rip off. We have a big dolly. Besides, I do stuff for those two boys all the time and they owe me," said Donna. "If I give each of them twenty bucks, they'll be thrilled."

I had a bad feeling about this delivery. So, when our secretary buzzed my office at work later that day, I wasn't happy to hear that it was Donna on the phone.

She was hysterical. "Paula, you've got to help me. The Sub-Zero got loose from the dolly. It bounced down a few steps and is jammed sideways on the landing. The boys can't budge it an inch. One side is scratched and I think there's a dent in the freezer door. Bob's going to kill me, Paula. What should I do?"

It was tax season at our office. Everyone was tired, especially the CPAs. No one was in the mood for dealing with one of Donna's dilemmas, and Bob was in no mood to hear that the expensive Sub-Zero they had just purchased was stuck on the stairs and had possibly been damaged. Holy crap. I didn't know what to say. Finally, I did know what to say.

"Call the delivery guys, Donna. They are your only hope. And for God's sake, don't tell Bob until you have it figured out."

It took four guys over an hour to dislodge the new appliance from where it was wedged on the narrow landing. Two hundred fifty dollars later, plus the forty dollars she had paid her boys, I could hear Bob and Donna talking on phone. She was on speaker.

"Are you kidding me? They did what? How big is the scratch? A dent? Where? I don't want to hear another word about it!"

I heard Bob slam down the phone.

Later, over lunch, Donna did her best to put a positive spin on what happened. "You can't even see the scratch on the side of the refrigerator because it's set into the cabinet.

And I hung a tea towel on a magnet over the dent on the freezer door. Honestly, it's really not bad at all."

Donna's New Mercedes

Life with Donna has been an ongoing challenge for Bob. Despite it all, and because he is a forgiving and loving husband, Bob surprised Donna with a new Mercedes for her sixty-fifth birthday. It was dark blue, with a gray leather interior. Donna was thrilled with the gift.

When Donna told me they were going to Hawaii for part of the summer, I asked what she was going to do with her new car. She told me LAX had a very nice, safe parking lot. She planned to cover the car and leave it there. Her garage at their beach house was overflowing with crafting stuff and supplies for entertaining, so the lot at LAX was her only choice.

As I mentioned, Donna loves a bargain. It didn't surprise me one bit when Donna decided to buy six cases of beer when they were on sale. "We can use the beer for our big Fourth of July barbecue," she told me proudly. "It was a real bargain, almost half price."

What I didn't know about the "bargain" was that Donna had decided to leave the beer in the back seat of her new car. Her trunk was full of luggage and, since the beer was heavy and Bob wasn't home to help remove them, she thought the cases of beer would be fine in the back seat of the Mercedes until she got home from vacation.

The day Bob and Donna left for Hawaii, Los Angeles was having a heatwave. For almost two weeks, the temperature was over 100 and one day it hit 103 degrees.

According to Google, on a 90-degree day, the inside of a closed car can reach 160 degrees. I can't imagine how hot Donna's car got, covered and sitting nearly a month in excruciating heat. Of course, it never occurred to Donna what might happen to those six cases of beer in a stifling hot car. But physics always wins, and the cases of beer exploded. By the time she returned from Hawaii, the beer had soaked through her beautiful leather interior and dried sticky and hard on the seats, windows, ceiling, and dashboard. I don't know if it was from the hops or yeast, but the car also had a sickeningly musty smell.

"It smells like dirty sweat socks or a filthy brewery floor," Bob told Alan one morning while they were eating breakfast. "Honestly, it's horrible."

Donna, the eternal optimist, told Bob not to worry. "I'll get our boys to clean the leather."

"The hell you will," Bob said with an authoritative tone he seldom used. "Call a professional and see what can be done."

Donna did call, but the car was never the same, even after the "professional" was finished. No amount of freshener or odor-removing products eliminated the stench. They just had to live with it until the car was finally sold.

Donna, Donna, Donna. What are we going to do with you?

24

The Realtor

> **1978**

After many years working real estate in my home town of Seal Beach, I was worn out. Business was terrific, to the point that I couldn't even work in my front garden without someone stopping his car to ask me about the real estate market. It was a blessing and a curse at the same time. Also, the pet shop that I owned with my sister Alice was taking up more time than I wanted to work. I needed a break and wanted to spend more time with my family. I was ready to move on.

Mission Viejo was a large master-planned community about thirty miles South of Seal Beach, known for its broad avenues and lush greenbelts, and it seemed like the perfect place for our family. It had something for everyone: good schools for both kids (an obvious priority), plentiful parks for the dogs, gorgeous golf courses for Alan, wonderful horse facilities for Natalie, and lakes for our bass fishing son, Roger. Also, I longed for the adventure of living in a new environment. Seal Beach was a charming small town to grow up in but, at thirty, I wanted to see what else California had to offer.

What we knew about Mission Viejo was what we had learned from ads and from a casual drive through the various housing developments one Sunday afternoon. A big decision like moving warranted further exploration. So Alan and I drove down again to meet a few realtors who had homes listed in the enormous Multiple Listing Book I carried around (this was pre-computer and cell phones).

In all honesty, I was not excited about having another realtor represent us. Many realtors seemed more interested in the money than putting out the effort it took to help clients find the homes of their dreams. I think that is one of the reasons I was very successful. The money I earned was secondary to the joy I received from finding the perfect fit for a family.

But I had to be realistic. Sure, after thirty years, I knew Seal Beach like the back of my hand. Mission Viejo was a bit of a mystery and it was, with traffic, about an hour away. Plus, the sheer size of Mission Viejo was challenging. With at least ten housing tracts in various stages of development (some were complete, but some were still under construction), I needed help figuring out the place. Alan agreed, so I made a few appointments and we headed down south.

The first realtor just didn't listen. In advance of our appointment, we gave him our must-have list, which included a dining room (among other things). We entertain quite a bit and have a big family. But the houses he showed us didn't have dining rooms. He kept saying, "This home has a family room. You don't need a dining room."

Each time he said it, he'd look toward Alan for agreement.

"Don't look at me," Alan responded. "She's the one you need to make happy." Realtor #1—gone!

Realtor #2 kept showing us houses with only three bedrooms instead of four (a must-have), and one house didn't have a swimming pool (another must-have). Because we needed an office, we asked to see houses with four bedrooms, and, because it's hot in Mission Viejo and we all loved to swim, we wanted a swimming pool.

"The family room has plenty of room for a desk, you won't need an office." (At that time, a family room was a relatively new concept in home building, and I don't think some realtors understood its purpose.) And the missing pool? "Lots of your neighbors will have pools. When your kids make friends, you won't need a swimming pool. Besides, they are expensive." Another non-listener, and who the heck was he to tell us we didn't need a swimming pool? Realtor #2—gone!

Frustrated, we stopped for lunch and reviewed the ad from the last realtor we were meeting. "On the Mission Viejo Golf Course: fully loaded, four bedrooms, three baths, gourmet kitchen, and sparkling pool." Sounds almost too good to be true, I thought to myself.

"1720 Reymalino Drive, there it is Alan," I said, as we turned onto the tree-lined cul-de-sac that bordered the Mission Viejo Golf Course. Because they are dead-end streets, cul-de-sac streets are safer for kids and very desirable.

"Wow. I love this street. Look at all those trees."

Tall, slender, and impeccably dressed in black, The Realtor stood leaning casually against his Mercedes as we made a wide U-turn and parked in front of the two-story Spanish Colonial he had listed. Even as we parked, The Realtor stayed laidback against his car, seemingly unimpressed by the arrival of potential buyers. As we approached, we began to introduce ourselves, at which point The Realtor pulled himself away from his car and swaggered toward us, setting his feet in a stance like a cowboy preparing for a duel. Then, in what was obviously a well-rehearsed and familiar routine, he raised his sunglasses above his eyes with one hand and patted his hip with the other, saying coolly, "The name is Skutsky. I have a beeper on my belt and a pulse on the market."

It took everything in my power not to laugh out loud.

In all my years, I had never met such a pompous and self-absorbed jackass. His new beeper, one of the first electronic gadgets used by salespeople to receive messages, was obviously mentioned to impress.

"I hope you have some good properties to show us," I said, trying to disguise my amused reaction to his ridiculous behavior.

"Don't need any others," Skutsky answered smugly, as he fiddled with the lock. "This house is just what you need."

Giving Alan a sideways glance, I whispered sarcastically, "Oh sure it is," under my breath.

Skutsky, beeper and all, showed us through the house, pointing out the must-haves from our list and talking incessantly about how lucky we were to have met the "hottest Realtor in town."

Did I mention he had a pulse on the market? Did I mention that he had mentioned it?

Adjacent to the eighth fairway of the Mission Viejo Country Club, the house had stunning views from the kitchen, family room, and the kidney-shaped pool in the backyard. A low, wrought-iron fence, covered with radiant climbing roses, separated our lot from the lush green fairway and golf cart path.

The home was exactly what we were looking for: four large bedrooms, a dining room, and swimming pool. The guy was a jackass but he *did listen*, and he did seem to have his "pulse on the market." After all, the other realtors had the same must-have list and access to the same Multiple Listing Book, and yet, they hadn't shown us this property. No effort. No sale.

I have said before, "You can't keep a buyer from purchasing the house of her dreams if you find it and she can afford it." Because Skutsky, despite his pomposity, had done his homework and found the house that matched our wants and needs, he would make the sale.

Within just a few hours of first meeting Skutsky, we had signed the purchase agreement and were headed back toward our car. He walked beside us, admiring his reflection periodically in the large windows on the front of the building, adjusting his posture and pulling in his stomach as needed to accentuate his lean build and full chest. This guy had no idea he was such a jerk.

Just as we started to close the car door before leaving, I recognized that The Realtor was about to proceed with his well-rehearsed routine. When he raised his sunglasses above his eyes with one hand and patted his hip with the other, I quickly interjected, "I know: you have a beeper on your belt and a pulse on the market." Skutsky, unfazed by my mocking, simply pointed his finger at me sharply, and said, "You got it, girl." Then the narcissistic ninny turned on his heels and was gone.

Later, Bill Skutsky and I ended up working for the same broker there in Mission Viejo. It turned out Skutsky had a horrible reputation in the community, beyond his dopey theatrics and spiel. "He's a liar and a cheat," one of his clients shouted loudly as he stormed into our office searching for the "crook who sold me that house." I understood the seller's anger; unhappy Skutsky patrons were a common occurrence in our office. We used to kid him when he stopped by the office to get his mail, because he always looked from side to side to make sure he wasn't walking into an ambush.

The problem with the rat race is that even if you win, you're still a rat.

—LILY TOMLIN

"Hey, Bill, another one of your satisfied customers dropped by."

Also, I had firsthand experience with the guy. Skutsky had told us the house we bought was fully loaded, with air conditioning throughout. We didn't discover he was lying until the weather turned hot. Home inspections came later in real estate history. But, it was my error; I should have checked. When I reminded him that his listing ad said fully loaded and that he had told us *flat out* that the house had air conditioning, he looked me straight in the eyes and lied, "No I didn't." Not a moment's hesitation.

The weird thing about Skutsky was that he hadn't needed to lie. We would have bought the house anyway. Lack of air conditioning was not a deal breaker. The guy who had called him a crook was furious because Bill had assured the client that the seller would replace the broken dishwasher before the escrow closed. When the deal was done and the dishwasher was still broken, the buyer felt cheated. When Skutsky avoided him and wouldn't return his calls, the buyer became enraged.

At first, I didn't understand Skutsky's behavior. After all, a broken appliance is an easy fix compared to the hit a realtor takes to his reputation with an unhappy client. But that never seemed to matter to Skutsky. He got a strange high from the swindle and, like a sociopath, lacked empathy or remorse. He loved to "freak people out" and thought being a con artist was cool.

Looking back on the situation, as mad as he made folks, I'm surprised he never became one of those awful headlines Dad used to read to us kids in the morning, "Local Realtor Shot Dead by Disgruntled Client."

25

Amazing Mugsy

1978

It was 7:00 a.m. when we arrived at the Earl Warren Showgrounds in Santa Barbara, California, where my daughter Natalie was competing in a horse show. From Mission Viejo, where we lived, the trip to Santa Barbara was less than three hours. But, in California, the traffic is unpredictable, so, like the rest of the folks from the Mark Mullen Barn, we spent the night in Santa Barbara, just a few miles from the Showgrounds.

Upon arrival at the showgrounds, we unloaded all our gear: saddle, show clothes, brushes, boot rag, saddle pads, crop, and riding boots, and headed for the Mark Mullen Barn, our daughter's current riding trainer. Slender, handsome, and suave, Mark was a talented equestrian himself. He greeted our daughter, Natalie, with a friendly hug and the rest of us with a big smile.

During Natalie's riding career, she had several gifted riding coaches. All of them were wonderful, but her first teacher, when she was about six years old, was Don Swan, and he was my favorite. What I loved about Don was his cowboy demeanor and down-home attitude toward hunter jumper training. He dressed like a cowboy in the movies, with a broad-rimmed, sweat-stained Stetson and well-worn leather boots. He didn't take kindly to any rich-kid attitude toward the Mexican grooms who did the heavy work around the barn.

"Nobody in my barn is better than anyone else," he used to tell the ten or so little girls who were under his riding tutelage, "and nobody is above getting her hands dirty."

The whole Thomas family was in attendance for the show, because Santa Barbara was the biggest show our barn participated in that year. We were all excited, especially Mugsy, a brown, black, and white border collie mix that somebody had dumped as a puppy at the barn and whom we had fallen in love with when Natalie brought her home. Well mannered, gentle, and highly intelligent, Mugsy was our constant companion for over twelve years and was snuck in and out of some pretty fancy hotels.

Horse shows were tons of fun. They were full of good food, lively companionship, and exciting riding competitions. The food choices ranged from county-fair food, like funnel cakes and popcorn, to high-end barbecue and prime-rib sandwiches. Mugsy, like her human companions, enjoyed the smells of the various vendors and the occa-sional snack we shared. More than that, I believe, she loved the smells of all the other creatures in attendance. Along with horses, people brought their pet dogs, goats, and even pigs to the show. Also, I believe Mugsy knew she was an integral part of the family and being taken there, to the horse show, proved that fact. We all adored her furry face, and she was seldom left behind.

As excited as I was about the competition, I dreaded the long day we were facing. Natalie, our little eques-trian cutie, was entered in multiple hunter jumper and equitation (the art of riding and horsemanship) classes throughout the day. The first was at 8:30 a.m. and the last was at 4:30 p.m. With July heat, dusty horse arenas, and long times between classes, I knew the day would be fun, but also exhausting.

Among the horse show supplies we unloaded was a bright orange, terry-cloth hand towel we used to clean Natalie's boots just before she entered the ring for an event. Because of the dusty arenas and dirt-filled barns, a boot rag was a necessity and used repeatedly throughout the day. Riders were judged on appearance as well as equi-tation, so clean boots were critical and the orange boot rag was an important and useful tool.

Growing up as I did in a big family with very little disposable income, I never dreamed my daughter someday would own a horse and be competing in the Santa Barbara Horse Show. It was with great pride that I watched the events as the day unfolded. Natalie made us so proud. She won her equitation class on Rise and Shine, her beauti-ful, thoroughbred chestnut filly. We screamed and yelled in the stands like crazy folks as she was presented with a giant ribbon she later attached to the horse's halter.

Hearing the ruckus we were making, Mark Mullen looked over and said in a dry, sophisticated manner, "Try not to act like it's the first prize she's ever won." I'm not sure if Mark was kidding or not.

It was late in the day when Natalie's final class concluded. We gathered up our supplies and, with tired feet, dusty hair, and sweaty clothes, headed happily toward the car. Mugsy was tired too and walked at my side with her long, pink tongue hanging slightly out of one side of her mouth from the heat. All of a sudden, Mugsy broke from my leash and ran full blast toward some people walking about a hundred yards away. I looked up and started screaming, "Mugsy, Mugsy!," yelling at her to stop.

"What on earth is Mugsy doing?" Alan yelled, as I looked incredulously at the hand that no longer held a leash. I really had no idea what she was doing. Mugsy had never done anything like this before. Squinting in the direction Mugsy had headed, I tried to see what or who had caused Mugsy to bolt. Then I saw it:

A young man was walking along, casually swinging a bright orange rag back and forth into the air with each step. I yelled to the folks in the distance, trying to explain why our dog was running at breakneck speed in their direction.

"It's our boot rag. You have our boot rag," I yelled with cupped hands, to no avail.

Just then, Mugsy reached the startled boy and, with a small leap and quick jerk of her jaw, she pulled the boot rag out of his hand. Then she quickly turned and headed straight back in our direction with the orange boot rag held securely in her mouth.

"Sorry about that," I yelled at the boy, who was watching the receding dog and rag.

With pride for a job done well, Mugsy dropped the rescued boot rag at my feet and stood smiling and panting as she looked straight into my eyes. (Oh yes, dogs do smile.) Her sweet furry face and soft brown eyes told the story.

"See, Mom," she was saying without words, "I did my job. I protected our things."

The boot-rag retrieval was just one of the amazing things that Mugsy did during her lifetime. On a camping trip to Catalina Island one summer, Mugsy probably saved my life.

We were sleeping on the beach in a little cove a few miles north of Avalon, the island's major city, when Mugsy heard something approaching from the rocks above our campsite and she let out a low, loud, menacing growl. It was a rattlesnake, which are plentiful on the island and cause havoc to campers on occasion. Because California was suffering from a drought, the snake was probably just searching for the water we had left in a bowl for Mugsy. The bowl was next to my sleeping bag, near my head, where Mugsy's bed was laid. My husband, having grown up on Catalina Island, was very familiar with the distinctive sound rattlesnakes make. Mugsy's warning growl awakened Alan and within seconds he had a flashlight pointed in the direction of the sound. Mugsy's growl turned to a frantic, constant bark as the light exposed the snake, which was poised to strike. Instantly, Alan jumped

Mugsy and I had a very special bond. She knew my moods. If I was upset, Mugsy would nuzzle her soft nose under my hand and offer herself for petting.

into action and killed the unwelcome visitor with a shovel.

The frightening incident was over in a minute, but none of us could immediately go back to sleep. Alan and the kids decided to swim out to our thirty-five-foot Scarab boat, which was anchored close offshore. Since we didn't have a dinghy, they piled their dry clothes and towels onto float rafts, put on their bathing suits, and swam out in the cold water to bunk the rest of the night in the safety of the Scarab's forward cabin. Not me. I wasn't about to get in that cold water this late, and, besides, the rocking of the boat would make me sick. I would make a lousy pirate.

Instead, I made a fire and hot coffee and sat on the shore petting my sweet savior, Mugsy, as the sun slowly came up off the California coast.

Thank God, Mugsy alerted us to the approaching danger. And thank God, Alan was swift to recognize the danger and quickly kill the threat. If not, my "potluck" of a life might have been reduced to a snack and first course, at best. I can see Dad now, sitting at the table reading the headline, "Local Women Dies from Snakebite on Catalina Island."

26

Holy Crap

It doesn't get really cold very often in Southern California. Since I am a "hot-blooded" person who gets easily overheated, I rarely wear warm clothes. Most days I wear sandals, cotton tops, and lightweight pants. But this particular morning was unseasonably cool, so I wore a new long-sleeved, one-piece pantsuit I had just purchased. It was a beautiful blue color, and the top was attached at the waist to the bell-bottom pants that were the rage at the time.

If I wasn't busy and I was in a crafting mood, one of my weekly treks was to a wholesale craft warehouse about forty-five minutes from home. I loved the place. It was filled with crafting items. You could buy five hundred different types and colors of ribbon. You could buy design items for any event, from a wedding to a bar mitzvah and everything in between. It was impossible for me to spend less than three hours in the place, and I never left without two hundred dollars' worth of great stuff that I had just purchased cheap. It was paradise for creative types like me.

On this cool morning I arrived early, as usual, with a hot cup of java and quickly showed my membership card to the lady at the window. I grabbed a big green shopping cart and headed down the first aisle. No dedicated crafter would start anywhere else. At the front and end of each aisle was a themed display made by some talented designer who frequents the place. Today, the first aisle featured a jungle theme with wild-animal printed ribbon, textured decorated balls, and cages with stuffed animals and birds. Honestly, the designs were amazing. Anyhow, at the very end of aisle one was the only ladies' lavatory in the place. Before I filled my cart, I decided to make a quick stop, because the hot coffee had begun to work wonders in my intestinal tract. I left my empty cart by the bathroom door, grabbed my purse, and headed into a stall. Ah, just in time, I thought. Thank goodness I hadn't tried to postpone the inevitable.

The rest of the warehouse is cold, regardless of the outside temperature, because the ceilings are high and the place is enormous. The nice Asian family who owns the warehouse makes a concerted effort to keep the comfort station comfortable, but the bathroom today was hot. Because I'm always so hot-blooded, I was happy to quickly pull down the top of my pantsuit and sit there in just my bra. When I was finished, I reached back to pull up the sleeves of my top. But, Lord Almighty, my top had gone into the toilet bowl. Yes, that's right. The lovely blue top of my one-piece pantsuit had become an accidental toilet bowl liner and the receptacle of my bodily waste.

"Holy crap," I stammered. "Are you sh . . . ting me?"

Now, it's one thing to have a little human excretion in your undies or a bit of dog mess on your shoe, but it's a total disaster to have a quart container of urine and poop in the top of the outfit you have pulled halfway on. Yep, I could feel the warmth and wetness ooze down my back into my undies and start down my legs. Oh, my God. It was a disaster. Okay, I have a pioneering spirit. I was raised in a family with seven kids and a mom who could make a masterpiece for dinner out of a bag of noodles and a pound of hamburger, so I jumped into action. I removed the foul-smelling garment and filled the sink with water. This will work, I thought plausibly: I'll wash it out, dry it with the electric wall hand dryer, and then put it back on.

Nope, nope, nope. NO FRIGGING WAY! The bathroom filled with an odor I have never endured before or since, and there was no way all this waste would empty down the sink. There I was, your typical Orange County housewife, standing naked, except for my bra, next to a sink filled with what was left of my food intake for the last few days. I was mortified! Enough self-pity, it was time for Plan B. I went to the bathroom door and peeked out, hoping to see a nice average lady like myself heading toward the rest room.

"Yoo-hoo," I whispered, toward a shopper coming my way. "Can you come help me, *please?*" With only the top half of my body slightly visible, I coaxed her toward the door.

The look on her face was quizzical to say the least. She was obviously trying to determine if I were a damsel in distress or some weirdo looking for a thrill. Thank God, she turned out to be trusting. She advanced to the door, and I quickly explained my dilemma. The odor wafting through the doorway was proof positive that my story was real. She became an angel of mercy and quickly asked how she could help. I handed her my car keys, told her where my car was parked, and asked her with all the humility I could muster to *please* bring me my gym bag from the trunk.

While I waited, almost naked, an old Chinese lady entered the room. She didn't speak English and I don't know a word of Chinese. Standing there, with my handbag covering my crotch, I pointed to the sink and then back at me. Having absolutely no idea what I was trying to convey, the Chinese grandma fled the restroom in fear. After what seemed like an eternity, my angel of mercy returned. I did the best I could to clean my back and backside, threw on my dirty gym suit, and fled to my car with a foul-smelling stench following me like a shadow on a sunny day.

I can't imagine what the janitor eventually thought when he discovered my filthy pantsuit stuffed inside the sink. I'm sure (I hope) my angel of mercy laughs when she shares this story.

I did, I think, learn a valuable lesson from all of this. I do not own and will never wear a one-piece pantsuit again.

27

My Hippocampus Was Hijacked

1980

My husband is one of those folks who can remember peoples' names. He knows the names of all the caddies at the golf course. He knows all his clients' first and last names and the names of their wives and kids too. It's flabbergasting to watch him at a social event. Once introduced to new people, their names are stuck in that incredible brain of his as if adhered with Gorilla Glue.

Not me. There is something missing from my brain. My brain is a sieve when I am introduced to a stranger. Five minutes after being introduced, the person's name is gone like water draining through loose spaghetti. It's so bad that when I play golf, I always immediately write down the name of the person I'm playing with. Honestly, it's that embarrassing.

That's not the only problem. Sometimes my brain will instead behave like a clam. Once a name gets inside, it's hard to open up the clam and insert another name. For example, Julie was the name of my son's first girlfriend. She was adorable, and so I adored her. However, the clam shut tight, and his subsequent girlfriends didn't appreciate being called Julie. Go figure. It didn't make me popular with my son.

My brain is sort of like the Bermuda Triangle. Stuff goes in and it's never found again.

—ANONYMOUS

Also, my brain will tend to combine names. My pet pig was named Beethoven, and for eight years that sweet swine was the love of my life. Beethoven mixed with Peyton, my granddaughter's name, and eventually came out of the clam as Peytoven. This did not sit well with my granddaughter or her mom. Nobody in the family is surprised to be called by the dog's name. I swear it's a brain problem and I've suffered with it for years.

I asked my husband how he does it, and he told me to add a silly visual picture of each person to his name when you are introduced. For example, he says, if the person's tall and his name is Jack, he will think Giant Jack and visualize him as a giant, like in the beanstalk story.

Okay, that sounds easy enough. The problem with this is that when I next meet Jack, I call him Giant. I tell you it's a brain issue and has nothing to do with the fact that I'm slightly scatterbrained. My hippocampus, the region of the brain associated with memory, has been hijacked.

A few years ago Alan and I went to my high school homecoming. It was a blast sitting in the bleachers again and watching Huntington Beach High School play our big rival, Anaheim Hills. I had been a cheerleader for three years at HBHS, so I brought a lot of spirit to this reunion. When the "vintage" cheerleaders were invited down on the field at halftime, it was pure nostalgia. Seeing all my old friends again brought tears to my eyes and a smile to my face that lasted for days.

During the homecoming game, we sat next to a dear old friend of mine, Jerry Long. Jerry and his family had lived across the alley from my family in California. We became fast friends because we both loved to dance. Every day after school, for months on end, we'd fire up the record player and dance to The Del-Vikings hit "Come

That's me the year I graduated from Huntington Beach High School, Class of 1961.

Go with Me" and Jerry Lee Lewis' "Great Balls of Fire." It was 1957, and my life then was a mirror of many of the scenes from the 1973 movie *American Graffiti*. It was an innocent time. *American Bandstand* was the rage, and nobody we knew smoked or drank.

"Jerry," I squealed when I saw him in the bleachers, "Oh my gosh, how long has it been?" Enveloping him quickly in a big bear hug, I continued, "Where's Virginia?"

Now you have to understand that all through high school, Jerry and Virginia had been an item. She wore his class ring around her neck on a chain and his letterman jacket during the games. They were like the king and queen of the prom and the very epitome of young love. Jerry and Virginia, everyone knew, would get married after graduation and live happily ever after. They were legends. It just had to be. Jerry quickly explained that he and Virginia had broken up after high school and that his wife, Sheri, was at the snack bar getting drinks.

"Oh," I winced slightly, "sorry about that. I always loved Virginia."

Soon Sheri returned, and Jerry introduced me to his beautiful wife. "Hi, Virginia," I instantly blurted out. I swear, my brain sucks. Anyhow, this misnaming continued all evening, with my calling Sheri "Virginia" and then apologizing. Again. And again. It was so embarrassing, and I'm sure she thought I was either doing it on purpose or that I had mental issues.

When the evening concluded, I got Jerry's address and promised that an invitation to our annual Christmas party would follow. And it did. In preparation for their attending the party I practiced their names, like a politician preparing for a speech. "Jerry and Sheri. Jerry and Sheri. Jerry and Sheri," I mumbled to myself, as I went about the house, tidying and making preparations. "Jerry and Sheri." I was determined to get this right even if it killed me.

The evening finally arrived. I was excited to see everyone and Christmas was in the air. When the doorbell rang, I could see it was my very special guests through the glass in the door. Prepared, and having bolstered my confidence with a glass or two of wine, I threw open the door and gave each of them a hug. Then I walked them together into the family room and proudly introduced them to the other partygoers.

"Everyone, this is one of my very best and oldest friends and his wife. I'd like to introduce Sheri, and her husband, Virginia."

I give up. My hippocampus has been hijacked. If you could all just wear name badges, that'd be great.

28

Cutie Pie

1984

Lisa Anderson was our daughter Natalie's very best friend. They were freshmen together at my old alma mater, Huntington Beach High. At the time, we were living in Huntington Harbor, a nice neighborhood where everyone owned boats. Our house was small compared to others in the area, but we lived on the water. For our family, this was heaven on earth, or at least heaven adjacent to water. Across the main highway, on the beach-side of the town, was a very nice little market. It was high-end and expensive, but because it was close to our house we shopped there quite a bit. Lisa and Natalie had a crush on a handsome young man who worked there. I called him Cutie Pie. He was the boxboy and worked as cashier sometimes.

One day, I overheard Natalie and Lisa hatching a plan to make contact with the handsome boxboy, and they eventually asked me to drive them to the market. Their plan was to ask Cutie Pie to help them find all the different ingredients to make chocolate chip cookies. Making cookies was the perfect ploy. Since I needed milk and a couple of other items for dinner, I was happy to help.

"Mom," Natalie instructed me quite adamantly as we got in the car. "Don't say anything stupid in the market. Just shop and don't embarrass us." The girls were at that age when parents, even just the sight of them, were embarrassing.

"I won't," I assured her.

"And don't sing either," she added. "You know I hate when you sing. It's embarrassing."

"Okay, I got it Natalie. I'll just go about my business and you won't even know I'm there."

The girls were both adorable in their youthful fluster. Lisa was a tiny little thing, under five feet, and cute as a button. Typical teens, they spent most of their weekend getting dressed up, fixing their hair, and practicing putting on makeup. In fact, they were totally dolled up as we left for the store.

When we got to the store, they immediately spied Cutie Pie restocking the shelves. "There he is. There he is," they whispered, as they grabbed at each other like a pair of little kittens. Turning red in his mere presence, they said "hi" softly as we passed him by.

"Go talk to him, Lisa," Natalie coaxed her friend. "Go up and ask him where to find something we need for the cookies. Go ahead. Do it before he goes in the back or something."

Watching and listening carefully, I stood quiet as a mouse, as ordered. Finally, Lisa, at Natalie's urging, got up her nerve and approached the handsome boxboy who was standing on a short stool. Because Cutie Pie was up on a stool and Lisa was short, her face was right at the height of his belt buckle.

With her bright eyes sparkling, Lisa looked up and blurted out, "Can I see your nuts?"

"What?" Cutie Pie answered, obviously confused.

I broke out into laughter. "That was real smooth, girls." I said, in hysterics, as the teens turned red and fled around the end of the closest aisle.

"They are looking for walnuts. They're making chocolate chip cookies," I added quickly, trying to salvage their plan.

When I recovered from laughing, I collected the food items I needed and headed up to the checkout stand. The girls had recovered somewhat and were following me. Working as the cashier, Cutie Pie began to add up my items on the machine. Suddenly, he cocked his head slightly to one side and looked at me with a giant smile of recognition on his face. "I know who you are. You're Rags the rabbit," he stammered. And he was right.

When all of our kids were in grade school, my sisters and I used to put on plays at their school. Dressed in bunny suits, we were Peaches and Rags, characters in stories written by my talented sister Sharon. The stories were clever and funny and always had a valuable moral or lesson for the kids to learn. Kids loved these stories and we became celebrities of sorts with all the children in town.

"Those stories meant so much to all us kids. You made school fun. I'll never forget you Rags." And with that, Cutie Pie leaned across the counter and gave me a big hug. Within seconds, Natalie was at my side. She threw an arm around my waist and said proudly, "That's my Mom."

Life can change in an instant. One minute you are an embarrassment to your kids and the next minute you are their hero.

Above: That's me, Rags, in blue, standing next to Momma rabbit, Yvonne Ansdell. Sheri McGraw, a cousin rabbit in the story, is standing next to Peaches, my sister Alice, in pink (without her ears.) Right: I loved playing the frisky and sweet little boy character, Rags the rabbit, in the programs our family and friends presented at Zoeter Elementary School in Seal Beach. Being that character, allowed me to act funny and interact like a little kid with the other little kids in town. There is no doubt in my mind that I enjoyed being Rags as much as the kids enjoyed our performances. My sister, Sharon Russell, gave the children in Seal Beach a very special gift by writing those stories. Thanks sis!

29

Thanksgiving

> 1986

Thanksgiving was approaching, and I remember wishing it would be different this year. I was longing for the sort of Thanksgiving Day I had enjoyed when I was a little kid. I wished my children were excited about the big bird in the oven, and I wanted our Thanksgiving to be like one I had celebrated at Betty Boultinghouse's home when I was nine or ten. That particular year, on the night before Thanksgiving, a bunch of my siblings were gathered over at Betty's cozy little wood-framed cottage next door. It was Southern California-cold outside and Betty's heater was broken, so she had the stove turned on for heat. We were all dressed in un-matched, faded pajamas with thick socks for slippers. Betty, our unmarried neighbor, was a second mother to our family and her sweet, simple home was a peaceful repose for our large and hectic clan.

Betty was sitting in front of the television with a giant metal roaster perched in her lap. My youngest sister, Alice, and I were sitting on each side of her breaking stale bread into little pieces for the stuffing. Kay and Judy were talking about the fresh cranberries on the kitchen table as they sipped cold milk and munched Oreo cookies, our favorite. Rex was laying on the ground, wrapped up like an Indian papoose in Grandmother Strother's multi-colored, hand-crocheted afghan. We were all talking excitedly and we were all talking about Thanksgiving.

"I like the stuffing best," someone was saying.

"Not me," added another, "I like the turkey sandwiches the next day with cranberry sauce."

"Remember last year, when we forgot the mashed potatoes in the oven?" Rex added with a laugh.

We were all talking and remembering the special smells and tastes of Thanksgiving.

Some memories are unforgettable, remaining ever vivid and heartwarming!

—Joseph B. Wirth

"Boy, that turkey roasting in the oven smells incredible. My mouth is watering just thinking about it," Judy added.

"Are we having chocolate cream pie this year, Betty?" Kay asked.

A big meal with a lot of special dishes meant a lot to our family. After all, we were a big brood, two adults and seven kids, plus our grandmother lived with us a good deal of the time. We always had enough to eat but we ate that kind of simple food which, as mom always said, "went a long way." We ate lots of stews, soups, casseroles, and lots of vegetable dishes with veggies from our garden. We never went out to eat. In those days, nobody took nine people out to dinner, and about the only thing we ever had for dessert were home-made cookies or cupcakes.

So, a big, fresh turkey stuffed with homemade dressing, mashed potatoes, gravy, handmade pies, vegetables, candied yams, cranberry sauce, rolls with real butter, and Dad's famous scalloped oysters sounded pretty wonderful and elegant to a bunch of constantly hungry growing kids. And the day-long anticipation of the meal made the big event even more memorable. In my mind, every Thanksgiving was a glorious feast indeed.

We enjoyed so many wonderful Thanksgiving holidays in Mammoth Lakes, California. Here we are on the way to Mammoth Lakes. Alan, Roger and Natalie in the back, me and amazing Mugsy in the front.

Thanksgiving meant more to me than just sharing a wonderful meal with my family. I cherished how we sang together as a group. "We Gather Together to Ask the Lord's Blessing" was our family prayer and, to this day, brings tears to my eyes whenever I hear it sung. Even though we didn't share an organized religion, or go to church on Sundays, I always felt our family was spiritual. Mom and Dad reminded us often that we had much to be thankful for, and we were thankful in turn.

Looking back on those Thanksgiving memories made me want more for my children. I wish my children could know all those wonderful feelings I knew as a child. I want them to know the excitement of anticipation and to savor the flavors as we did. But most of all, I wish my children had more sisters and a brother whom they could sing with.

I am not sure what Thanksgiving means to my family. We don't talk about it much. I don't remember one of them ever looking into the hot oven to see how beautiful the turkey looks as it crisps up at the end of the cooking time. In fact, last year, when I asked if anyone wanted to watch me baste the bird, they all looked up from the television at once and someone said, "What for?"

"What for?" I protested back. "To watch the juices bubbling down the darkened skin, to smell the delicious aroma, to snitch some dressing! That's what for."

"Oh," Alan answered quietly. "How about we do that at halftime?"

How could Alan appreciate the sheer joy of looking in the oven at the cooking turkey? The "poor" fellow had grown up with such abundance that he never knew want the way I had. The first time I had dinner with his family was the first time I had ever seen meat left over on a platter after everyone was served. It was an amazing sight for me, seeing big pieces of fried round steak sitting unwanted at the end of the meal. What a concept. With nine people at our table, there were never leftovers in our family, and certainly not *meat* leftovers.

So, I guess I am stuck; stuck with my happy memories of Thanksgivings gone by in my childhood. I should be thankful, and I am, that my children have never known hunger or food monotony. About the only time anything went missing in my children's lives is when I hadn't had time to shop for fresh milk or bread.

More and more, with every year that passes, I realize that life is full of trade-offs. I've traded the fun and excitement of craving a giant special feast on Thanksgiving for having good eats on a regular basis. I've been very lucky and I've had them both. I have been hungry enough to appreciate a really fine meal, and, later, I've been so full of good food that I actually welcomed, and had to insist on, some lean meals. Having little makes you appreciate a lot—in a way that growing up with a lot probably leaves you no room. It's a funny thing, but in looking back, it is the looking forward to that is sometimes better than the having.

30

Call the Police

My mother was in the Seal Beach Women's Club, a philanthropic organization that did all kinds of wonderful things in our community. Because they did so much for others, I invited the members to our home for a luncheon a couple of times each year. There were about thirty-five ladies, and they ranged in age from sixty-five to ninety.

I like to believe that my luncheons were memorable events. One time, I hired a professional chef to present a cooking lesson. Another time, I invited a former college professor in her seventies to give a talk on gardening. Olga Lewis was an expert, with multiple books on the subject.

In February, I invited the club ladies for a Valentine's party, and it happened to be right after we returned from our vacation. We had been out of the country for a few weeks, so when I got home I had to get busy and get the food organized and the house decorated for the occasion. Since I liked to make special gifts to place at each spot on the table, the week of the party was a whirlwind of work.

The only problem with living in Huntington Harbor was that the parking rules were strict. You had to move your car to one side of the street each Friday for the street sweeper and move it back for the garbage truck a few days later. If you didn't move your car, you had to pay a fine. Since we had remodeled our garage into a man cave for our adult son, Roger, we only had off-street parking for two of our four cars. It was a challenge to keep the parking fines at bay.

Returning from our vacation, we had multiple parking tickets on the cars. In our haste to leave for the airport, we had forgotten to move our kids' cars to our neighbor's ample parking area. The fines came to over two hundred dollars, and the tickets were still on my desk the morning of the party.

"Have you paid the parking fines?" my husband asked, as he finished off his last bit of breakfast coffee.

"Oh, good Lord, no! I forgot to pay those darn fines," I answered.

It was out of character for me not to pay parking fines. I'm a worrywart, so I immediately started getting upset at this reminder.

It didn't help when my husband added, "You know, if we don't pay those parking fines, they are liable to throw our butts in jail."

And with that, he was out the door to work.

"I've been super busy this week with the party, IN CASE YOU HAVEN'T NOTICED," I yelled after him.

Soon the guests arrived and the ladies settled into their seats. Anna, who cleaned our house weekly, was working that day and helping me serve drinks. The house looked festive, and the ladies were commenting on the lovely boxes of candy they had received. I was feeling proud of myself and I knew my mom was proud of me too. All of the sudden the doorbell rang.

"Are we expecting another guest?" I asked Mom, looking back at the table and seeing that all the chairs were full.

"No," she answered. "Everybody is here."

I opened the door and there stood a policeman.

"Paula Thomas? Are you Paula Thomas?"

"Yes," I answered quickly. "Is there a problem, officer?"

"Yes, I'm afraid there is," he said sternly. "I'm here about your multiple unpaid parking tickets. We take parking fines very seriously here in Huntington Beach, and your fines are grossly overdue."

I hurried to explain that we had been on vacation . . . we forgot to move the cars . . . didn't think of it until we were almost to the airport . . . I got back and was super busy with the party . . . I was planning to pay them. . . .

The policeman interrupted me mid-sentence. "What's going on in there?" he asked, as he jerked his head in the direction of the sounds coming from my living room. I hadn't noticed that the ladies had gotten loud.

"Oh, it's nothing, officer. I'm having a luncheon," I stammered. "Here, come and see for yourself."

The policeman followed me into the house, walking close behind me. Once inside, and without warning, he grabbed my wrist and handcuffed me to a chair. I looked at him, startled. "Don't move, I'm calling for backup," he said seriously, as he went back to the door.

I turned and looked at the club ladies. They had stopped talking and were staring at me handcuffed in the chair. I could see that they were startled too. Suddenly, I heard music. The "policeman" had grabbed a boombox from where he had stashed it outside the door. He started gyrating to the music and began taking off his clothes. Ok, I hate stuff like that. I mean, I knew plenty of ladies who went to Chippendales, the strip club for women, but I would never go. The idea of guys pulsating seductively around me, half naked and putting their crotches in my face, sounded disgusting. I sure as heck wouldn't put money in some guy's thong.

Sitting in my front room, stone sober, with a strange guy taking off his clothes was not my idea of fun. When he wrapped his shirt around his bottom and started pulling it from side to side, I started turning red, as red-faced as those candy boxes I had just given as gifts. Oh, I knew who had done this to me.

"I'm going to kill my husband," I thought.

My next thought was for the ladies. What in the world would they think?

I needed haven't worried. They were loving it and loving him. After embarrassing me completely, the policeman danced toward my guests. He was cavorting around their chairs playfully, thrusting his "nightstick" back and forth to the beat. Some ladies were covering their eyes and squealing, but most ladies were clapping and laughing. Louise grabbed some money and tucked it into his thong, and another gal actually pinched the "officer's" butt. When that happened, the ladies went wild; okay, wilder. The more they yelled and clapped, the more provocatively the policeman pranced. After the melee was finally over, and "all charges were dropped," I looked around the room. I could tell what the ladies were thinking. This crazy party had just beat the heck out of some ol' gardening lesson. My husband could hardly wait to hear how he had embarrassed me. The unpaid parking tickets were, of course, the perfect ploy. He had gotten me good, that's for sure. But, more importantly, Alan's ridiculous policeman stripper had put a ton of fun in some special ladies' lives.

31

The Rental Car

> **1986**

At one point in life, our son, Roger, was going to school in Utah. One February day, I got a call from that school. Roger was in the hospital and was going to have surgery the following morning. Bang, I got on an airplane and flew off immediately to be at his side.

When I arrived in Salt Lake City, it was snowing like mad. Just getting to the rental car dealer was an ordeal. Snow that day was several inches deep and the wind temperature was well below freezing. Like the other Avis customers in line, I was relieved to hear that Avis would take us by shuttle right to our cars. Thank goodness! Sloshing in the snow, looking for some strange vehicle, didn't sound like fun to me. I was already nervous since I had never driven in snow before.

The struggles we endure today will be the "good old days" we laugh about tomorrow.

—AARON LAURITSEN

When I told this to the guy at the counter, he gave me this advice: "Just slow down when you go over bridges and watch for black ice; it can be treacherous." Good to know. I'd watch out.

All customers had to wait until everyone was checked in, and so the shuttle bus was full when it left for the car lot. As cold as it was, it was worth the wait. I was one of the last people in the shuttle and was standing opposite the middle door, hanging onto a metal rail which ran the length of the ceiling of the bus. The shuttle jerked to a start and I had to quickly catch myself from falling on the handsome young man beside me. Down the driveway we headed to the waiting snow-covered cars. The wind was swirling about and it was difficult for the driver to find the numbers on the various vehicles. Finally, the shuttle bus turned onto aisle 3 and stopped. A bundled-up guy got out, fumbling with his luggage to exit. A giant swoosh of freezing air and swirling snow came through the bus door, jolting all the other customers to attention.

Suddenly the driver yelled back toward me. "Lady, you're a celebrity, right?"

I had no idea who he was talking to. I pointed at my chest with a gloved finger, looked from side to side and said, "Me? Are you talking to me?"

When he nodded yes, I answered, "No, I'm not a celebrity."

By now, every other person in the bus was looking around to see who the celebrity was whom the driver was talking to. The driver now raised his voice slightly and it was obvious he was irritated.

"You. Lady. You're the celebrity. Right?"

Now all eyes were on me and I could feel myself turning bright red at the unwelcome attention.

"No! Honest, I'm not a celebrity," I said emphatically.

The driver lost it. He yelled, "Did you, or did you not, rent a Chevrolet Celebrity?"

I felt like an idiot. He was talking about a car. I had never heard of that make of car, and I certainly had no idea I had rented one.

"I guess so, if you say so," I said feebly. Freezing or not, I couldn't wait to get out of that bus. Delivered to my patiently waiting Chevrolet Celebrity by my not-so-patient shuttle driver, and now alone with my thoughts, I started the car and sat there wishing Alan were with me. It was the beginning of tax season and he was already swamped at work, so I said I'd go alone. But I was afraid. It was now after dark and I was about to drive off into the middle of what looked to me like a blizzard. No car phone. No Google Maps. Nope, they hadn't been invented yet. Just me and that damn Celebrity driving to Provo, Utah, which was about fifty miles away, with those "treacherous bridges and the black ice" to worry about.

Considering the weather, I was sure the trip would take me well over an hour. I just knew that I wanted to get there in time to see Roger before his surgery the next morning. That was my goal. The blizzard would make it near impossible to get to the hospital for visiting time that night. I could call him as soon as I got to the hotel. That's if and when I found it. I'm horrible with directions, especially in the dark and under stress. Surprisingly, I made it to the hotel. Alive, even.

When I checked in at the front desk, I was emotionally exhausted. "How was your trip?" the attendant asked cheerfully. "Oh, it was fine after I got out of the airport. My sense of direction is awful. I had to hire a cab driver to guide me to the I-80 East exit. He was a nice guy and wouldn't take a dime. Anyhow, I'm here and that's all that matters." The attendant was sweet and told me she was happy my ordeal was over.

"I just have one question," I continued, as she handed me my room key. "Where the heck are these bridges Avis warned me about? I didn't see any bridges and I never saw any black ice either."

The gal laughed. "We don't have any bridges. The guy was talking about metal cattle crossings. That's where you see the black ice. Well, you don't actually see it. You feel it while you're driving."

Okay, I get it. You can't see black ice, because it's black and so is the blacktop. So, it's just invisible ice. Is it just me or isn't it a bit silly to tell someone, "Watch out for black ice," because if you *can't* see black ice, there is nothing to watch for. That's why it's *black ice*.

Anyhow, with the black ice issue settled, sort of, I got up to my room and immediately called Roger. He was in good spirits and was happy I was there (well, in town). It was wonderful to hear his voice.

"I'll see you first thing in the morning, sweetie. I love you," I said, as we finished our call.

It was 10:30 p.m., and I needed to decompress. Maybe I could get an appetizer and a glass of wine at the bar. I headed down to the reception area and looked around.

"Where's the bar?" I called to the gal behind the desk.

"You're in Utah. Remember? But I can get you an apple and some cookies and milk."

Which, to be honest, sounded delicious. No longer stressed out, I realized I was quite starved.

The next morning, at the crack of dawn, I was already at the hospital. Roger was talking to his anesthesiologist as I entered the room. The surgeon came out to meet me. Then I gave Roger a big hug and told him I was sure everything would be fine. As they wheeled my handsome son through the surgery doors, I waved happily as tears filled my eyes and a lump of fear formed in my throat. I so wished I weren't alone.

Thank God, the surgery went well. Once Roger was released from the hospital and back at school, I loaded up my rental car and headed back toward Salt Lake City. The trip was uneventful. Knowing my son would be fine, absent a blizzard, and in the light of day, the fifty-mile trip was a breeze. I even saw some bridges along the way. I returned my rental car at Avis and hopped on the shuttle bus for the trip back to the airport. The driver helped me with my bag. Then he looked at me, laughing.

"I know you. You're the celebrity!"

"Yep," I said smiling. "That's me."

32

Lisa's Wedding

After my daughter graduated from high school, Lisa, her best friend, became a local hairstylist, while Natalie went off to college in Colorado. Not long afterward, we received an invitation at our home to Lisa's wedding, but the timing didn't allow for Natalie to come home and attend. My mom and I decided to go to Lisa's wedding and represent the family.

Lisa got married in a beautiful little church in Laguna Beach. She was a stunning bride and the groom was handsome. After the ceremony a buffet reception was held at the newlyweds' home on a hill above Laguna Beach. Mom and I were thrilled to find a parking spot just a few blocks from their house. Laguna is a charming place, but parking on the hillside is tricky to say the least. We parked and starting walking up toward the house, following the path marked by pink and white balloons. It was a beautiful day and not too hot. My new pink wool dress was perfect for the occasion. I had accessorized the dress with pearl earrings and a very long strand of large pearls that hung with a knot in the middle, almost to my waist. As always, Mom was stylish in a flowered silk dress.

At the door we were greeted by the bride and groom and Lisa's parents, whom we knew from previous occasions. After the usual pleasantries, we surveyed the surroundings for seats. The house was already full of people, and I was lucky to find a place on an upholstered bench overlooking the water below.

"Wow," I said to Mom, "This is quite a place." I was pleased that Lisa had married well.

The buffet line was up a few steps in the dining room. I suggested that I go fill us some plates so Mom could guard our precious seats. She agreed and settled in as I got in line for the buffet.

The spread was fabulous. There were sliced ham and turkey, several kinds of fresh salad, and an array of vegetables and potato dishes. A selection of breads and crackers were stacked high on silver platters to one side, and there was also a lovely assortment of cheeses and condiments. In the center of the table was an amazing selection of fresh fruit with a glass container of wooden skewers. The idea was to select the fruit of your choice with the skewer and dip it into the melted chocolate in the giant silver chafing dish nearby.

I looked over at Mom and mouthed, without actually saying it, "The food looks great," and gave her a friendly thumbs-up. I knew she would not be able to hear my words above the background noise and people talking. I filled up her plate with lots of delicious goodies, then I bent way over the table and started pointing toward the fruit, mouthing, "Do you want fruit?"

I wasn't sure about the fruit, because Mom had mentioned some stomach issues and I didn't want to waste it. She put up both hands and I thought she was signaling no, as her hands went back and forth. I thought maybe she was saying no to the bananas in front. I bent over the table again and skewered some pineapple instead and held that up. Mouthing again, "Do you want pineapple?" This seemed likely, as pineapple was her favorite fruit.

She just started waving again, this time more frantically. I thought maybe that meant no fruit at all. "What?" I mouthed again, this time pointing to the strawberries. "Do you want strawberries instead?" I felt like we were playing charades, and I was totally confused.

The back and forth went on for several minutes until Mom mouthed, "Look down, look down," and pointed in an exaggerated fashion toward the floor. When I looked down, I stammered loudly, "Oh, my God." *Now* I knew what she was waving about.

When I had bent over the table, my long pearls had draped into the container of melted chocolate. Each time I straightened up, my chocolate covered pearls followed like a pendulum. Yikes! What a mess. I had dark melted chocolate all down the front of my new pink dress, and chocolate was running onto my shoes. There was also chocolate all over the table. I was so embarrassed and I felt like a fool. The hostess came running over and tried her best to mop up the dripping chocolate, but the more she patted the chocolate, the more it spread around. Others tried to help too, but they just made the matter worse. Soon, chocolate covered the front of my dress and was on my sleeves, on my hose, and even sticking to my toes inside my shoes. I felt ridiculous and my dress looked like a child's finger painting. We had no choice but to leave the party, and do it fast.

As we passed arriving guests on the way back to our car, they looked at me with horrified expressions. "Oh, my Lord, what happened to you?" a lady asked mystified. What could I possibly say?

"It's a long story," I laughed. "Just be careful at the buffet."

33

Roman Holiday

> ### 1987

Unless you are one of those gifted folks who speak multiple languages, most tourists traveling to Europe experience an occasional language problem. I speak some broken Spanish thanks to my alma mater, Huntington Beach High School, and a few Italian and French words, mostly related to food. But not knowing how to pronounce the name of the hotel you are staying in or remembering the name of the street it is on can create an adventure when you are in a foreign city and trying to get back to your room.

Our friends, John and Carolyn Rose, joined us one year for a trip to Rome. At that particular time, the world was unsettled and a bit scary, so we chose our hotel carefully. Not one of the big fancy American places for sure, because if you stay in an American chain hotel, you might as well stay home. Instead, like always, we chose a smaller hotel with lots of Italian flavor in the Old City, not far from the Piazza Navona, an area that features important sculptural and architectural creations, baroque fountains, and delightful cafes and trendy restaurants. We wanted a quiet, out-of-the-way place that was frequented more often by Europeans than other Americans. I can't remember the exact name of the hotel, but I know it had at least four words in the title, something like Alla Corte degli Angeli. I had no idea what the words meant, but I was pretty sure they weren't the names of pasta.

Anyhow, we arrived late afternoon, lunched at a friendly little family restaurant recommended by the front office staff, and then settled into our comfy rooms for naps. Later, we met for dinner at a restaurant that Carolyn had read about in the Los Angeles Times' Food Section. This restaurant, according to Carolyn, featured "quintessentially Italian repast." I had no idea what all that meant, but it sounded delicious. Carolyn is a food expert of sorts and a terrific cook, so we were sure the meal would be delicious and probably expensive.

We took a cab to the dinner spot, which was every bit as fancy and tasty as the name suggested, and, yes, every bit as pricy. The "sumptuous repast" took almost three hours to consume and included the *aperitivo*, a small appetizer of olives, nuts, and crisps, which was eaten at the bar along with a cocktail. Once seated, we were served the *antipasto*, salami, prosciutto, fancy cheeses, and other charcuterie products. Next, was the *primo* course, non-meat dishes. We all had pasta. Then came the *secondo*, or meat course. I had steak. The *contorno*, which is a side dish of vegetables, was added to the meat plate, and *insalata*, a fresh garden salad, followed all of that.

At this point in the meal, I understood why it was said that Romans used a vomitorium to voluntarily throw up during feasting times, just so they could return to the table for a second round of roast. Actually, that's a misconception. A vomitorium was not a room used by Romans to evacuate their meals. They were large passageways used to evacuate big crowds at the end of a performance at an amphitheater or stadium. What did we do before Google?

Back to the repast: *Formaggi e frutta*, local cheeses and fresh seasonal fruit followed the meat, vegetable, and salad course, and then *dolce*, or dessert. I had tiramisu. Caffè was served after the meal, followed by a *digestivo*, such as grappa or limoncello, a liqueur meant to ease digestion after a long meal. Boy, did we need that!

Stuffed to the gills (and we didn't even order fish), and three bottles of Italian merlot and a couple of cocktails later, we stepped out of the restaurant into the cool, fall evening air, and headed toward our hotel, which Alan said was due east. The walk was just what we needed; but four blocks later, I wasn't so sure. An hour later still, we admitted we were lost. None of us could even pronounce the name of our hotel, and east turned out to be a big destination. Thankfully, just as we were at our wit's end, John recognized the distinctive blue lights of our hotel's sign in the distance. Tired and relieved to be at our home-away-from-home, we said, "*Buona notte a tutti*" (good night, all), and headed up to bed.

Up bright and early the next morning, we met for a typical Italian breakfast, not that we were hungry. Like a continental breakfast, there was lots of hot espresso, with or without milk, along with bread, butter, and jam. Bolstered by five times as much caffeine as I would typically drink at breakfast in California (according to Wikipedia,

"Caffeine is a central nervous system stimulant of the methylxanthine class and the world's most widely consumed psychoactive drug"), I was wired-up and ready for a Roman Holiday.

The first thing we noticed as we exited our hotel was a cadre of armed Italian soldiers, dressed in black flak jackets and carrying Uzi submachine guns. Ignoring our greetings, they were serious-minded and paying close attention to the entrance of the hotel.

"What's going on out here?" I asked a travel agent who was waiting for a group of tourists.

"The prime minister always takes the top floor of this hotel when he's in town. He came in late last night and will be here for the next few days."

So much for choosing a low-key hotel.

Carlos, our guide, who had been recommended by friends from the States, was waiting in his car across the street from our hotel. To assure that we wouldn't get lost again, I carefully wrote down the name of our street and the name of our hotel inside the cover of my trusty *Frommer's Italy* guidebook, or the Bible as we called it.

Born and raised in Rome, Carlos was the best guide anyone could ever have. In his late sixties, bald, a little pudgy, and handsome, he had charm and wit, and kept us laughing all day with stories about notorious nuns and intrigues of the various popes who had lived in Vatican City. Under his wise tutelage, we walked the Roman ruins in the forum, saw the Temple of Venus, and explored Palatine Hill and the Arch of Constantine. None of us remembered much Roman history, and it was embarrassing to admit our educations were so lacking.

Afterward, in the hills above Rome, we lunched on a vine-covered patio at a restaurant owned by a family friend of Carlos. "Besta fooda ina Italy," Carolos told us smiling. "*Molto buono e molto delizioso.*" He was so right: it was very good and very delicious. Carlos chose the wine, Orvieto Classico from Umbria, Italy. "It's the sun of Italy in a bottle," he told us proudly, before adding another Carlos story: "Eighteenth-century Pope Gregory XVI was said to have requested that his body be washed with Orvieto prior to burial."

It was late in the afternoon when we drove back toward the hotel.

"Please," I pleaded, "we need to walk off that lunch." I was stuffed and didn't want to crash for a nap without burning off a little wine and a whole lot of homemade pasta.

"No problem," said Carlos. "Your hotel is just a few blocks away. Take a left on the next street." With that, we hugged Carlos, said *ciao*, and waved as he drove away.

"There's our street, right there," I said proudly, checking the spelling I'd written down in the "Bible." Off we went toward our street, reminiscing about our amazing day, and feeling a little less woozy and a little less full with each passing step. Our street turned left, like Carlos said it would, and we followed it, chatting and laughing again about that one story of the nun who was evidently a bit of a floozy. On we walked, continuing to follow our street as it twisted and turned, eventually enjoying the walking less and getting irritated that our street seemed to go on forever.

"We've walked a dozen blocks. Where the heck is our hotel?"

Our street turned again, and Alan said, "Wait a minute. There's another street right there with the same name."

"That's impossible," I stammered. I walked over to a cabdriver who stood outside his cab, waiting beside a residence for his fare.

"*Scusa mi fai parlare?*" That was one of the sentences I had memorized before leaving home. I was praying he'd say, "Yes. I speak English." And he did.

By this time, the rest of the group was standing beside me as I brought out the "Bible" and showed the cabdriver the name of our street.

"Senso Unico. Our hotel is on Senso Unico."

The Italian cab driver looked at me as if I were an idiot, which it turns out I kind of was.

"That's not a street name," he said blankly. "*Senso unico* means one-way street!"

Whoops.

The cabdriver kindly directed us back to our four-name hotel, and, once there, we each took a hotel business card and stowed it for future use. From then on, getting to and from our Italian abode was easy.

I eventually found out that Alla Corte degli Angeli means "Court of the Angels."

When we travel with friends and family, we make it a habit to spend one day together and the next day adventuring by ourselves. It keeps us from getting sick of each other and makes it more fun, because on our days apart we see different things that we can share later.

"We have to find a tailor today," John told us over his third espresso. He had busted the zipper of his black pants and, since he only had two pairs on the trip, it was a must-do on the day we were spending apart. The front desk, always helpful, gave him the name of a good tailor in the vicinity of our hotel.

Later that night, when we met for dinner, John was wearing his black pants, so we assumed all had gone smoothly. In fact, as we left the restaurant, John thought he spied his tailor going down the dark side of the street across from the restaurant we were exiting. John wanted to say "hello" and thank the fellow for doing such a nice job on his pants. Unable to speak the language, John called out the tailor's name, Ricardo, and started running toward the guy, pulling his zipper up and down, trying to signal with this pantomime, "It's me, the guy you fixed the zipper for." But it was dark. And it was late. And the poor guy didn't recognize John and started walking away from us at lightning speed, wanting nothing to do with this guy making obscene gestures in his direction.

Caroline started running after John screaming, "No. No. No. That's not the guy. It's not Ricardo," which only added to the bewilderment of the late-night drama. Who knows what this innocent Italian guy thought this American was up to, just running at him screaming.

"That poor guy," Caroline snapped at John. "He probably thought you were a pervert, trying to sell your wife for sex, and she was screaming NO."

Zippers and one-way streets aside, Italy is a fabulous destination. The people are friendly, the sights are amazing, the history is captivating and the food—oh, my gosh, the food!

It's funny how, when you travel, you rarely remember or talk afterward about the accommodations you had, unless they were horrible. You know: no air conditioning in your room when it's unbearably hot. Sure, you might say the view was stunning, or the room was spacious, or the breakfast buffet was grand, but those things are secondary to the experiences you have and the people you meet. When the language is foreign, buying a train ticket from a machine or trying to find the right bus can create a challenging experience, especially if the bus you want to take is the only one that day and is about to leave.

Life is either a daring adventure or nothing.

—HELEN KELLER

My son still remembers the time in Italy when he got daring and ordered a *"Pizza con l'uovo sulla parte,"* saying, "I want to try eating outside of the box" (pizza box, that is, the joker). None of us had the slightest idea what he was ordering and laughed out loud when his pizza arrived; it had an egg on top. Then there was the time in Switzerland when we ate Chinese food. When we travel with our kids, we take turns choosing the dinner spot. The evening that it was her turn, Peyton, our granddaughter, chose Chinese. Not a word in the menu was written in English. Not a single word. Now that I think about it, how do I even know it was a menu? Anyway, we all just pointed at stuff and ate what came. It was one of the best meals ever.

Getting outside of your comfort zone, trying something new, doing something daring—that's what makes travel exciting. It's mostly the funny experiences or the scary ones or even the stressful events that keep the vacation alive in your mind and in your heart. I, for one, will never forget those moments. *Ciao.*

34

The Spritzer Boy

1987

My husband and his buddies are avid golfers, so I wasn't surprised when Alan asked me if I would like to do a long golf weekend in Palm Springs with our friends, Cliff and Mary Lee Sharp. The initial plan was for the guys to play golf each day, while Mary Lee and I would lounge by the pool and probably get facials and "lady" stuff like that. We have lots of fun with Mary Lee and Cliff because, like us, they like to dance, eat, and drink. A weekend at the desert sounded sensational.

When we arrived at the hotel, our husbands kissed us goodbye and left immediately for the links. This was not surprising; they had already dressed for golf before we left home. Mary Lee and I checked in and were escorted to our suites by a friendly and very short young man dressed in khaki Bermuda shorts, a starched white shirt, and khaki ball cap with the Desert Springs' logo (a hummingbird) embroidered on it.

"Afternoon, ladies. My name is Bert, your bell captain. Please, can I carry your bags?"

Bert walked ahead of us, carrying our bags, pointing out the entrance to the pool, the exercise facility, and "our world-renowned" health spa.

Trying not to act too eager, I asked, "Do you have a bar?" Mary Lee chuckled.

Bert told us that the hotel had three separate bars, and set down our bags so that he could point out their locations.

"And of course, there is the disco lounge, which opens at 11 p.m.," Bert added proudly.

Did I mention that Bert was also wearing knee-high socks and white tennis shoes? Because of his height and those knee-high socks and ball cap, Bert looked like a Boy Scout. Maybe a Cub Scout. A Cub Scout who was happily encouraging us to drink alcohol and disco dance, not that it took much encouragement.

The Desert Springs Resort is huge, and it seemed like we walked forever to get to our rooms. At last Bert opened our doors, got us fresh ice, and showed us the minibars and safes inside our rooms.

Alan had tipped Bert before the guys left for golf, and Cliff had told Bert, "Make sure you take good care of the girls." I loved that Cliff referred to us as girls, because at that point in our lives we were well past our prime.

Anyhow, Bert did as he had been instructed and got us settled in nicely. Then, with a quick salute, our loyal little troop leader was gone. Mary Lee and I agreed to meet out by the pool for lunch. Mary Lee said that she wanted to unpack their things and get organized.

"Okie dokie, Pinocchio," I said, already getting in a playful mood. "How long will you be?"

If we were animals, Mary Lee would be a tortoise and I would be a hare. She takes her time and is methodical. I do everything fast. When she said thirty minutes, I knew it would be forty-five minutes or more, because a tortoise takes her time. I decided to head out early. It was hot out by the pool, probably eighty-five degrees. I mean, that's why people go to Palm Springs. I asked the pool boy to put down towels on two chaise lounges for us, as close to the pool as possible. It was a Thursday and already the resort was getting packed. After tipping the pool boy, I lay out like a lizard across one of the big soft towels, using the second towel for a pillow.

"This is the life!" I said to myself. It was so peaceful and the hot sun felt great.

I checked my watch and calculated when to expect Mary Lee to show. Then, I signaled the poolside bar attendant and asked him what he would recommend we drink?

"The mai tai is the signature drink here at Desert Springs Hotel," he said helpfully. "Everyone loves our mai tais."

"Then that's what we need," I answered. I asked him to please deliver two Desert Springs signature mai tais at 1:15 p.m. sharp. I was sure Mary Lee would have arrived by then, and her drink would be ready and waiting for her. This was going to be fun. Time passed and I was getting hot. I cooled myself by slipping in and out of the pool several times. Despite the quick dips and the nice big umbrella we had as a cover, I was starting to sweat. I kept looking toward the door that opened onto the pool from the hall near our rooms. Where was my beautiful friend? At 1:15, on the dot, the mai tais arrived. I was glad to suck up the glorious combination of liquors. They went down smooth and cool. I tried sipping slowly and ate the fresh pineapple that decorated the top of the giant tumbler. The drink was cold and delicious. I could see why it was the resort's signature drink. Before long, my mai tai tumbler was empty. And Mary Lee's was just sitting there on the table, getting hot. A travesty. I couldn't bear to let that marvelous concoction go to waste, so I picked up her drink and started sipping. When Mary Lee finally arrived, her drink was gone, and her drinking buddy was slightly gone as well. I don't usually drink a cocktail before lunch, and I certainly never drink two sixteen-ounce mai tais.

"Where's my drink?" Mary Lee demanded playfully, putting her hands on her hips.

"Well, you took so long I *had* to drink it. It was too yummy to go to waste," I answered.

As I got up to greet my buddy, I realized the drinks, the sun, and the sweltering sweating had taken a toll on my sense of balance. I swayed slightly as the bar attendant arrived. We ordered Mary Lee a mai tai and I asked for a big glass of water. As we ordered, I mentioned to the waiter that I was getting too hot.

"I'll send over Jake. He's our pool spritzer boy," he said.

"Thanks a lot," I said slurring my words slightly.

Anyone familiar with Palm Springs is familiar with pool spritzer boys. All the hotels have handsome guys whose job is to traverse the pool deck and spritz overheated guests with ice water. We had seen them before and had commented how especially attentive they were to the young bikini-clad beauties who decorated the pool. By the time Jake arrived, the full force of my two cocktails had hit me. Mary Lee and I were sharing stupid stories, entertaining each other and laughing loudly like a couple of fools. Jake, the spritzer boy, was not a boy at all. He was a man, and tall, dark, tanned, and handsome beyond belief. He wore short white tennis shorts, flip flops, and dark aviator glasses.

"Oh my God, look at this guy," I whispered loudly in Mary Lee's direction. "I bet he makes a fortune in tips."

Jake flashed a big handsome smile and held up his plastic spray bottle filled with ice water. "Anyone for a spritz?" he asked in a flirting tone.

I was drunk as a skunk and hotter than Hades. So, with all my inhibitions washed away on a mai tai sea, I threw open my legs and yelled, loudly, "Spritz away!"

Poor Jake. I startled him. Turning red as a cherry, he fled away from our lounge chairs as fast as his tanned, muscular legs could carry him and he never returned all day. We couldn't stop laughing for twenty minutes. The ghost of mai tais past still seemed to be gaining strength in my system and I was beginning to feel really dizzy.

"Mary Lee," I slurred, "Maybe we should order lunch." Which helped.

Stuffed, drunk, and happy, we decided we needed to take naps. We headed back through the door near our rooms, and I started fumbling to find my key. Being a hare, and not a tortoise, I had rushed out of my room without my key. Upon discovering my dilemma, Mary Lee took charge.

"Stand against the wall. Don't move. I'll go find Bert to open your room."

I agreed to wait. I was in no shape to take the long walk back to the reception area. I leaned against the wall, as instructed, and tried to act sober, nodding occasionally to the nicely clad guests who went in both directions through the hall. Slowly, gravity took over, and I began to slide like an inebriated noodle down the wall. My feet slid forward and in no time I was prone, ass on the carpet, blocking the path. It was much more difficult to pretend I was sober when people were forced to step over me.

Dear alcohol, We had a deal where you would make me funnier, smarter, and a better dancer. I saw the video. We need to talk.

—Unknown

"I'm fine. Really. Just resting." I said ridiculously, as a couple looked down in concern.

Finally, Mary Lee returned and, with the Boy Scout's assistance, helped me into my room. "I just hope my husband won't be mad at you, Bert," Mary Lee joked, faking a stern demeanor. "You were supposed to take care of the girls, and look at her: she's a mess."

I did try to find Jake, the spritzer boy, to apologize the next day. I was embarrassed to death by my drunken behavior. But Jake never reappeared anywhere near me. I'm sure that after that experience he stuck to spritzing young bikini-clad beauties and stayed away from ladies past their primes.

35

Hedonism II, Jamaica

> **1988**

The first time Alan and I went to Hedonism II ("Hedo" to the locals), it was by accident. We knew nothing about the place except that it was a "Super Club" and it was in Jamaica. Super Clubs are all-inclusive: you pay one price for airfare, room, activities, and all the meals and drinks you can consume. The club offers sailing, scuba diving, tennis, aerobics, dancing, and entertainment every night. It is really a travel bargain if that kind of stuff sounds good to you. Our travel agent recommended this Super Club and said they had open reservations if we wanted to go. We said yes, and the trip was on.

A few weeks before the trip, we mentioned our upcoming vacation to some business associates one night over dinner. The wife spoke up promptly and asked if we'd mind if they tagged along.

"We haven't been anywhere alone without the kids in ten years!"

I looked over at Alan and I could tell he didn't mind.

"Sure," I said, "the more the merrier." I thought it was probably the wine doing the asking, but I was wrong.

The next day Mary called me at the office. "We're all set. I called your travel agent and she got us reservations. We'll meet you at the airport on the twentieth."

Now, I really didn't know Mary and her husband very well. Alan worked with Don, Mary's husband, and we had been to a couple of Christmas parties at their office. But, other than an occasional dinner out, I knew very little about their family.

I asked Alan if he wanted to drive with Don and Mary to the airport. He was adamant. "No. Don is a last-minute guy and I'm not waiting around for him. He'll be late for his own funeral," Alan added.

Alan was so right. Just as Jamaica Air announced they were closing the airplane doors, Mary and Don came running down the aisle.

As they settled into their seats, Mary explained why they were tardy, "We don't have passports, so we had to drive to the courthouse in Santa Ana to get a copy of our voting records so they would let us into Jamaica."

"That is how Don operates," Alan whispered in my ear.

Upon arrival in Montego Bay, Jamaica, all us tourists heading toward the various Super Clubs were loaded onto big, air-conditioned busses for the trip to Negril and spots along the way. The bus would stop and drop folks off periodically at the different clubs as it progressed through the steamy, tropical countryside. We passed small villages of huts and a sprinkling of larger homes as we drove. Goats, horses, chickens, and kids ran free and seemingly happy along the roads.

The two-hour bus trip gave Mary and me a chance to get acquainted. I noticed she carried a Bible in her bag, and I learned that she was a strict Catholic and was trying to convert her husband, Don.

"I'm not having much luck," she admitted. We laughed. "I knew Don wasn't religious when I married him," she added, "but, I'm not giving up. I read the Bible every day."

Everybody on the bus was in a good mood and seemed as excited as we were about getting a week away from work. We began to chitchat with a couple sitting in the seats in front of us.

"Where are you headed?" the guy asked in a friendly manner.

"We're staying in Negril Beach at Hedonism II," I answered. "How about you?"

"Oh, my God. Are you really? You're going to Hedonism II?"

The guy got so excited, you would have thought I had said we were going to the moon. The guy stood up in his seat and yelled to some of his friends in the back of the bus as he pointed at us, "These guys are going to Hedonism II."

"Why are you so excited? What's the big deal about Hedonism II?" I asked him quickly. Before he could answer, I turned and looked at Mary. "Alan and I do things spontaneously, Mary. We didn't investigate the club. We just took the travel agent's recommendation. I have *no idea* what this club is like."

I wanted to let her know all this right up front, because I was getting a little concerned by the guy's reaction. The fellow proceeded to tell us all he knew about Hedo.

"It's just the wildest place in Jamaica. Everybody runs around nude."

"What?" I laughed. "Are you serious?"

Oh, he was serious all right and filled us in about other things he had heard.

"You guys must be wild types. Are you swingers?" he asked brightly.

I turned again to Mary. "Honestly, we didn't know the place was for swingers. Alan and I like fun, but swinging and nudity are not what we were expecting."

Alan thought this news was terribly funny and said, "I can hardly wait!"

Don wasn't worried either, but I could see concern growing in Mary's eyes.

"For goodness sakes, Mary, we're adults." Don said. "I think we can handle some topless women running around."

Negril Beach is on the west end of Jamaica. In those days, there were just a few big clubs in Negril and some small restaurants and motels along the way. It's the home of Rick's Café, a famous spot where local kids dive off the rocks for money and tourists get hurt when they are drunk and try to do the same thing to show off. Hedo was the last stop for the bus.

"You're just in time for lunch ladies," the handsome Jamaican said, as he put out his hand to help us off the bus.

A beautiful, fully clothed, Jamaican lady handed us tall rum drinks as our luggage was unloaded. The steel band playing near the reception area was welcoming and made me feel like we were walking into a party already in full swing. People of all shapes and sizes were milling about. Some people were wearing bathing suits and, so far, none were naked or even topless.

"Maybe the guy on the bus was exaggerating," I thought.

When we checked in, the clerk asked, "Do you want rooms on the nude side or the prude side of the club?"

"Prude," I interjected, because I could see Alan was giving the question some thought.

"Your rooms will be ready shortly. Please have some lunch while you wait. The Lunchtime Spin is about to begin."

We wandered into the enormous eating area. The dining tables were outdoor furniture with big, soft, cushioned seats. Music was playing loudly and wild Jamaican blackbirds squawked and flew about. There was a round bar in the corner of the room, covered with a palm-thatched roof. Lush, green, and beautiful, Jamaica is a world apart from California. So far, everything at the club seemed perfectly normal to me. Nothing weird was going on. As we got in line for the lunch buffet, we spotted a few scantily-clad ladies at the bar with a group of guys from Australia. They were talking loudly and laughing, and we could hear their Aussie accents. They appeared to be playing some kind of a drinking game.

Suddenly the winners of the game screamed, "Pants on your head. Pants on your head." A guy, obviously the game's loser, took his bathing suit off and put it on his head.

Okay, the guy on the bus wasn't lying. This place was going to be different.

As we settled into our seats with a plate of delicious food from the buffet, the Lunchtime Spin began. The spin was different each day and included some kind of entertainment on the big stage the tables were facing. The schedule said that today's event was a drinking game of sorts and asked for volunteers. Tomorrow was a talent show. Perhaps seeing a bit of concern on our faces, our waiter told us complete nudity was not allowed in the restaurant. I'm not sure why he didn't count the Aussie wearing his pants as a hat, but with that welcome news, and bolstered by another rum drink, we began to relax and have fun.

Our rooms were sparsely decorated in a tropical theme, with fragrant red hibiscus flowers scattered across our pillows and a large window that opened onto the turquoise sea. We hung up our clothes, changed into our bathing suits, and quickly joined Mary and Don at the "prude" beach. After Alan signed up for scuba diving the following morning and we ordered a round of piña coladas, we took a sailboat out and glided along the pristine bay, passing the nude beach as we sailed. The nude beach was packed with bodies of every description; some resting on lounges and others involved in sports and game activities.

[Note to self: Do not go to a nude beach when you are in your eighties.]

[Second note to self: Don't play volleyball nude, ever.]

Over afternoon drinks at the bar, we studied the activity schedule, which was the same for the nude and prude sides of the club. Mary read them off.

"Prude beach volleyball, nude beach volleyball. Prude aerobics, nude aerobics. Prude dance lessons, nude dance lessons."

"Good Lord," Mary squealed. "They have nude Twister at three."

Twister is a game that challenges you and your friends to contort around each other and put your hands and feet at different colored places on a floor mat without falling over. The image of Twister being played by butt-naked bodies was too scary to even consider.

At first, Mary was extremely uncomfortable at Hedonism II, and I was worried about her. As the days passed, and her liquor consumption increased, Mary definitely loosened up. Hedonism II is a wild place when compared to a typical beach resort hotel, but nobody has to do anything they don't want to and we spent most of the time belly laughing at the ridiculous antics of others. It turned out to be a really fun week.

Our last night at the club was Toga Night, and all the guests dressed in togas for dinner. The club left extra sheets on the beds for making togas and gave lessons on how to do it during the Lunchtime Spin. We anticipated a typical toga party like college kids have, think *Animal House*.

We arrived for dinner in our togas and immediately noticed a group from the nude side of the club coming our way. After a week at Hedo, you knew which folks were nudes and which were prudes.

Anyhow, Mary said in a surprised manner, "Look, the nudes are dressed normally." We had thought for sure that the nudes would be provocatively attired.

We smiled and greeted the nudes as they passed our table.

"You spoke too soon, Mary. Take a look at them now," I suggested, as they passed our table. Their togas were tied in the front around their necks only, like necklaces. The backs of their togas were completely open and flying free, like hospital gowns, but . . . sexier? Butts galore were visible.

"Isn't that cute," Mary said. Boy, had she had changed in a week.

Our second trip to Hedo was years later, in late April after tax season, and we took my sister Alice, who was working in Alan's accounting firm at the time. We knew the Hedo experience would be lots of fun with Alice because she has a great sense of humor and fun people flock to her like flies. Plus, because we are sisters, we act like goofy little kids when we're together. From the moment we arrived at the LAX airport to the moment we arrived in Jamaica, the three of us were already having fun.

When we arrived in Montego Bay this time, we took a small airplane to Negril Beach in lieu of the two-hour bus trip. The flight over the sparsely inhabited lush jungle was just thirty minutes long. As before, we arrived at the club around lunchtime. During lunch, we met the nicest young men from England. There were four of them and, like us, they had just arrived at Hedo. We met them again at the beach later and ended up being friends and companions all week.

At night, Alice and her handsome English escorts would go over to the piano bar that separated the two sections of the clubs. That bar opened after dinner and entertainment had ended, and stayed open until the wee hours of the morning. The piano bar had a wonderful pianist and also offered karaoke. Alice has a beautiful voice and quickly became a popular addition to the bar. Alan and I were usually too tired to go late barhopping and would head off to bed after dinner and entertainment. We looked forward each morning to hearing about the adventures of Alice and her English escorts on "The Dark Side," our nickname for the nude section of the club. One morning they told us about an attractive gal who had announced to everyone at the crowded bar that she wanted to do a striptease for her husband to celebrate their anniversary. Alice suspected, and probably rightly, that the anniversary was just an excuse to get naked, but, with that announcement, the gal got up on the grand piano and started doing her thing. Okay, it's an adult environment. How bad could it get? William, one of the English boys, could not believe his eyes.

"Blimey, mate, the bird took off her panties and was thrusting her bum toward the crowd."

Alice said the boys from England were totally embarrassed by her dancing and their faces turned bright red during the impromptu amateur show. For her finale, the gal squatted down slowly on the piano, pointing her bare butt toward her husband and the blushing boys sitting on either side. It was too much for one of the fellas, and he jumped up and ran out of the bar.

Later he told us, "That bird's stripping was not my cup of tea."

After our aerobics class that morning, Alice saw the stripper gal walking with her husband. Alice wanted to acknowledge that she'd been in the bar the night before and had seen the gal's striptease.

Without thinking, Alice said, "Hey, I caught the tail end of your act. Literally." We all walked away in hysterics.

At the conclusion of each evening's events, one of the English boys always escorted Alice safely to her room. One night Alice was walking back with Jarrett when they were stopped by a gal in her late forties. She was with a younger woman, who turned out to be her daughter.

"Say, I noticed you're hanging out with a bunch of young guys. How about sharing?"

The mom went on to explain, "We work like sort of a tag team." As she said this, she was pointing at her daughter, with a seductive look in her eye. Alice had no idea what she was talking about and sure didn't want to learn more.

"No thanks," Alice said, and she pulled Jarrett away by the hand in a protective manner.

We found out later from some other Hedo vacationers that the "tag-team twosome" had quite an erotic reputation on the nude beach. We didn't ask for all the gruesome details. How on earth does something like that get started?

People at the club were attracted to our little group because we were laughing so much and obviously having so much fun. One guy, Terrence, frequented our general area and was kind of an awkward fella who didn't really fit in. He constantly told everybody in earshot how many e-mails he was getting each day, but no one really cared. I guess the e-mail count was to make us all think he had lots of friends or was an important businessman back home. In any event, we felt sorry for Terrence and tried to be nice, but it wasn't easy because he was such an oddball. Anyhow, one day Alice and I were out by the ocean lounging and tanning, when I heard a familiar voice.

"Could you rub suntan cream on my back?"

"Sure," I said, flipping over.

I thought it was one of the English boys, but it wasn't. It was Terrence. I didn't really want to touch Terrence, but I had already said I would, so I felt obligated.

Terrence pulled off his shirt. Oh, no. Terrence had thick black hair on his back like a bear. When I started rubbing the cream on him, it felt creepy. It was like rubbing cream on a big furry sweater that was sweating. Alice, watching me wince as I rubbed, laughed out loud.

One thing we learned quickly at Hedo was to *never* volunteer for the games they played during the Lunchtime Spin. The games always sounded innocent, but always turned into something very embarrassing and usually risqué. A good example was the scavenger hunt. The announcer asked for volunteers and then directed the volunteers to retrieve a red lipstick from someone in the audience. The first person to bring back a red lipstick to the announcer won a prize. At first the game was cute and the players seemed to be having fun. The announcer went from asking the players to find lipsticks, to finding pencils, to eventually condoms, and then sex toys. Like I said, regardless how any game started, it always turned risqué.

On this particular day, the announcer asked the players to locate, "A true redhead and bring her to me." Well, we knew what the announcer was getting at: these "scavenged" redheads would be asked to prove they were *natural* redheads. That, of course, could only be done one way: the ole "Does the carpet match the drapes?"

The players started fanning out among the crowd looking for redheaded women. Alice and I both have red hair, so we sunk down in our seats as low as possible. There was no way in *hell* we were going up on that stage to prove whether our red hair was or was not natural. Alan wanted to embarrass us and started pointing toward us, yelling to the announcer on the stage, "Here's a couple of redheads."

Hearing Alan, a few players started running in our direction. Just as they got to our table, I yelled, pointing toward the stage, "Too late. Too late. A redhead has already been found." I was lying, of course, but I didn't really didn't care.

A different redheaded victim was quickly located in the audience and was being dragged reluctantly toward the stage. Then, just as we suspected, the next step of the game was on.

For those left wondering, she was a natural redhead.

Another day, Alice and I were sunbathing while Alan was out scuba diving on the boat. It was hot and Alice had gone up to the beach bar for a second round of piña coladas. I was lying face down on my lounge and a handsome guy in his late twenties approached and asked gently, "Would you like me to rub tanning oil on your back?"

"That would be nice," I said, with an embarrassed smile covering my hidden face. The guy had an Italian accent and he was a hunk. I was all giddy to think a guy who looked like that would want to put oil on my body. He sat down on the side of the lounge as I moved my thigh over a bit. He squeezed the tanning oil into his hands carefully and began to rub my back in a firm manner. Up through the center of my back and over my shoulders his strong hands glided. Alice returned with the next round of piña coladas just as the guy was finishing.

"Thanks so much," I said, with a silly, flirty tone.

"Anytime," he said sweetly. "I've been watching you two all morning. You remind me of my mother and her sister back home."

I was totally deflated, and Alice began laughing.

One night at dinner, Terrence came over to our table and asked me for "a big favor." He was leaving the next day and wanted badly to sing during karaoke. He begged me to come over to the piano bar and take his picture while he was singing. "I have a couple of songs picked out and I really don't want to go to the karaoke alone. Please."

I looked toward Alan, hoping he would agree to accompany me. "Not me," Alan said quickly, "I have plans with the boys," meaning the guys from England.

Truth be told, Alan was going to bed, but even if he hadn't been exhausted from diving, there was no way he'd voluntarily go to karaoke *with* Terrence.

Oh, brother. I really didn't want to go to karaoke with Terrence. The truth was I didn't want anyone thinking I was with Terrence. If only Alice were around to go with me, but she had a little stomach problem and had gone back to her room.

"Okay," I said reluctantly, "but, I'll only stay for one or two songs."

Terrence was thrilled and thanked me profusely. "I just have to get my sunglasses back at my room." He was planning to sing with them on so that he would, in his words, "look real cool." Great. This was going to be so embarrassing.

I waited for Terrence and then the two of us went over to the bar. Terrence picked up a lyric sheet for the song he was planning to sing; I think it was a Billy Joel song. We had to sit through a couple of other would-be entertainers and finally it was Terrence's turn at the mic. Terence put his shades on "so he'd look real cool" and handed me his camera. I stood ready to catch him in his act.

When the music for his song began, Terrence was facing away from the audience. He started to sing. I mean, I could hear his voice, but he didn't seem interested in turning around to face the audience. He kept singing while facing the wall. Finally, when the chorus came around, so did Terrence. He spun around and said/sang, "Yeah, yeah, yeah." Then, just as quickly, he turned back toward the wall. The only time he looked out at the audience was when he sang the chorus line, "Yeah, yeah, yeah." Three times the "Yeah, yeah, yeah" came up and three times he turned to face the audience. On the last turn, I snapped a single picture. The audience sat there incredulous. What the heck was this guy thinking?

After the song was over, Terrence came back to where I was hiding next to a large planted palm. "I think that went pretty well. Don't you?" he asked, with a big smile on his face. I said nothing. I was speechless.

I was just reliving my karaoke experience with Alice the next morning when we saw Terrence talking to a couple of girls at the breakfast buffet. "Yep," he told the girls loudly, "I went over to karaoke last night with a bunch of my friends and we closed the place down."

Poor Terrence, I thought, he is clueless. Alice and I looked at each other with sad faces. We actually felt sorry for the guy.

"Bye, Terrence," I yelled in his direction as Terrence boarded the bus for Montego Bay. "You were awesome last night at karaoke," I added, as Alice joined in waving. Terrence broke into a broad smile. We had to throw the poor guy a compliment. He was such a sad character, and completely delusional.

The disco lounge at Hedo was on a section of the patio set below the swimming pool. At night we could hear the sound of disco music blaring even from our room near the bay. The back of the bar in the disco lounge was glass, so that people in the bar could sit and watch people swimming in the pool above them. I'm sure most folks in the swimming pool had no idea that their antics were visible in the bar. Use your imagination.

The swimming pool saw a lot of action during the day with games such as pool volleyball and water aerobics, but, at night, the swimming pool took on a bizarre dimension. Some drunk was always falling into the pool or throwing another guest into the water. Mating rituals and hanky-panky were common place. Couples would cavort around together in the water, unaware that they were putting on a show for the voyeurs who frequented the disco bar. It was hilarious to see the expressions on their faces when someone in the bar got their attention and they found out.

The beachside bar opened at 10 a.m. and was the watering hole for beachgoers until very late afternoon. On a typical day in Jamaica, tropical rains would start around 3:00 p.m. Our group would huddle under the big thatched roof of the bar and visit with each other, telling stories and getting further acquainted.

The Jamaicans who work at Hedo were absolutely delightful. Always smiling and friendly, they made Hedo really fun. Jake, our bartender, was a fantastic example. He kept the drinks flowing and the music playing at the bar. Hedo is a "no-tip" environment, but Jake got plenty of tips.

"I thank you and my children thank you," he would say quietly and graciously.

One rainy afternoon, a gal who had just arrived from New Jersey came out to the beach bar. She immediately started whining to all of us about her horrible experience getting to Hedonism II. None of us really wanted to listen to her. We were in Jamaica—no problem, man—but she didn't care and she loved wallowing in her drama. I dubbed her "the Drama Queen."

"First, my flight was delayed two hours. I just hate that airport. You can't get decent food. Then the overhead compartment near my seat was full, and some lady had the nerve to move my bag. Then I had to sit next to this horrible guy and hear his life story. He was a jerk and really a bore." Irony much?

"Then, I was sure the airline lost my luggage. It took forever before my bags came down the conveyer belt and when they finally arrived I couldn't find a porter to carry them to the cab stand. Ugh, those Jamaicans are so rude. Then my cab didn't have air conditioning so I was dying of heat all the way to the club. Of course, they couldn't find my reservation at check-in and now it's raining." Blah, blah, blah, blah, blah.

Jake, our Jamaican bartender, listened patiently to all of the Drama Queen's ramblings, and then suggested a drink to "make your problems disappear." It was a special concoction Jake had invented that fell somewhere between a mai tai and a "strip and go naked," a drink made of lemonade, vodka, rum, gin, and beer. He quickly presented the Drama Queen with a double and suggested she drink it down really fast.

"This is the first good thing I've tasted in this stupid country," Drama Queen said obnoxiously. In a few minutes, she was sipping her second.

We continued our friendly banter with the people in our group, doing our best to ignore the Drama Queen, who would retell her story of woeful travel to each newcomer who sidled up to the bar. Blah, blah, blah, blah.

"Shoot me if I ever do that," I told Alice.

By the time Drama Queen started drinking number three, she was clearly listing to one side of the bar stool, like a ship about to tip over on its side. Her story started to sound garbled; she was slurring her words and repeating herself. Eventually, Drama Queen fell right off the bar stool and laid there lifeless, like a beached seal, and someone covered her with a towel.

Jake paused momentarily from his duties and said good-naturedly, "I told you I could make your problems disappear."

A few hours later, we saw some of the Jamaican house staff dragging Drama Queen to her room. Her feet were like two anchors pulling through the sand and her head was down toward the ground. She was still passed out cold. After this, we didn't see Drama Queen for several days. Then I spied her at lunch, and she was talking again.

"I don't know what happened to me. I was perfectly fine and then I passed out. I probably got a flu bug or something on that stupid airplane. I've been stuck in my room for two days."

I'm sure our Drama Queen was thrilled to have new material to whine about for the rest of her vacation.

Hedonism II is not for everybody. At our ages—we were in our late fifties, it was an experience "outside of the box," as they say. Most folks we met there were perfectly normal and, like us, had arrived at Hedo unaware of the club's wild reputation. Others sincerely subscribed to nudism and wanted to vacation naked in the sun. Still others were straight-up exhibitionists.

I did a little online research and it seems that over the years Hedo's reputation has gotten even raunchier. I would not go there today, but at that time and place in our lives, Hedonism II was a lot of fun and an experience we shall never forget.

36

Peace Corp Thanksgiving

> **1989**

During one of our many trips to Jamaica, we met a wonderful young man who worked in the scuba and sailing shop at the Hedonism II. Almost daily, Devon Hendricks, a strikingly handsome and muscular Jamaican, took my sister Alice, my husband Alan, and me sailing in the turquoise waters near the club. During those adventures, we had the opportunity to learn a lot about life in Jamaica and about Devon's family.

Devon earned about fifty dollars per month at Hedonism II, which he considered a "good-paying job." He was married to Marsha, a beautiful young woman with a smile that lit up the room and a magnificent singing voice. Devon and Marsha had a girl, Shevel (age six), a boy, Devon Jr. (age eight), and Ramona, their nine-month-old. Devon's family lived in Green Island, a small community filled with wooden shacks, a sprinkling of larger homes, and a small commercial district. Green Island was a twenty-five-minute cab drive from the Hedo. Devon was proud to tell us that he was building a new house for his family with the tips he received from visitors at the Club. Hedonism II didn't actually allow tipping, but generous folks usually slipped the working guys and gals a few dollars on the sly as they left for home at the end of their vacations.

Devon used the bulk of his tips to buy cinder blocks, and he had been building his new home for over two years, "a few cinder blocks at a time." Devon told us that Americans are by far the most generous of the resort's guests. "And, thanks to all you good folks, I have completed my house, except for the roof."

We learned that most Jamaicans don't earn enough to buy and own their own building tools. "I rent a hammer and wheelbarrow from a neighbor a mile or so down the road." That's how it is done in Jamaica. Even the wood framing for his roof would be "rented" from another Jamaican in town.

When we left for home two weeks later, we tipped Devon enough to put the cement roof on his house and promised to return again with gifts and tools for his family, but we couldn't promise when that would be. As it happened, our next visit was at Thanksgiving, about six months later. Our grown children had plans to have Thanksgiving at their in-laws that year, so a Thanksgiving vacation in Jamaica worked out well. As we had promised, we returned to Jamaica bearing gifts.

We brought six enormous duffle bags filled with new and used clothing, tennis shoes, sandals, baby supplies, household items, backpacks containing writing tablets, crayons, marking pens, books, and tools, and a computer and printer for the children's school. The customs agent stopped us, looked in our bags, and immediately spied the computer and printer at the bottom of the biggest duffle bag. "What is the computer for and why do you need a printer? And why so many bags? How long are you staying in Jamaica?"

I was concerned from her tone that we might have to pay duty on all the goodies we were importing.

Alice and I arriving in Jamaica with supplies for the Hendricks family and their kid's school. In addition to the carts we were pushing, we had two additional carts that were overloaded with giant duffel bags too heavy to carry.

"We had to bring our computer and printer so we could work while we're on vacation," Alan quickly lied.

"And all the other bags?" the agent continued.

"Most of the other stuff is my sister's makeup," I insisted, laughing.

The agent got a big smile on her face. "You sound like my big sister," she said, and she raised her hand and waved us through. That agent knew we were up to something and could have easily charged us duty on all the new items we were bringing into the country, but she chose to let us pass. God clearly works in mysterious ways.

When we arrived at the beach, Devon saw us coming and ran toward us with a big smile on his face and tears in his eyes. "I was just praying to God last night for help. The kids need shoes, Christmas is coming, and little Ramona has been sick. God sent you here and answered my prayers." With that, Devon enveloped Alice and me in a big hug, as Alan looked on, smiling happily.

Since it was Thanksgiving week, we asked Devon if we could go with him to Green Island and meet his family and take him shopping for food. "That's what we'd be doing at home," we told him, "spending time with family." He was thrilled with the idea and brought his best friend Benny, a local cabbie, to Hedo on Thursday, to drive us to his little town. Benny wasn't licensed to drive tourists, so he couldn't drive onto the resort grounds to pick us up, and it was against Hedo rules for employees to meet club patrons outside of the establishment, so Alice and I walked outside the hotel complex and across the busy road to where Benny and Devon were waiting patiently in the rain.

Jamaica has licensed cabs that are insured and safe for transporting tourists around the country. In addition, certain privately-owned vehicles are allowed to take Jamaicans about the island. Because the buses are crowded and without air conditioning, the privately-owned cabs are quicker and are also used for out-of-the-way locations that bus routes don't serve. In our case, we were helping our friend, who wasn't licensed to transport tourists, earn a little extra money on his day off.

The first stop was the food market in Green Island. This market was about the size of a large 7-Eleven store you would find at almost any gas station in the U.S. It was dingy on the outside, and trash was strewn about the entrance. Inside, the market was well organized but poorly lit by lights that blinked on and off sporadically. We had each of the guys grab a shopping cart and we told them to fill the carts. Both were very timid and respectful and, at first, would only buy the smallest boxes and quantities of each food item. It took a lot of urging from us to get the fellas into the swing of things.

"That's no good," we said jokingly. "Get the ten-pound bags of rice and beans." It was that way with all the items they grabbed.

Up and down the aisles we went, until the carts were packed and stuff was falling onto the floor. Flour, sugar, cereal, jam, spaghetti, meats, eggs, and bread. I couldn't tell who was having more fun, Alice and me or Devon and Benny. We even attracted a crowd of onlookers who followed us around the store laughing, sincerely happy for their neighbors' good fortune.

When the groceries were at last loaded into Benny's small cab, we continued our journey to deliver the Thanksgiving bounty and meet the families.

Benny's house was not too far from the market, so that was where we stopped first. The road to Benny's house wasn't actually a road, it was just a dirt-and-rock-lined path with an assortment of shanties on either side. Benny's home was a small, wooden hut in faded red with ragged cloth curtains flapping out the tiny window in the rain that fell relentlessly. We trudged with our shopping bags up to the front door. Benny's wife, a sweet faced and tiny young woman, was startled as we peeked around the door to say, "Hi." Their bed and a small T.V. set were the only furniture visible in the single-room hut they shared with two school-aged kids and a new baby. Benny hoisted the newborn into the air with pride. Since the bed took up almost all of the room, the front door only opened wide enough to stuff the bags through and for Benny's kids' heads to peek out in bewilderment at these gift-bearing strangers.

Back in the car after making our first delivery, Alice and I held hands for a moment and gave each other knowing smiles. We already felt the blessings of Thanksgiving. Seeing Benny's home and family put all our lives' concerns in order. Ten minutes later we arrived at the fork in the road that led to the small hill where Devon lived.

"We have to get out here and walk the rest of the way," Devon explained. "Cars can't drive this road." It only took a few steps to see why. The road was filled with ragged rocks and boulders, and there was water running in rivulets toward the base of the hill the car had just climbed.

"Don't carry more than you can handle," Devon warned us kindly. "Benny and I can come back for the rest of the stuff." Weighted down with what we could comfortably carry, we started our climb to the top of the hill. Devon told us later that the top of the hill was cooler, which is why he had built there, and also safer than being close to town.

Jamaica will give a plot of land to anyone who can build a home on it. Electricity can be connected if the occupants install their own poles through the jungle and wires up to the city main. Once installed, the homeowner is billed for electricity usage and charged a small fee for the land.

On the walk up to Devon's house, we passed the compound in which Devon's parents and some of his siblings lived. High bamboo-like fencing separated their huts from the rock-filled road. Hearing his voice as we approached, Devon's parents and younger siblings came outside to meet us and thanked us for all the gifts we had brought, which Devon shared. Devon's dad shimmied up a palm tree and cut down a coconut with his razor-sharp machete and opened it with the blade so we could taste the sweet milk inside.

When we finally arrived at Devon's house, we were greeted with hugs and giant smiles of gratitude by Marsha and the kids. Within moments, Alice was

Within minutes of arriving at the Hendricks' home, we felt like family. That's me in the back, behind Marsha and little Ramona. Alice is holding Devon, Jr. (aka Cruz) and Shevel.

holding sweet little Ramona, and Shevel was on my lap playing with the bracelets on my arm. Devon Jr. (Cruz) looked like his father and smiled shyly, not quite sure what to think. Quickly, we felt like family.

The Hendricks' home was spotless and the children were dressed in clean clothes and obviously well cared for. The only picture on the walls was a calendar, an advertising piece from the local gas station. As soon as Devon completed building his new home, the two-room wooden shack they were currently sharing would be vacated and rented to another family.

"I am almost finished with the new house," Devon told us smiling. "Soon-coming," he added.

Located just up the hill from their rented shanty, their newly built house was much larger, with a kitchen, living room, bathroom, and one large bedroom. The two older kids would sleep in the living room on beds that doubled as couches during the day. Little Ramona would sleep with her parents. The kitchen had a stove, a small refrigerator, and a sink.

"Look," Marsha showed us excitedly, "we have a faucet." The faucet was a big deal, because in most Jamaican villages, a group of huts would share a common kitchen build under a lean-to outside.

"What about running water?" I asked. "Do you have a water heater, or what?" I was informed that once the family had enough money, they would buy a hundred-gallon water reservoir for the roof and they would have running water. Because the reservoir basin was painted black, and the Jamaican sun so consistently hot, the water would be heated warm enough for showering.

We met Devon Hendricks, a sailing instructor, at Hedonism II. While sailing with Devon, we learned about his family and how hard he worked to support them. Alice with the family in their two-room home.

Devon explained that Jamaica has clean water available at spigots placed sporadically throughout the villages. "There is a water spigot close to my parents' home." Villagers can either carry fresh water home for drinking and bathing purposes or, like Devon was planning, attach series of hoses to the spigots and during the night, when the use of water is greatly reduced, fill their water reservoirs for daytime use.

It was obvious the Hendricks' new bathroom was their pride and joy. It had a tub and a toilet, but no plumbing fixtures. "Plumbing fixtures will come later," Devon told us, "after we have the reservoir." Until then, the family would use the outhouse shared by other families in the vicinity, along with an outdoor shower Devon had rigged up "for the girls" (Devon and Cruz both used the nearby stream for bathing).

When I asked Marsha what took up most of her time each day, she answered quickly, "laundry." Marsha washed the family laundry by hand at the stream and then carried it uphill to the clothes lines Devon had attached to and strung away from the house. The lines were full and the clothes hanging were still wet from the rain. "No problem, man, the sun will dry them for us again."

I looked at Alice and whispered, "Makes you realize being out of fabric softener is no big deal."

While we ate a snack of fruit, gathered fresh from the jungle, we made a list of the items the Hendricks' still needed most. We told the family that if we couldn't return again to Jamaica, we'd send what we could by parcel.

We headed back to Hedonism ll in Benny's cab. The entire family was tucked inside for the return trip. The guys were in the front and Alice and I each had a child on our laps, while Marsha held little Ramona. With a nursing mother at our side, we whistled down the road, hot and humid, with the windows down and wind rushing through our hair.

I whispered to Alice, "I think this is what it would be like if we had joined the Peace Corps."

"So, how did the trip go?" Alan asked, as we flopped down at a comfy table near the bar. Alan had begged off

Shevel, Ramona, and Devon Jr., the year we enrolled them at Harding Hall School.

going on the visit, saying he thought he might be catching a cold and didn't want to risk spreading it to the children. Later, he told me the truth: "I was afraid I would cry just seeing how they lived." But he didn't need to tell me that, I already knew how he felt.

Over dinner the three of us discussed how best to continue helping the Hendricks. Alan suggested we look into schooling options.

"Education is their only hope," he said. We agreed and knew he was right.

Marsha, the children's mom, is beautiful on the inside and out. Hard-working and smart, she insisted that studies came first.

A few days later, we visited Harding Hall School with Marsha and the children. It was a wonderful private school run by a wealthy English woman who was married to a Jamaican. Attached to her spacious home, the school was nestled in a quiet valley, safe and far away from the noisy, congested, and sometimes dangerous town. For the cost of a few fancy meals a month, we were able to enroll Shevel and Cruz and, eventually, little Ramona at Harding Hall. I am proud to say that Cruz graduated from Harding Hall, then from high school, and then took a two-year college course in computers. He now works for one of the "Super Clubs" you see advertised on T.V. Shevel graduated from Harding Hall as well, then high school, and she completed a two-year college program in hotel management. Instead of working for one of the resorts, however, Shevel works as a bartender and waitress at the American Club. Because she is absolutely gorgeous, she makes a fortune in tips, easily taking home five times what she'd earn working in an office, sitting at a computer. Like the others, Ramona attended Harding Hall and went on to high school. She graduates this May (2017) and will enroll in the police academy in September.

"I am so happy," she texted me recently. "I'm at the best school in the area and I'm at the top of my class."

Ramona and Shevel checking out their new computer tablets.

Devon Jr. was the first person ever to graduate from high school in their large family.

Student placement in the various district schools is dependent upon testing scores. The smartest kids get assigned to the top schools. Harding Hall gave the kids a wonderful foundation and they all tested above their grade levels.

Devon was a hard-working and devoted father, but it was Marsha who kept the kids' education alive in the family. She insisted that "studies come first" and kept us in the loop about doings at school for all the kids.

"Do you think we could send the kids to summer school? They would really like to go," she asked. And later, "The kids would really benefit from a laptop. I know you already do so much, but any chance you could get them each a laptop?"

Always looking out for their best interests, Marsha knew if she planted the seed with us, it would eventually grow. In short order, all the kids had their own computers and were excelling in school.

Graduation from high school is an amazing accomplishment for the Hendricks family. Devon Jr. was the *first* person to graduate from high school in their large family. Public schooling is free in Jamaica, but classrooms are crowded and the graduation rates are extremely low. Teen pregnancy is also rampant, a big contributing factor to drop-out rates. Textbooks are shared by students, and the overall conditions at the public schools are lacking, to say the least. Harding Hall School was far superior to public school. Their students had computers, language and science labs, a small cafeteria, and a swimming pool. Despite the fact that Jamaica is an island, most kids don't learn how to swim! Thanks to Harding Hall, the Hendricks kids are swimmers.

A devoted and hard-working woman, Marsha braided hair for customers in her home to supplement the family income. A talented braider, Marsha had quite a following of regular patrons. When the city discovered she was unlicensed and wanted her to close her home business, she asked if we might help her get her beautician's license. We helped with the small fees, and she eventually opened her own shop.

Many folks we knew ended up pitching in to help the Hendricks family. Our staff at Thomas & Fees, the accounting firm my husband and his college friend, Bob Fees, started, were extremely generous and donated clothes, shoes, and jewelry for the Hendricks. Enid, our retired secretary, left Nancy Hice, our current secretary and Enid's successor, several boxes of good costume jewelry.

"I know Enid would want this donated," Nancy told me as she opened box after box of very nice earrings, necklaces, bracelets, and pins. It was a treasure trove of saleable items. We sent Marsha a few display racks and she was able to sell all the jewelry in her shop.

Alan and I enjoyed searching garage sales on the weekends, and we found some terrific items at cheap prices to send the family. We bought a full set of Noritake china for twelve, serving pieces and all, for just thirty dollars.

"The china was Nana's," said the gal selling the china. "We don't do much formal entertaining, and I'm sure

Nana would be happy that her beloved china went to such a deserving family."

Comments like that came frequently when we were shopping for our Jamaican friends. People hearing about our project would donate additional items to help the cause. One guy donated a whole box of shop tools.

In the beginning, we sent all donations by mail, but that limited what we could send and became expensive. Then we discovered that we could ship full fifty-gallon drums for forty-seven dollars each (unlimited weight) to Jamaica from Miami. Nancy ordered me four drums at a time from U-Line, and two or three times a year I'd fill them to the top with donations: linens, toys, books, and lots and lots of food. The drums allowed us to send building supplies too, like locksets for their doors, long lengths of water hose, a medicine chest, plumbing parts, and tools.

"I can hardly lift these drums," our delivery boy told me as he hefted the drums into our Traverse for the drive to Miami. "I bet this one weighs three hundred pounds."

Helping the Hendricks family became a rewarding experience for everyone involved. We laughed and high-fived as we shipped off more drums and anticipated how the new bounty would be received. We could imagine the smiles on the distant faces we knew so well as they sifted through the enormous drums and found a place in their home for all the food and the beautiful Noritake China.

"I feel like a princess," Marsha later told me. "I never thought I would own such beautiful things."

It felt wonderful to know we had made a difference in the lives of another family. Because the Hendricks undoubtedly shared what they received, we knew our contributions impacted, at least in a small way, an entire community. One family helping another, and not a penny spent was wasted on administration.

I love this saying from the Bible: "To whom much is given, much is expected" (Luke 12:48). And because our family has been given much, my husband and I try to live by that motto. It's pleasantly ironic to me that when you give, you also tend to receive. I guess it's the old "what goes around, comes around." I always felt that the sheer joy, excitement, and appreciation

My craft room was the perfect place to store the items we purchased for the Hendricks. Once we collected enough to fill four barrels, we'd have them delivered to the port in Miami Beach for transport to Jamaica.

of the receiver more than paid back any cost of our generosity, many times over usually. I'm sure some brilliant person has written something very poetic about that. I simply say, "In giving, we get again."

37

The Vet Convention

1989

My sister Alice was going through a divorce, and, even though it was a friendly enough divorce, she was going through some difficult times emotionally. To help her out, I hatched a plan to take her to Hawaii. My sister Kay and her children were planning a trip with my mom to see our brother Rex, who lived there, so the timing seemed perfect. Rex and Sharon, his second wife, were transplants to Maui from California and had been living there, with a couple of sweet dogs, for many years. The first week of our trip to Hawaii was spent in Maui with them.

After visiting Rex in Maui, the rest of my family flew back to the mainland while Alice and I continued our vacation, heading to the Big Island, Hawaii. We picked up our rental car and drove to one of the splashy resort hotels on the coast. Our room was on the fifth floor of a hotel built on lava from one of Hawaii's three active volcanoes. We could hear the powerful ocean waves hitting the rocks and see the splashing water periodically from our balcony.

I immediately got on the phone to the front desk. "Hi, this is Paula Thomas, in room 511. I'm here with my sister who is getting a divorce and is kind of depressed. I want to make sure she has a fabulous time. What kind of appetizers do you have?"

The lady on the phone was very friendly and recommended some hot pupus, which is Hawaiian for hors d'oeuvres. "Wonderful," I said enthusiastically. "Send up a tray of hot pupus and a bottle of merlot."

I was getting the party started while Alice was getting dressed for the swimming pool.

When the hot pupus and wine arrived, we sat on the balcony and took in the beauty around us. I'm telling you, this was the life: two sisters, who were also great friends, sitting on the balcony of a lovely hotel in Hawaii enjoying all this abundance—crystal blue water as far as we could see, an ocean breeze in our hair, and the sweet smell of the sea splashing high against the rocks with all the fury Mother Nature could muster. We felt so blessed.

Relaxed and refreshed, we took the elevator down to the beachside swimming pool. It was close to 3:00 p.m. While Alice arranged for lounges, I went over to the bar.

"Hi. I am Paula Thomas, in room 511. I'm here with my sister Alice who is getting a divorce and kind of depressed. I want to make sure she has a fabulous time. What would you recommend we drink?"

The bartender kind of smiled and suggested a Long Island iced tea. I had no idea what that was, but I knew Alice liked tea. So I told him, "Make us two of those tea things." And, "What the heck," I added. "We're on vacation, so make them doubles." I have never adhered to the principle that less is more. I firmly believe that more is more.

What I didn't know at the time was that a Long Island iced tea is typically made with tequila, vodka, light rum, triple sec, gin, and a splash of cola, which gives the drink the amber hue of its namesake. It looks like tea. Trust me, it's not tea.

The pool boy put fresh towels on a pair of lounges for us up near the pool. Alice and I laid down and I began looking around, noticing that the pool area was packed with adults but very few families. Most of the folks we did see were reading some kind of a thick book.

"Who are all these people?" I asked the bartender delivering our drinks.

"It's a veterinarian convention. There are two hundred vets staying at the hotel." That's probably why no one wanted to chitchat, I said to myself. From their looks, I concluded they were serious types and had studying to do.

Our teas were delightful. "Just what the doctor ordered," I told Alice, giving the animal doctor sitting next to me a smile. Her response . . . was no response. Irritated by my intrusion, she only buried her face in her book.

Like I said before, I'm the type of person who does everything fast, so my drink went down quickly. Within a short time, I was already feeling the tea's effect.

"I think I'll cool off in the pool," I told Alice, as I made my way carefully toward the water.

I noticed some of the people in the swimming pool were floating on colorful plastic rafts. I went over to the towel shack and asked where I could get a couple. The attendant took my room number and said he'd bring the rafts to me poolside. "Make sure you bring the rafts back to me when the pool closes, otherwise you'll be charged twenty dollars per raft."

When the rafts arrived, I lay down on one and pushed off from the side of the pool into the center of the swimming area. The cool water rolled up over the sides of the raft where my body was heaviest and it felt wonderful. I *was* feeling a little dizzy as the water rocked gently from side to side, but then the water calmed and I began to float on liquid heaven and my eyes began to close. With Hawaiian music in the background, I felt peaceful and serene. Just me, the water, and a belly full of Long Island iced tea; I floated off into oblivion.

The next thing I remember was being poked with a pole.

"Lady. Lady. Wake up, lady."

I was hearing a voice from a distant land. Then the pole hit me in the side again and the voice insisted.

"Lady. Wake up, lady." I felt another jab.

I opened my eyes very slowly and tried to focus. I was face down, staring at brightly-colored plastic. I slowly turned over. The towel shack attendant's face eventually came into view.

"What?" I asked, confused. "Why are you waking me up? Why are you poking me with that metal pole?" I had no idea where I was or what I was doing.

"I need your raft, lady. I need your raft. I can't leave the pool area until I get all the rafts."

I looked around and the place was nearly empty. Alice was still there, sound asleep on her lounge. A couple of vets still had their heads stuffed into books. I was the only one left in the pool.

I paddled toward the edge and surrendered my raft to the attendant. "Sorry about that." I must have passed out, I thought to myself. I could feel my back and legs were sunburned. Hot and groggy, I collected Alice from her lounge and the two of us stumbled up to our room.

The rest of the evening, my sunburned body was wrapped around the toilet bowl. I have never been so sick. Long Island iced teas are on my "never again" list, as are the hot pupus that returned with the tea. At least I had achieved my primary goal: Alice was no longer depressed. Now she was sick.

Day two on the Big Island was alcohol and hot pupu free. We got up late, had a *sensible* breakfast and lay under a covered area next to an indoor pool. Crackers and water is all we ate for lunch and by the afternoon we were feeling slightly better. A guy we had met the day before came out to the pool where we sat reading. He was in his thirties and obviously attracted to Alice. Mike was from New Jersey and was definitely *not* wearing Hawaiian attire. He wore new blue jeans and a white tee shirt rolled up at the sleeves. One sleeve held his cigarettes and he wore some kind of black leather shoes. He had curly hair that was almost shoulder length and it almost, but not quite, covered a snake tattoo on his neck. It looked to us like Mike had just had a permanent wave, which was popular for guys at that time.

Mike told us he owned a concrete driveway business in Jersey. Since it was snowing there this time of year, he had decided to take a trip to Hawaii. "People told me Hawaii was packed with girls and had lots of nighttime action. This place seems kind of dead." We explained to Mike that the Big Island was not where he should be. "You should be in Honolulu if you are looking for night-life and chicks," I advised him frankly.

When Mike sat down next to us, I had been reading aloud to Alice from Cosmopolitan magazine. Cosmo targets contemporary women and features beauty, fashion, career, and sex advice. The article I was reading out loud was "Sex Test—How Do You Rate?" We were laughing out loud at some of the ridiculously embarrassing questions. The idea of the quiz was to give yourself a score on each answer and total your score at the end. Then you were supposed to compare your totals to the included chart and see how you rated on each section of the test. The sex test had questions like: "What's your best come-on line for attracting the opposite sex? How do your arousal techniques compare? How do you tell your sexual partner what you want and need in bed?" We thought the test was kind of silly, but, since cell phones and "Words with Friends" hadn't been invented yet, it was a way to pass the time and have some laughs.

I continued reading the test aloud until the very end. Then I asked Alice, jokingly, "Okay, what's your score on sexual arousal techniques?" Before she could answer, Mike spoke up, "My scores are ready; do you want my scores now?" He asked that question with such sincerity on his face that I didn't have the heart to tell him we were just kidding around about the test.

"Sure, I guess so," I said hesitantly, with a sideways glace toward Alice.

Oh, great. I had to figure out how to create a description of this guy's sexual prowess from a bunch of numbers and a chart in this stupid magazine. For all of his bad-boy talk and looks, this guy's self-esteem seemed fragile and his ego was in my hands. He was undoubtedly good at concrete, but I had the distinct feeling from the way he talked that Mike generally struck out with women, and I certainly didn't relish the idea of discussing the pros and cons of his sexual preferences in bed. I pretended to study the magazine for several minutes, to compare his scores with the answers on the test.

"How are my scores? Did I do ok?" Mike asked in earnest.

Alice looked at me with concern and widened her eyes.

"Okay, let's see. Give me a minute here, Mike." I was stalling for time. "Yeah. Okay. Yeah, that looks good. Yep, this section is good. Okay. Okay. This is very good. Yes." I could see Mike was getting nervous, hanging on my every word.

"Well, how did I do? Tell me!" he begged again. I could see he was getting very concerned.

"Excellent," I said, matter-of-factly. "Your numbers are amazing. You did awesome on every section of the test." And with that I threw my hand up in the air for punctuation. "Obviously, you have lots of girlfriends. I'm surprised you're not married and why are you vacationing alone?" (Change the subject, Paula!)

Mike's eyes lit up at these answers and he got a huge smile on his face. He was clearly proud.

"That's a relief," he said sighing. "I wasn't sure what to answer on a couple of those questions. I'm sure glad I did okay." As quickly as I could manage, I threw the magazine and Mike's scores in the trash can and followed it with a giant glass of ice water I had mostly finished drinking. I was afraid Mike would ask to see the magazine and the results for himself.

Later, as we left the pool area, Mike asked if he could get a few pictures with Alice.

"I'd like to show the guys back home my girlfriend in Hawaii."

He threw his arm around Alice, who looked terrific (not depressed) in her bathing suit, and we took several shots. The final photo was of Alice kissing Mike on the cheek. He was beaming like the stud he was in his imaginary test results.

Mike offered to take us to dinner, but we weren't in the mood. Alice declined nicely and walked away. I gave Mike my usual spiel about Alice. "My sister is getting a divorce and has been kind of depressed." Mike understood but was disappointed. "Darn. I was going to ask Alice for her phone number."

Mike thanked me for the advice about going to Honolulu.

"Can I make one last suggestion?" I asked Mike gently, as he was leaving.

"Sure. What is it?"

I told him his clothes were perfect for New Jersey. In New Jersey, his look fit right it. But he needed to dress differently in Hawaii. "You know the saying, 'When in Rome, do as the Romans?'"

His eyes lit up. "What should I wear?"

The next day, we saw Mike getting into the airport shuttle. He was wearing flip-flop sandals, a Hawaiian shirt, and Bermuda shorts. Even with untanned legs protruding from his Bermuda shorts like white fingerling potatoes, Mike's new Hawaiian attire surpassed his New Jersey getup by a few thousand miles, and his cigarettes were now resting in his front pocket, not rolled up in his sleeve.

"I'm off to Honolulu like you recommended," Mike yelled, waving.

"You look great. Have fun and take it easy on the ladies," I yelled back.

Mike walked onto the bus like a new man with confidence in his step. Maybe that Cosmo test wasn't so silly after all.

38

Honolulu

Alice and I took the short flight from the Big Island back to Oahu and checked into our hotel in Honolulu. We had one last night of vacation and we planned to spend it dancing. Both of us absolutely love to dance, and there was a popular disco on the top floor of our hotel. We did some last-minute sightseeing in the capital city and then went to an early "touristy" luau for dinner. After that, we went back to our room to change.

When we headed up to the Blue Disco Club, it was still early in the evening. Discos don't get going until after 11 p.m. and we were early, so we found a table near the dance floor and began to look around. The crowd was varied. There were tourists and locals and folks in Honolulu on business. Some were obviously prowling for "hook-ups" and some, like us, were just there to dance.

I felt so awkward sitting in a nightclub without my husband. I hadn't been to a bar without Alan in twenty-five years. The awkwardness I felt there made me have a lot more empathy for Alice. It *would* be depressing to go back to dating when you had been comfortably married for so many years. The idea of entering the dating scene would depress anyone.

Because I wasn't in the dating scene, any time a guy would ask me to dance I felt compelled to level with him. "I'm happily married. I'm just here because my sister is getting a divorce and is kind of depressed." I didn't want the guy to waste his time with me if he were expecting something more than dancing.

I must have said this to a half dozen guys, when one finally answered back, "For God's sake, lady, I don't want to marry you. I just want to dance."

Alice heard me talking to this guy and started laughing.

"Paula, you don't have to give a guy your life story," she stammered, "and for goodness sake, QUIT talking about me and my DIVORCE!"

As it got later and the Blue Disco Club got more crowded, we were asked more and more often to dance. Each time, despite my sister's instruction, I shared the reason why I was there. Either that or I'd start talking about my dog back home and my family. I was sure a conversation like that would keep the guy from getting the wrong impression about me and he'd know I was only there to dance.

One of my eventual dance partners was a policeman in Hawaii, and he showed me his badge to prove it. After our dance when we returned to the table, since I had been talking about my dog Mugsy, he opened his wallet and showed me a picture of his German shepherd, Luke. Alice took one look at the two of us sharing dog photos and said to me laughing, "Boy, it *has* been years since you've been in a bar."

During one of the breaks in the music, Alice and I wandered to the ladies' room. It was crowded with young gals putting on makeup and ladies our age trying hard to stop Father Time. "I feel ancient," I said to my sister later. "My God, I don't even remember being as young as those girls."

As we headed back to the bar, we passed seven or nine guys leaning on the rail overlooking the dance floor. Just as we passed, I couldn't help but let out a big series of farts. That's probably why they call them hot pupus. This made me crack up laughing, and I started trying to get my sister's attention. She couldn't hear what I was saying because of the music and because she was a few steps ahead.

"What?" she asked quizzically. "What happened?"

I was belly laughing so hard by then I could barely stand up straight and spit out the question she hadn't heard me yell.

"You know how you can tell you're getting old?" I asked Alice, in hysterics.

"How?" she asked, already laughing because I was laughing.

"When you fart next to a cute guy and you don't even care. That's how."

Whoever said, "Laughter is the best medicine," was a genius.

You can't deny laughter; when it comes, it plops down in your favorite chair and stays as long as it wants.

—STEPHEN KING

39

England—A Pilgrimage With Mom

1990

It was my mom who introduced me to *All Creatures Great and Small* by James Herriot, the beloved English veterinary surgeon and writer who told heartwarming stories about his life in the Yorkshire Dales in Northern England. His real name was James Alfred Wight, or Alf to his friends. Because advertising of any kind was frowned upon in his profession, he took the pen name of James Herriot, after a Scottish goalkeeper he admired, and he wrote a collection of books that Mom and I loved dearly. James Herriot authored many books, but *All Creatures Great and Small*, *All Things Bright and Beautiful*, and *The Lord God Made Them All* were our favorites.

His stories were not just about the animals he cared for in his veterinary practice. James Herriot wrote about their owners and the close interaction they had with animals. His honesty and tenderness in storytelling made us roar

Mom and I on top of the Arc de Triomphe in Paris, France. We stopped there for a week after England. We felt so blessed to have taken this trip together.

with laughter on some occasions and made us cry at others. He had keen insight into the human condition, and he gave his readers a close look at the amazing connection people had with their pets and the animals they cared for on their farms.

"What say you and I go find James Herriot?" I asked Mom one morning over coffee. I had read he was still alive and still tending to his patients, part-time, at 23 Kirkgate in Thirsk, the town he lived in, close to the Yorkshire Dales and North York Moors. "Maybe we can meet his wife, Helen." I added, half kidding. After reading so much about James Herriot's life, I really felt like we had become friends.

It was the days before cell phones, computers, and Google, so I had to go to the library to investigate what I needed to make this trip happen. But I was determined and, eventually, so was Mom, to make our pilgrimage to meet the man whom we felt we already knew and definitely adored.

On a crisp spring morning, bundled up in warm coats and boots, we arrived in London, England, after a long, exhausting flight. Forgetting that this was Mom's first trip to Europe, I lacked, for a few minutes, the proper enthusiasm upon our arrival. I was focused on finding our luggage and getting directions to our hotel. Then, I looked over and saw mom's eyes glowing and her face smiling as she spotted one of the famous black hackney carriages parked to pick-up airport passengers.

"Look, Paula, look!" mom said, with almost child-like enthusiasm.

I adjusted my attitude pronto, slowed down, and got into the spirit of the moment. "Aren't they adorable? What do you say Mom, shall we grab one into town?"

And we did.

The entire ride to our hotel was magical for Mom, and also for me, just sitting at her side. She was looking out the window, calling out the sights we passed. "Big Ben, Buckingham Palace, the Tower of London . . . oh, my gosh, Paula, I can't believe we're here." My heart was pounding and I was getting excited just watching her reaction to London's sights.

Our hotel was in the heart of London, so we were able to walk to the restaurant the desk attendant recommended. Over a glass of wine and classic cottage pie, minced beef in rich gravy and covered in mashed potatoes, we discussed our plans for the following day. We had arranged for a bus tour that had been recommended by our travel agent. It was perfect for Mom, and me, with lots of friendly folks to talk to. The bus tour was an efficient way to cover a lot of important sights easily, in our limited amount of time.

The evening of the bus tour, we attended the stage show *Phantom of the Opera*. WOW! What a musical! Playing at Her Majesty's Theatre in London's West End, Andrew Lloyd Webber's masterwork had a "scintillating musical score, unconventional love story, and extravagant costumes and sets," which, according to Google, has made the musical "the most successful theatre show in history." To say we loved it is an understatement on a grand scale. A fun side note to the event was that our airline pilot, whom we spoke to briefly before our flight to England, was also at the theater! He recognized us and insisted on buying us wine during the intermission. Handsome and charming, the attention the pilot gave us made us feel special.

The following morning, after a delightful *full* English breakfast at our hotel (and they do mean "full"—orange juice, cereal, stewed fruit, bacon, eggs, sausages, grilled tomato, baked beans, tea, toast, and marmalade), Mom and I waddled down to the Tube, London's fantastic underground subway system. So easy to maneuver, the Tube is a fast and efficient way to get around London and much less expensive than those adorable black taxis. We quickly arrived at Hyde Park, one of London's best-loved parks, with its large lake, rose gardens, delightful walking paths, and more than four thousand trees.

After a stroll along the lake, we sat on a park bench and quickly struck up a conversation with an older English gentleman who claimed to have been in the Queen's Guard at Buckingham Palace. His attire was clean, but well worn, and his charming accent and manner were, well, very English. He could tell we were tourists by our typical tourist attire. We each carried a large purse, with maps and tour books visible, and we both had a camera hanging around our neck. (Note, this is all attire recommended by travel agents.)

As we chatted casually, he asked if we had yet visited St. Paul's Cathedral, "London's most beautiful cathedral." When we answered "not yet," he expressed concern.

"You can't possibly visit London without visiting the 1,400-year-old cathedral and seeing the Stone and Golden Galleries." Then he asked if we had purchased our tickets for the galleries. Evidently, because the galleries are so popular with tourists and Londoners, the ticket lines can be long and tiresome. Never having been to the galleries before, despite having visited London previously (shhhh, don't tell!), I was happy he shared the information with us and was even more delighted when he offered to be our escort, since he was heading toward the cathedral, which was near his home.

"Getting tickets for the galleries can be tricky, but I have a friend who works there," he said.

As we walked and talked with our self-proclaimed guide, he described points of interest and pointed out good spots to take pictures. We wanted to take his photo, to create a pictorial history of the event, but he adamantly declined, which Mom told me later she thought was odd.

To make a long story short, when we arrived at St. Paul's Cathedral, I gave our guide twenty pounds to purchase the tickets from his friend for the galleries he had recommended. Since I was unsure of the cost, I tried to give him more.

"No," he said. "This is enough."

The old gentlemen found us a bench to rest on while he went up the stairs and around the corner to the ticket booth. We sat and people watched, waiting for his return.

After about twenty minutes, Mom looked at me and smiled, a bit smugly.

"You know, Paula, he's not coming back."

"What?" I protested.

But she was right. I can be so naïve. That charming old former Queen's Guardsman scammed us out of twenty pounds. Later, over tea, we dubbed that adventure the "Twenty-pound tour."

After a whirlwind tour of Cambridge, a dinner cruise along the Thames, a shopping spree at Harrods department store, and a visit to the horrifying Museum of Medieval Torture, we boarded a three-day bus tour to Wales, and from there took the train to Manchester, only ninety-five miles from Thirsk.

On the train, we were seated across from twins; two retired spinster schoolmarms who were returning to Manchester, "after their annual holiday in Wales." The portly pair wore identical, tired-looking, chartreuse wool overcoats that hung well below their knees, with thick brown stockings and sensible brown leather shoes. On their heads were matching pillbox hats covered in chartreuse bird feathers.

When I commented on the bright feathers, the talking twin said smartly, "These hats are forty years old, and the reason they look pristine is because they have had excellent care." Her twin sat there, silently, just nodding in agreement (not unlike a wooden bobblehead doll.) I am not making this up!

Immediately upon discovering we were Americans, the talking twin began to quiz me on my knowledge of history. I have no idea why, unless it was to expose my inadequate American education, which I exposed without effort.

"Which king of England agreed to the Magna Carta, in what year was it signed, and why?"

"Have you got anything to drink?" I whispered to Mom, as she sat there trying not to laugh as my interrogation continued.

At last we pulled into the Manchester train station and said farewell to the talking twin and the bobblehead. I tried to sound sincere as I said, "It was nice to meet you," but because I was feeling like a double-dunce, my words fell flat. The double-sized duo disembarked before us, and I helped unload their matching leather bags. As they waddled off toward the station, I could see they were talking and I am sure it was all about me. When I say "they" were talking, I mean I could see that the one twin's mouth was moving and the other was bobbing her head continually in agreement.

Our hotel in Manchester was the former home of some famous duke, or count, or fifth cousin, or such like, to the Prince of Cornwall. After a while, because England is so old and there were so many dignitaries, the names run together like brown gravy. Besides, I'm an idiot about English history, remember? Anyhow, we checked into the small hotel near the park, which was festooned with purple and yellow crocus beginning to sprout forward into the spring. The host carried Mom's bags and escorted us up two flights of narrow, wooden stairs to a cozy room above the reception area.

"Mom, do you mind if I take the first shower?" I asked as we were getting settled. "The cold weather has chilled me to the bone."

The shower had a small rectangular box in the corner of the low ceiling, which was the water "heater," so they said. Anyhow, I took off my clothes and got into the small plastic stall and reached for the handle, which was attached to the heater with a long metal hose. Standing naked now, I was really getting cold. I turned on the faucet and a trickle of lukewarm water began to run out. I turned the knob further, and the water increased to a triple-trickle and still was lukewarm at best.

Slowly, ever so slowly, the water began to heat. Finally, as I stood there shivering, it reached a temperature above lukewarm. I held the shower nozzle over one shoulder for a few seconds, warming that section of my back while the other side of my back stayed frozen. Then, I would move the nozzle to the other side for a few seconds, to thaw it out, freezing the opposite side as the warmth disappeared. I won't even discuss the difficulty I had washing my backside.

"Mom," I screamed playfully, "I think this shower is something we missed at the Museum of Medieval Torture."

After our train adventure, we decided to hire a driver for the short trip to Thirsk. The train platform was not easy to navigate because of all the steps and all our luggage and the packages we had accumulated along the way. So, bright and early the next morning, we were picked up at the hotel by a charming Scottish gentleman for the two-hour trip to James Herriot's hometown, Thirsk.

"EyemenameeyScottie," our driver said in a Scottish brogue so thick we first thought he was speaking a foreign language. For the entire trip to Thirsk, our Scottish driver chatted as Mom and I just smiled and nodded, which was a technique we had learned from the bobblehead twin. We were acting like we understood what he was saying. As he drove through the beautiful English countryside, Scottie pointed out places of interest and added enthusiastic banter, all of which was in English but sounded like Greek to me. It was a relief when we finally arrived in Thirsk and bid our Scottish friend a fare-thee-well. We can't be sure, but we think he said, "Have a grand trip."

Just before we left for England, *Life* magazine had published an article about James Herriot's life in Thirsk, with pictures of some of his friends in their favorite English pub. Mom brought the magazine along and we read it during our flight. When we arrived at the Three Tuns Hotel, to our delight and sheer amazement, we discovered the hotel featured in the article was the very place we were staying. Three tuns means three large flasks of wine or beer.

"Oh, my gosh!" I said excitedly. "Our hotel bar is James Herriot's favorite pub."

"Look who is sitting there," Mom said quietly. "It's Herriot's good friends, Bob Climey and Bill Foggitt. See?"

Mom pointed at the article she had just pulled out of her valise. She was right. James Herriot's friends were there in the hotel lobby, sitting on the very same ladder-back chairs shown in the article, wearing the same clothes they wore in the article, and Bill held the same scruffy, wire-haired terrier on his knee. They were the photo in *Life* magazine. Mom and I bravely introduced ourselves and showed the magazine to the gentlemen. They had not yet seen the printed copy and smiled as they stood to greet us politely and shake our hands. We told them the story of our pilgrimage, and our love of James Herriot's books and his Yorkshire Dales. Within minutes, we had made plans to meet them later that evening for a "pint or two of stout." They would try, but couldn't promise, to "bring Alf, the good doctor, around."

Up in our room, overlooking the center of Thirsk, Mom and I sat at a small table by the window, looking down at

Thirsk is an old-fashioned market town in North Yorkshire and the destination of our pilgrimage. It was called Darrowby in the late James Herriot's books that Mom and I loved so much. The Three Tuns Hotel, where we were staying, is the brick building just behind the clock on the left.

the town we knew from the books we had read. We could see the city clock tower that chimed off the hours, and the place where the townsfolk gathered for the fresh food market on Saturday mornings. We were inside one of Herriot's books, talking about how blessed we were, sitting and sipping English tea. Before dinner, at the cozy Red Hawk Inn, we walked the town and found Skeldale House, the doctor's veterinary clinic, and also the apartment he had lived in as a bachelor and later shared with Helen, when they were newlyweds.

"That's the window she waved the dish towel from each morning as the doctor left for work," I said, reminiscing. We visited the church where they got married and we walked the paths Herriot described so aptly in his books.

Traveling with my mom, without my husband and children, gave me a freedom I seldom enjoyed as a mother and wife. I was me, Paula Thomas, the woman I had grown into, without the labels that defined my life back home. With no one but Mom to concern myself with, I was able to concentrate on my feelings, my wants, and my needs, without the responsibility that often overwhelmed me in my other distant existence.

Sitting in an English pub, drinking stout, feeling totally free to be me and laughing with folks I somehow felt I knew was one of the most enjoyable evenings of my life. It was unfortunate that during the timing of our visit, James Herriot was out of town, but our new friends made sure his absence didn't dampen our spirits. At our next pub meeting, we met Herriot's next door neighbor and several other good friends. One asked, "What is it about his stories that have caused you to travel thousands of miles to meet him?"

"Our shared love of animals," is all I could answer.

Bill Foggitt was the local weatherman. His family has kept records of the weather in Thirsk for over one hundred years. He filled the evenings with hilarious stories about the "one-eyed woman from Witbey" who turned out to be "a bit of a thief," and about characters he'd met who, like us, had traveled from points around the world to meet Thirsk's famous author. Bill told us how Herriot, a very private and soft-spoken individual, was overwhelmed one night by a big, heavy-set Texan who yelled, "Howdy, Doc," and hugged Herriot so hard it pulled him right off his feet.

"You should have seen the look on poor Alf's face when it happened."

The Texan's wife took Bill aside later and explained, "My husband has terminal cancer and before he dies he is determined to visit and take a picture of every place he read about in Herriot's first book, *All Creatures Great and Small.*"

On our last day in Thirsk, we visited the Skeldale House Veterinary Clinic. Jim, his son and also a veterinarian, runs the clinic with his famous father and was attending patients on the day we were there. Mom and I waited in the reception area with an array of small animals and their owners who were also waiting to be seen. After the animals had been tended to, Herriot's son, like his father did almost daily, welcomed in fans of the books.

Once in the operatory, we introduced ourselves, explained about our pilgrimage, and told the young veterinarian how much we loved his father's books. The younger doctor wasn't surprised at all that two ladies had traveled all the way from America and waited in his clinic to meet him.

"I guess I'm second best, as Dad isn't around," he told us, smiling. "It happens all the time." The young doctor looked like his father and could not have been more gracious. "Thanks for dropping by ladies. I'll tell my dad you were here."

We left the clinic with tears in our eyes and walked briskly toward the White Horse Café, which was said to have the best high tea in town. Seated at the front table, we kept smiling over the conversation we had with the doctor, while the waitress brought a ceramic teapot full of steaming Earl Grey tea and put it down carefully on the table, next to the mismatched cups. Next, she delivered a variety of fresh warm scones, lemon curd, and a mound of

The Yorkshire Dales behind our hotel.

clotted cream. This was followed by cucumber sandwiches with Stilton cheese and homemade petit fours.

"Oh, we can't possibly eat that much," we said laughing. Wrong! We had to ask for "just a tad more clotted cream."

Back at the Three Tuns Hotel, Mom opted for a nap and I decided to take a walk, hopefully near the sheep pastured in the beautiful green dales behind our hotel. Unsure exactly where to walk, I stopped at the front desk, carefully stepping over Marni and Jan, the owners' beautiful golden retrievers, who decorated the office like golden, furry rugs.

"A beautiful walk?" Ellen asked from behind the counter. "Just head around the building on the right and the path will take you right out to the dales." Ellen was a lovely lady who had been raised in Thirsk and had only left to "attend university."

"Seeing your sweet doggies, makes me miss mine," I said, as I stepped back over the sleeping dogs and started toward the exit.

"Would you like to take the girls walking?" Ellen asked happily.

"Really?" I asked in amazement. "You'd let me?"

As soon as Ellen brought out their leashes, her dogs were up on their paws and ready to go. "How will I know where to go?" I asked quickly, as Marni and Jan dragged me toward the door.

"They'll take you where you need to be," Ellen yelled after me, "and when Marnie sits down, you'll know it's time to turn around and come home."

Meandering the northern Yorkshire Dales, Herriot Country to me, with a pair of sweet canines panting at my side was one of the highlights of my trip. It was such a welcoming place, with rolling green pastures of grazing sheep, trees beginning to bloom, and flowers bursting up through the scruffy clumps of grass along ancient stone fences. A gentle breeze and the occasional sound of a bird caught the air. My heart was full of love, and I felt total peace and in harmony with myself and with my life. As God is my witness, I felt for a time like I had died and gone to heaven. My pilgrimage was complete.

40

~~~~~~

What I Learned from My Mom's Passing

> **1991**

When my mom died, I remember thinking that I didn't want my children to suffer the pain I was feeling at her death. There I was, hurting from a spot in my chest I didn't know existed, sobbing my heart out, and thinking about my children and wanting to spare them the same suffering one day. There was so much I never had told Mom. Oh sure, we went on trips together, we shopped all over, we did crafts in her room, we spent hours over lunch, but we hardly ever spoke of real things. I questioned myself, upon her death, why hadn't I told Mom how *much* I loved her? Not the "love you, Mom," you end a phone conversation with, but the "love you" from way down in the place I was suffering. With both Mom and the opportunities gone, the unspoken words leave me wounded and bleeding inside from regret.

This is my mother's high school graduation photo. Her necklace is a chain with two basketballs that Dad received for playing varsity basketball for the Ashland Tomcats.

So, what advice can I leave with you, my children? What can I tell you to spare you the hurt and sadness I carry to this day? I guess the answer is that this is how life is meant to be. We all live out our days the very best we can. We feel each moment only to the limits we can bear to feel when that moment arrives. We are seeing each moment only within the scope we can bear to see. We are doing each moment only what we have strength right then to do.

If we don't stop and hear the other person who needs or wants our attention, or remember to apologize for our shortcomings, or think to take the time to express our deepest thoughts, it's not because we lack love, or because we are merely selfish, and it's certainly not because we want to hurt. God knows that is not our intent. It is because life is a cup filled to overflowing with the tasks of living. We can't put anything more in our overflowing cups, even should we want to. That's the way of life, and it is okay and we are okay.

I didn't know much about my mother. I know she liked to make things, read books, cook, and that she was cultured. I know she loved my dad. Always, she loved Dad. I know she loved her darling little dog, Moggins—she carried his picture in her wallet until the day she died—and I know she loved all of her children. A day didn't pass that one of her children was not in the center of her thoughts. For forty-eight years, Mom loved me and yet, I can only write a paragraph or two about her before I realize how much I didn't know.

Maybe this disproves all I am saying. I worry that here was this person, this awesome lady I loved with all my heart, and because I like to tell stories, I feel cheated because I can only write a few lines about her. How many lines do I need if writing, "My mother loved me," covers nearly half a century of loving her and being loved in return? God knows my love for Mom was deep and He knows my love was true. If I can only write a few lines about this person who meant the world to me, it must be the natural order of things. Surely words are the wrong way to measure how well I knew her. What I hadn't said to Mom was not left unsaid. She knew and felt my love. Even without the words spoken or shouted or whispered out loud, she knew.

So, my dearest Roger and Natalie, don't ever feel regret or sadness about the past. There is nothing you ever did or said, or failed to do or say, that needs explaining or telling in the end. You are the best children any parent could have ever had: two sweet, perfect, little humans filled with love and aspirations. You came into my life and began living life as it should be lived; imperfectly, with equal turns of excitement and bewilderment. All you need to know is that I loved you from the moment you were expected. I cherished your sweet faces and your pure, caring souls. You are the one thing in life I did perfectly. Having you was a gift to Dad and me and the world.

41

Close Encounters of the Critter Kind

> **2010**

Animals have always played an important part in my life. They offered me comfort, caring, and the attention I craved while growing up in a boisterous family where everyone was busy dealing with their own issues and trying to survive.

Mom carried a huge workload with cooking, washing, and cleaning up after nine people. She was a remarkable woman and always did her very best, but she couldn't possibly always have time for all the little things that make up the day-to-day existence in a kid's life. My animals never let me down and were never too busy to provide the attention and reassurance I hungered for. Having no clothes to wash or dinners to fix, my pets were companions I could rely on. On countless occasions, my critters were able to take away the tears caused by the sometimes sad, sometimes frightening, and sometimes seemingly unjust situations that impacted my life. It was from my pets that I learned much about living. It was from watching their births and experiencing their deaths that I learned about the circle of life.

Until one has loved an animal, a part of one's soul remains unawakened.

—ANATOLE FRANCE, WORKS OF ANATOLE FRANCE

All the animals in my life brought something different to the table . . . or should I say, stable? I have owned and raised white rats, guinea pigs, parakeets, fish, lovebirds, cockatiels, cats, horses, hamsters, and even a pig. Each creature had unique and special abilities, and they all had quite distinct personalities. Ok, I can't say I really understood all of those fish personalities, but they were all different! Some animals made me laugh at their antics, others just offered a soft pink nose or furry warm face for cuddling. I can't image how empty my heart would be without all their animal companionship.

Although I bonded closely with an array of animals, it was definitely with dogs that I felt the greatest connection. Between those Alan and I owned and the ones our children kept, I interacted with a large variety of canine creatures.

Our daughter, Natalie, owned two different Akitas. She had Zukkie while in college and Bear after Zukkie passed away. Large, powerful, and fiercely independent, both were affectionate, protective of their owner, and skilled hunters (Akitas were originally bred in Japan as hunters). Later, Natalie rescued another hunting breed, a Plott hound named Delaney. One of the least known breeds in the United States, Plott hounds are scent hounds that hunt in packs and were bred to hunt wild hogs and bear. Unlike the Akitas, Delaney was more emotionally needy and loving, but was every bit the hunter.

The hunting breeds have sharp instincts for the chase, and on numerous occasions they suffered from the intensity of those instincts. Only the sustained efforts of the owners could keep those dogs from exercising their instincts to escape the house or yard when they caught the scent of a wild animal. Many a rabbit, raccoon, squirrel, armadillo, peacock, and even feral cat became their prey.

No amount of scolding from us or the personal pain they brought on themselves could dampen these dogs' enthusiasm for the hunt. Zukkie almost died because she refused to give up trying to catch some ducks one winter in the icy waters of a reservoir near Truckee, California. Back and forth through the water she swam in pursuit of those Mallards. Finally,

Our daughter Natalie with her first Akita, Zukkie. Natalie was attending Western State College in Gunnison, and lived and skied at Crested Butte, Colorado.

Natalie was thrilled when she found a photo of a dog that looked like Delaney in a book. "I told you he was a special bred. He's a Plott Hound. See . . . I told you!"

Time for a homemade dog biscuit. Natalie feeding Chico (left) and Delaney in our kitchen at the farm.

exhausted and nearly frozen, she pulled her weary body up on the shore.

Bear, while chasing a rascally raccoon on our Florida farm, got stuck under a wooden walkway on a hot summer afternoon. If we hadn't been there to dig her out, she would have died of heat exhaustion. And Delaney, Natalie's Plott hound, has a coat riddled with scars and welts and is partially blind in one eye from running through the brush chasing wild pigs and other critters. Yet, despite those painful, harrowing, and near-death experiences, the hunting breeds are destined to hunt.

Then there is Chico, our adorable and feisty Jack Russell mix. Bred to hunt fox, his instincts have gotten him into trouble on more than one occasion. He was attacked by bees when he chased a squirrel into their hive.

"He ran straight through the hive," Alan told the vet, as she injected Chico's body with Benadryl and a steroid to bring the terrible swelling down.

Another time, Chico chased the horses, got kicked in the head, and needed seven stitches on his eyelid. We found out recently, during a vet visit to determine why

Chico wasn't feeling well, that in his pre-Thomas life he had been hit by a car. The x-rays that day revealed he had suffered a broken hip and tibia before he became a member of our family.

Despite all the pain he has endured, we have to keep Chico tightly leashed while on a walk. Otherwise, he'll see something moving in the brush and be gone. Headstrong and determined, his animal instincts far outweigh his fear (and my forearm strength!).

In all other instances of these dogs' lives, and with other vocal commands we've taught them—stay, come, sit, etc.—the hunters in our family listen and respond appropriately, but when their instincts kick-in all bets are off.

Hilariously, Chico has a very specific, adversarial relationship with golf carts. On the farm, we often exercised him and Delaney with our golf cart. I guess he thinks now that any cart he sees must belong to us and must be stolen and that he needs to protect "our" property. At our condo in Irvine, California, the parking ticket patrol use golf carts to ticket parking violators. During walks, at the merest sound of a golf cart, Chico's ears perk up and he goes into a berserk barking fit. He will try to track down and kill any golf cart in the vicinity. It's so funny and embarrassing. We've tried a variety of things to break the habit: we've carefully introduced him to the various patrol drivers, allowed him to explore the innards of golf carts parked nearby, picked him up and scolded him . . . but nothing works. It is obvious by his actions that, in Chico's mind all stray golf carts must be corralled and reacquired.

Some dogs are stick chasers, like Mercury, Natalie's big, black German shepherd (I think I see a trend here: Natalie

Mercury was addicted to sticks. On walks he would quickly find a stick to carry, the bigger the better. As he got older the sticks got smaller, but his enthusiasm for carrying sticks never diminished.

likes big dogs with attitude). Because of his size, speed, and downright determination, none of the other dogs in the family pack could compete with Mercury when a stick was involved. If they did, a fight would ensue. Not a vicious fight, just a friendly reminder of who was in charge. So the smart ones chased the stick but always let Mercury retrieve it, as if to say, "For goodness' sake, if it means that much to you, keep the stupid stick."

And stubborn. Did I mention yet that Mercury was stubborn? One time, during a walk in the forest, he carried around a thick, six-foot-wide tree branch, refusing to drop it when it was time to get back in the car. No amount of coaxing or prying could remove the tree limb from the tight grip of his titanic teeth. Again and again, he attempted to run and jump into the car with the branch sticking out three feet on each side of his mouth. Time after time, the branch would hit the car frame, rebounding Mercury back onto the ground with a ferocious thud. If the Three Stooges had owned a dog, Mercury would have been the fourth Stooge.

Ten times he did his run, jump, and thud routine until he figured out that if he rolled the branch sideways in his mouth as he jumped, he could get the branch and himself inside the car. Then, and *only* then, would he let go of his cherished "stick."

While Natalie preferred the powerful, dominant, hunting breeds, like her Akitas, our son Roger and his family loved Labrador retrievers.

Yes, labs are used for hunting. In fact, Snoopy, our first lab, was an accomplished duck and pheasant retriever. But not all labs are tornadoes wrapped in fur with highly developed instincts, like an Akita or Jack Russel terrier. Roger's lab, Wager, was one of the sweetest and most intelligent dogs I ever knew, and maybe more human than canine. When Roger and his family moved to Florida, there was "no way Wager was flying cargo." Roger convinced the airlines that Wager was a celebrity, a movie star dog, and bought her a ticket and her own seat in first class. After the flight, a fellow traveler told Roger, "You know, when we first got on board, I wasn't exactly thrilled to see a dog in the cabin. But, honestly, that dog of yours was better behaved than my kid."

Later, fate provided Roger with another lab, a lost and ragged-looking animal who showed up one morning on his front step. She was hungry and pitiful, with sores and bald spots all over her dingy coat. I asked if the dog were possibly a neighbor's pet?

"Well, I'm not asking around," Roger answered, without hesitation. "Anyone who takes care of an animal like that doesn't deserve to have one." I totally agreed.

Soon, Winner, as Roger named her—because she found a winning home and because Roger likes to bet on the horses—became a much-loved member of Roger's family. Wager and Winner became best buddies and, in no time, Winner was as beautiful on the outside as her delightful demeanor proved to be on the inside.

Roger instructing Wager, Lucky, and Riley about the rules for their upcoming walk.

Shadow was one of two labs my husband and I owned. Petite, as labs go, she was a replacement for Mugsy, who had died of old age and whose passing almost broke my heart. Only another dog owner can truly understand the grief of losing a beloved pet. I miss her even today, twenty years later.

Anyhow, when Mugsy passed, the thought of going through life without canine companionship was unbearable. So I went in search of another doggie "friend." Shadow, who was named that because she would not leave Alan's lab, Snoopy, alone, and who literally hung on her neck and shadowed her every movement, became that replacement.

Shadow was incredibly smart and lacked any recognizable hunting instincts. Loving and gentle, she was an escape artist and could open doors (lever doors were her specialty!) and even open the refrigerator. Any enthusiasm she had for hunting was directed toward people food. We returned one night from a restaurant to find our dogs lying in the kitchen surrounded by all the wrappers from the meat and cheese drawer in the refrigerator. Stuffed like ticks, the dogs smiled and wagged their tails lazily upon our arrival. You could just tell that Snoopy was so proud of Shadow's ability to open the refrigerator; Shadow was obviously her idol. After all, how many dogs can fix their own dinners?

Another time, I was expecting a plumber to the house, and I saw his truck pull up next to our fence. Since my plumbing problem was in the garage, I opened the garage door to let the plumber inside. But, he wasn't there; the plumber was nowhere in sight. A few second later, the plumber was instead standing behind me in the doorway.

"That's the smartest damn dog I ever met," the plumber said, laughing. "Your dog opened the door and let me in."

So, let's just say that Shadow was not a good watchdog. When she saw visitors at the door, like any intelligent and gregarious person might do, she opened the door and let them in.

The only hunting Shadow did was for people food. One Thanksgiving we discovered her standing on the top of the dining room table, with her paws carefully positioned between pieces of my best china and crystal, cleaning off the plates after the meal with her long pink tongue.

All the labs we owned were gentle and loving creatures, but not all of them were so bright. Roger and his wife Teri bought a lab puppy when their beloved Wager passed away. They named the puppy Derby, another nod to horse racing. Wager, Winner, Derby . . . get it? Derby was as sweet as pecan pie, but she was not the smartest tool in the shed, and she suffered horribly from separation anxiety. Whenever Roger and Teri left Derby alone in the house, she would chew up something, usually a rug. So Roger's family rescued a curly-haired terrier mix named Rascal to keep

Roger and Teri's dogs, Derby and Rascal, are playful, loving, and energetic, but, according to their owners, "are not the sharpest tools in the shed. I think those two dogs share a single brain."

Derby company. Playful and energetic, Rascal fit into the family beautifully, but Roger said, "I think those two dogs share a single brain."

Over fifty years of married life, Alan and I have owned and loved many remarkable canines. Some we owned on purpose and others came into our lives by chance. We were down to just two dogs when we moved to our five-acre farm in Florida. But with our grown children and grandchildren living close by, their dogs became our dogs and the farm became a "dog party," with six dogs scampering about on weekends or whenever anyone left for vacation or had to be away from home and leave their dogs for any extended period of time. Between the enormous screened patio that covered the swimming pool and a huge fenced area attached to the patio (with a doggie door), our ankle-biters had over seven thousand square feet of shaded space to run and play. The sign on our gate read, "Thomas Family Farm, where dogs run free." It must have felt like heaven for the pooches who frequented the place. (As a side note, that sign turned out to be an effective burglar deterrent. Visitors, who didn't know our animals, would call on the gate speaker to ask us to contain the dogs so they would be safe to enter the premises. To those folks that sign meant we had a pack of guard dogs

The sign on our gate read, "Thomas Family Farm, where dogs run free." Visitors, who didn't know our animals, would call on the gate speaker to ask us to "contain the dogs" so they would be safe to enter the premises. To those folks that sign meant we had a pack of guard dogs roaming about. Our happy yappers could not have been more different than what visitors imagined. Right: Chico is an excellent traveler and enjoys looking out the window during takeoffs, but only after the stewardess is seated.

roaming about. In reality, our pack of happy yappers could not have been more different than what visitors imagined.)

Now, since we've sold the farm, it's only Chico, who flies with us to California, to Florida, and to Ottawa, Canada, several times a year. His life is filled with chasing rabbits and squirrels in Ottawa and those goofy golf carts that infest his California domain.

Even though canine/human bonding is mutually beneficial for both parties, dog ownership is not for everyone. It takes a lot of time to care properly for a canine. Feeding, walking, washing, playing, and cleaning up are the practical time commitments. Veterinary expenses are an

Top left: We have had so many wonderful rescue dogs over the years. Lucky, left, and Riley, loved the farm and were a nice addition to our family pack. Bottom left: Thomas enjoying a "furry face" moment with Lucky and Shadow. Right: You can tell by Rascal's smile that he was happy to have a new home. Our granddaughter Peyton with Rascal, soon after he left the shelter.

additional consideration. Then there are the occasionally sad results of years of reciprocal love and emotional attachment.

I respect people who tell me they'd love to have a dog but just don't have the time or space to give them proper care. I totally get that. It would be selfish and cruel to have a dog you only had time to love and interact with on occasion. As someone wise wrote, "They may only be part of your life, but you are their whole life." Dogs are sensitive and devoted creatures whose health and wellbeing depend on human care. I feel blessed to have had the time and space in my life to own animals. For me, the joy of those relationships has always far outweighed the work their care involved. Like I've always said, "I'm a sucker for a furry face."

42

Santa Maria

2010

One summer our family took a vacation to Rome. In preparation for the adventure, I studied the internet and looked up must-see places to visit and charming Italian boutique hotels. After much discussion and investigation, I booked the four of us into Hotel Santa Maria in the Trastevere neighborhood of Rome. The Trastevere section is on the bank of the Tiber River and is one of the most charming and authentic neighborhoods of Rome's historic center. The hotel's website boasted of a rooftop garden and rooms connected by a monastic portico with orange trees, flowers, and Mediterranean plants. It sounded like a perfect setting for breakfast or just for relaxing after a day of sightseeing.

From the minute I read about Hotel Santa Maria, I started singing, "♫ ♪ *Saan-ta-a Maa-ria, Santa Maria. Saan-ta-a Maa-ria, Santa Maria* ♫ ♪." I don't know where I heard the song or where it came from, and I only knew the chorus. I just kept repeating the chorus over and over and over. It

Our family in Costa Mesa, California. Roger is standing behind Alan and Natalie. I am in the chair flanked by Snoopy, Alan's lab, and Mugsy, the sweet canine Natalie brought home from the stables.

got stuck in my head, like songs sometimes do, and I just couldn't stop singing it. It was beginning to really irritate my family. For weeks, I sang this chorus and I was still singing it on the night we arrived in Los Angeles for our flight. "♫ ♪ *Saan-ta-a Maa-ria, Santa Maria* ♫ ♪." We found our gate easily, and in no time Alitalia flight 1236 was announced and would be boarding in fifteen minutes.

"Yea," I said to the family, "it looks like our flight will be on time."

With that happy news, I got up to get a glass of wine from the bar. My idea was to drink a glass of wine and take a decongestant. That combination works wonders on me for beating jet lag. By combining the two drugs, I would be asleep in no time and would hopefully sleep through the eight-hour flight to Rome. After I drank the wine and swallowed the decongestant, I settled back in my concourse seat and began absentmindedly singing again. "♫ ♪ *Saan-ta-a Maa-ria, Santa Maria* ♫ ♪." The announcer came on and said there would be a thirty-minute delay because of a minor problem with the cabin's air conditioning.

"No biggie," I thought. "♫♪ *Saan-ta-a Maa-ria, Santa Maria* ♫♪."

"Mother, enough already with that stupid song. You're driving me nuts," my daughter said roughly.

"That's a ditto for me," my son Roger added.

A few minutes of waiting passed and I could tell my drug and alcohol combination was beginning to take effect. My eyes were getting a little droopy, and I was feeling extremely relaxed and comfortable. "♫♪ *Saan-ta-a Maa-ria, Santa Maria* ♫♪." It was at that point my husband gave me a dirty look and moved to another seat. A few more minutes passed and I decided I should use the airport bathroom before I boarded the flight. I figured with that business taken care of now, nothing would stop me from going right off to sleep like a baby once I was on board. The bathroom was on the other side of the bar where I had bought my wine.

"This is perfect," I thought to myself, as I walked toward the ladies' room. "Boy, I am really beginning to feel tired."

The restroom appeared to be totally empty, so I settled onto the toilet seat in the first stall and began my melodic serenade again, "♫♪ *Saan-ta-a Maa-ria, Santa Maria* ♫♪." The lyrical song had become my Italian mantra and I just couldn't stop. "♫♪ *Saan-ta-a Maa-ria, Santa Maria* ♫♪."

All of a sudden, out of the stillness, I heard, "Mom?" The single word came from a subdued, gentle voice and seemed to be wafting down from somewhere above my head. "Mom?" the voice called again, softly. Honestly, the voice sounded sacred, as if it were floating directly to my ears from heaven.

In my semi-drug-induced state, I thought I was having some kind of a religious experience. Perhaps my singing to Santa Maria had attracted a divine messenger from God or a ghostly spirit. Or, perhaps my singing had created some kind of celestial aberration in the Universe. I heard the voice yet again.

"Mom?"

"Yes," I answered softly, with all the appropriate reverence I could manifest into my voice.

"Mom, you're in the men's bathroom."

Oh my God, it wasn't God; it was my son Roger.

I'd like to say that's the first time that I've taken a seat in the men's restroom, but it's not. And I'd like to blame the mistake on the combination of wine and decongestant, but I can't. For some reason, I get the photos of a stick man and stick woman mixed up. I'm not sure why; I mean, the nice stick woman is *clearly* wearing a skirt. I really *do* know the difference.

When the Alitalia announcer came back on yet again, I knew I was in trouble. It turned out the cabin A/C problem on our plane was not going to be an easy fix and we were being directed to another gate to board, which ordinarily would not have been a problem, but, since I was a little woozy from self-medication, walking anywhere quickly, and in a straight line, was going to be tricky. I grabbed my husband's arm, steadied myself as much as possible, and we drifted together to Gate H-43.

"♫♪ *Saan-ta-a Maa-ria, Santa Maria* ♫♪."

43

Beethoven

When I saw the ad in the local newspaper, I was thrilled. "Natalie!" I yelled to my daughter, who was cooking in the kitchen. "There's a lady selling potbellied pigs for only forty dollars in Fellsmere. I'm going to call her." Anybody who has ever wanted a miniature pig knows that forty dollars was a *bargain*. In California, from where we had recently moved, potbellies sold for over seven hundred dollars.

"Shouldn't you ask Dad first?" Natalie questioned, intelligently. "No! You know your father; he might say no. So I'm going to surprise him."

I was sure that once my husband saw the adorable squealy piglet he'd be thrilled with my decision. Besides, if I asked him, he'd ask me a bunch of bothersome questions that would bring me down to the unnecessary realities of pig ownership. I was going to go with my gut (my potbelly?) on this decision.

Our grandson, Thomas Jones, the day Beethoven arrived at the farm.

First, the timing was perfect. We had just moved into our five-acre farm in Vero Beach, Florida, and I was ready for some animals. What's a farm without animals, after all? Besides, I enjoyed the idea of duplicating something from my youth: Grandma and Grandpa's farm, the farm Dick and Jane visited during their summer vacations.

You remember Dick and Jane? They were the two main characters in the series of popular basic readers used to teach children how to read from the 1930s to the 1970s in the United States. It was because of those books that I dreamed of owning a farm. Picturesque and peaceful, Grandma and Grandpa's farm looked like heaven to me. I was determined to replicate that idyllic farm for my grandkids. After all, I was a grandma now. So, within minutes, Natalie and I were in the car and heading north to an even more rural area, about thirty minutes from our new home.

Nestled among some lovely oaks on a dusty dirt road was the little farm the classified ad directed us to. There, in a large pen area, was a lovely black sow and her last piglet. We quickly named this piglet Beethoven, because he had a musical squeal. It was love at first sight . . . for me. I'm not so sure my new piglet agreed. All he did was squeal while the owner corralled him into an enclosed feeding stall so she could catch him. He was adorable and still so tiny at a mere six weeks old.

"He's the last of the litter and the runt," explained the seller, as she placed the darling animal in my hands.

After receiving very thorough swine care instructions, we headed home, with the piglet nestled on a towel in Natalie's lap. Of course, before we got home, we had to stop at the pet store for piglet supplies: a harness to walk him in, special low-calorie pig food, and a booklet on raising pigs that the seller had recommended. A more prudent person might have, no probably would have, purchased all that before actually getting a pig, but I'm not very prudent. Are you familiar with the saying, "Fly by the seat of your pants?"

Anyhow, all was well with our new pet, until a few weeks into owning Beethoven, when I noticed a foul-smelling foam forming around his mouth and snout. A quick internet search revealed a little something I didn't know about *male* pig ownership: male pigs, until neutered, put off a special odor that female pigs adore, evidently. (Pungent, to say the least, this odor was definitely not appealing to this grandma and certainly wasn't covered in the Dick and Jane books.)

Added to this, I quickly discovered that most vets don't neuter pigs, because anesthesia can be tricky with pigs. Neutering was thus considered a specialty procedure in our neck of the woods. Poor piggy. Beethoven and I had to drive over an hour to a vet's office to have his operation performed. Plus, the cost was another little something I had to explain to my husband. Happily, four hundred dollars later, the pig odor vanished. Thank God for vets.

Okay, I should confess that, because of my limited pig knowledge, I initially thought potbellied meant dwarf. I had seen a small pig in a movie magazine once and just assumed Beethoven was one like that. After doing my homework (a little late in the game, true), I discovered that "dwarf" with regard to pigs didn't mean exactly what I had thought it meant. Originally bred in Vietnam, dwarf swine are considered miniature *only* when compared to domestic swine, which can weigh from 600 to 1,500 pounds. Therefore, my little piglet, Beethoven, turned out to grow a teeny bit bigger than I anticipated. I was thinking, maybe fifty pounds, sixty pounds, tops. When Beethoven bloomed to over 350 pounds, I had no one to blame but myself. (FYI, the pig in that magazine was a teacup pig not a potbellied and, according to Google, teacup pigs are a bit of a scam.) But size, at least in this case, didn't matter one bit. I was charmed by Beethoven's intelligence, personality, and curious and playful demeanor.

Within no time, Piggy (his nickname) took over the farm and stole our hearts. Even my husband enjoyed his antics as long as we stuck to the rule, "No pigs in the house." And we did stick to the rule, except for one time when Piggy snuck up the back steps and into the kitchen in search of the brownies he could smell cooking in the oven. Let's just say that cloven hooves and slick hardwood floors don't mix. Poor little fella, one step off the doormat and all squeals broke loose. Unable to get traction on the wood floors, he looked like a short chubby Olympic gymnast doing a floor routine. He did the splits and started slipping and sliding into the counters. He made such a ruckus squealing that our neighbors came running to make sure an alligator hadn't gotten him. Quickly, I grabbed the doormat and some small bath rugs and laid them out in front of him so he could walk. The rugs gave him something his hooves could grasp onto, he calmed down and so did we, and we got our sweet swine back out the door. Good idea Alan: no pigs in the house.

Piggy liked to be with the family. Despite his short legs and portly pose, he joined us regularly on dog walks out to feed the horses. He would sit grunting beneath the stalled animals waiting impatiently for some of the sweet feed they were eating to fall out of their mouths and onto the floor. On the way back to the house, he would break into a run, on occasion, when he suspected food was waiting for him in his trough. Other times we'd find Piggy plopped by the front door, enticed up the steps by the smells wafting out the kitchen window from something tasty baking in the oven. On hot afternoons, Beethoven made himself comfortable on a pile of soft leaves under the giant oaks near the horse pasture, dreaming no doubt of his next meal.

Piggy was not like any of the other animals I have ever owned. With intelligence, second only to that of a dog, and an amazing sense of smell, Piggy could find me anywhere I was working on the farm. I'd be pulling weeds on the other side of the house and he'd find me. I'd turn around to the sound of a gentle grunt, his way of saying "Hello," and he'd be there, squinting and snorting gently. Then he'd lie down next to where I was working and wait until I was finished, and we'd walk together back to the house for a snack of fruit. Piggy loved cantaloupe, apples, and strawberries, but canned pumpkin was his favorite. My kids occasionally complained that he ate better than they did. That wasn't an exaggeration, they kind of had a point; I was very fussy about his diet.

One day I was grocery shopping and the checkout gal complimented me on all the fruits and vegetables I was

Left: Beethoven at about six months. I was sure he'd stay small; I thought I'd bought a miniature potbellied pig. Middle: Pigs have an incredible sense of smell. Beethoven could smell where food was being prepared and on numerous occasions, tried to follow me into the kitchen. Right: A kiss for piggy. It was love at first sight for Patricia Berman, a visitor to the farm, and Beethoven. "What a cutie pie!"

purchasing. "Boy, you feed your family healthy food," she said. I laughed, and so did she, when I lifted the veggies to expose a couple of frozen pizzas and cookies I was buying for dinner. "That's for us," I said, pointing to the processed comfort food. "The fruit and veggies are for our pig."

Beethoven was, well, a pig, and so he was unrelenting in his quest for food. He loved to eat and could get very persuasive (okay, aggressive) when he smelled the food our yard workers had purchased for their lunches. One day a worker yelled through the kitchen door, "Hey, Paula. Your silly pig just knocked me on my butt and stole my burrito." At 350 pounds, Beethoven rarely took no for an answer where food was concerned.

Piggy was particularly pesky during holiday events at the farm, when food was almost always involved. Apple-bobbing contests at Halloween were his forte. During one event, he took over completely, refusing to share the apples in the giant tubs with the thirty little kids assembled for the contest. Pushing the kids down and knocking over the tubs, Piggy shoved his dirty snout into the water and butted any would-be contenders aside. Swirling dirty water soon filled all the tubs and a girl started yelling, "Oooh, pig germs!" Kids started crying and the event turned chaotic.

Piggy was in hog heaven, as they say, and was not about to budge. Roger yelled, "Mom, get the popcorn!" and I knew what to do. I grabbed a bag of popcorn we had popped for the kids and lured Piggy away to his pen. Fruit was one thing, but he really couldn't resist the enticing smell of

When Beethoven got a scent of fresh apples, he charged the container, pushed our grandson aside, and took over the apple bobbing game.

fresh popcorn laid in a trail back to his sleeping quarters. Once Piggy was secured, and clean water refilled the tubs, the apple bob was back on.

Easter was even worse. When Beethoven got a whiff of candy during an Easter egg hunt, he charged out of the bushes, upending Easter baskets, pushing little kids down, and stealing anything edible he could find. I don't know where they learn it in the wild, but evidently pigs are ace at smelling jelly beans and chocolate. Getting him secured that day was tricky. Every short child carrying a basket was an easy target for Beethoven. It was actually easier to corral the kids than to corral Piggy. Afterward, for days, Beethoven scoured the yard, and he would leisurely stop periodically to retrieve a surprise jelly bean someone had left behind. He loved Easter.

The greatest challenge I had with Beethoven was when he needed veterinary care. Like dogs, Beethoven required regular shots for rabies and a variety of other vaccinations to ward off illness, along with worming (another little something I had failed to learn about prior to his purchase). You can imagine how difficult it is to give a 350-pound animal multiple shots that hurt. (Heck, a three-year-old kid can be difficult to inoculate, and that kid can't knock two adults to the ground.) Also, pig skin is tough (think footballs), and the vet has to really jam the needle hard to puncture the skin, making it hurt more.

Anyhow, the first vaccinations were no real problem. The vet who had neutered him took care of those while he was under anesthesia. Year two wasn't too bad, because he was still relatively small. However, by the time of his third birthday, it was a totally different experience; a total fiasco for the vet, for me, and, worst of all, for Piggy. Using a half sheet of plywood as a wall, we would corner Piggy in his stall. Then, the vet would reach over the plywood and inject him. Each time she did this, Piggy would come flying and butting out from behind the plywood. Everybody involved got trampled and muddy. I had a cloven hoof print imbedded on the top of my foot for weeks.

By the fourth annual veterinary visit, our handyman had built a super-strong, fully enclosed pen from heavy open fencing that the vet could get her hand through, without being butted or bitten or stepped on. After each visit, Piggy was rewarded with treats galore and the vet got a nice cold Red Bull power drink. Me? As the pig's parent, I was emotionally spent and had to go to bed.

At night Beethoven preferred the safety of his straw-filled pen. During the day he usually napped on the soft leaves under our big oak.

Owning Beethoven was nothing like the Dick and Jane books portrayed. Beethoven wasn't cute and pink and cuddly. He was big and black, with coarse hair that stood up on his back when it was cold outside or he got frustrated. He sort of looked like Elvis ("Thank you very much"), and he had beady little dark eyes. But he was a very special animal friend and his antics made me laugh.

Because he was so big, forceful, and stubborn when he wanted food, there were times I feared that I had launched myself into another one of Dad's headlines: "Florida Housewife Trampled to Death by Pig with Sweet Tooth!"

Beethoven: 350 pounds of sweet swine.

44

It's a God Thing

2012

I love a project. If you mention that you're looking for a theme for your party, my mind immediately starts racing and within minutes I have come up with six ideas, including the look of the invitations, decorations, and food. I guess that makes me an "idea person." Did I mention that my high school counselor was an idiot and never recognized my gifts? Anyhow, I love to create, so it was not surprising that an e-mail I received from my neighbor piqued my interest.

My beautiful neighbor, Tanisi, is from Brazil. She was planning a bat mitzvah for her adorable daughter, Hava, and a bar mitzvah for Emri, her handsome son, who was a former classmate of my grandson, Thomas. We had received the invitation weeks before. I knew she was planning events that spanned several days and included separate presentations for each child at the Temple Beth Shalom, to be followed by a separate luncheon for each, with a gala dinner and dance event covering both

Like my talented mother, I am an avid crafter.

Lucky, one of our rescue dogs, on guard at the craft room my husband had installed for me on the farm.

on Saturday night. All of this was planned for Thanksgiving weekend.

Since we're not Jewish, and since I have never attended a bar or bat mitzvah, I headed for the internet the minute we received the invitation. I learned that a bar mitzvah (in Hebrew: הוצמ רב; isn't that cool writing and don't I look cultured?) is the ceremony where a Jewish boy becomes recognized as an adult, on or after age thirteen. The ceremony takes place during a regular prayer service, usually on a Saturday morning. The boy leads or takes part in the service and is called to the Torah for the first time. A bat mitzvah (הוצמ תב) is the ceremony where a Jewish girl becomes recognized as an adult, on or after age twelve. For non-orthodox girls, like Hava, it is exactly the same as a bar mitzvah. This was going to be a very holy and special occasion for everyone involved.

Tanisi sent me an e-mail asking my advice about flowers for the events. My creative antenna went into overdrive and I gave her a call.

"What do you need, girl?" I asked enthusiastically.

I knew I could conjure up just about anything she needed for a party; my craft room was a giant trailer my husband had installed out by the barn (am I blessed or what?). My craft room is a virtual treasure trove of craft supplies and party elements. It contains the remnants of parties past and products I've picked up for use in future fun. It's paradise for a part-time artist and crafter like me. Anyhow, Tanisi started talking feverishly. She told me guests would be arriving from all over the world. It was obvious from the chatter that she was not just excited, she was totally overwhelmed.

"We have family coming from Switzerland, Brazil, France, and all over the US. I am cooking Thanksgiving dinner for twenty-three people all by myself *and* for the first time ever, and then we have the bat and bar mitzvahs on Friday and Saturday." No wonder she was overwhelmed.

"Plus," Tanisi added, "This is the first Thanksgiving most of these people have ever attended. It just has to be fabulous, Paula. Really, it has to be great!"

Tanisi still had shopping to do for Thanksgiving and guest pick-ups at the airport to arrange, and she needed to borrow serving pieces and a whole lot of other stuff.

Almost in tears, she said, "But that's not the worst of it, Paula. I don't have centerpieces for the tables for the parties. That's why I sent the e-mail. I was hoping I could just clip some of those colorful, how do you say, boogeyvillas, for the tables. Boogeyvillas would work, wouldn't they, Paula?" Tanisi was pleading for reassurance. "I'm not creative like you, Paula." (Tanisi is only a biologist, after all!) She continued frantically, "Boogeyvillas, wouldn't they work just fine?"

I knew instantly that Tanisi was talking about the colorful bougainvillea plants that climb and drape gracefully along our pasture fences. Bougainvillea bloom off and on all year and create quite a colorful show in the yard but when cut, they drop their flowers very quickly. After a few more sentences, I understood the challenge and my duty was clear.

Bougainvillea bloom off and on all year and create quite a colorful show in the yard, but when cut, they drop their flowers very quickly.

One: we needed a total of forty-two flower arrangements: twelve for Hava's event, twelve for Emri's Kiddush luncheon, fifteen for the evening gala, and three huge arrangements for the buffet table.

Two: we were working on a very limited budget. Tanisi said, "I ordered flowers for the temple, but they were so expensive I just couldn't do it for all of the other events."

Three: we were short on time. I had just a few days to design and make four different styles of arrangements.

And, four: they had to be as wonderful as the events were sure to be.

As noted before, I grew up in a large family and slightly poor, so creating much with little money was right up my alley, and the time frame wasn't a problem either (like I said, I'm a hare). I work fast. In the old days, kids were not diagnosed with attention deficit disorder. The teachers just said, "Paula has ants in her pants." So, fast is just my normal speed.

"No problema," I responded resolutely to Tanisi. I tend to speak Spanish when I am trying to communicate with someone from a foreign country, regardless of the person's language at birth. "When can you come by *mi casa* and see my sample arrangements?"

Tanisi and her sister, who had arrived from Brazil, were at the farm at 9:00 a.m. the following day. On the dining room table, I had assembled four sample arrangements for their approval. There was a masculine arrangement for Emri, with black olive tree branches and beautiful pinecones in various sizes. For Hava's luncheon, I used a clear glass vase with yellow ixora and sword fern. In the center of the vase, I tied a crisp yellow-and-white polkadot ribbon. Ixora may be the most popular flowering shrub seen in South Florida. Related to the gardenia, it blooms all year long and is long-lasting when brought indoors. We have tons of this fantastic shrub running around our curved driveway in yellow, gold, red, and orange.

For the Saturday night gala centerpiece, I used a slightly larger vase filled with more expansive cuttings of ixora, this time in red, along with ferns and several elegant peacock feathers. The feathers were homegrown and free as the birds that wandered back and forth from our house to their home next door. To pick up and accent the color of the feathers and the blue tablecloths Tanisi had borrowed, I sprinkled opalescent turquoise glass balls in the bottom of the vase. For additional pizzazz, I tied a shimmery blue ribbon around the curved part of the vase with graceful ends that puddled onto a mirrored square. The centerpiece was surrounded by battery-operated tea lights that Tanisi had supplied.

Next, and most challenging, was the sample of the large arrangements for the buffet. I used a twenty-four-inch high glass cylinder left over from my daughter's wedding. Inside the cylinder, I fanned out three palm fronds, cut in varied lengths, tropical greenery, and several pieces of ostrich fern. The ferns would support the tall peacock feathers I added later. For color, I again added ixora, this time in reddish-orange, along with clear glass beads at the bottom for stability. The final touch was a giant billowy bow in white that flowed down onto the table.

It brought me such joy to see the look on Tanisi's face when she saw the flower arrangements I had made.

"Awesome. They're awesome. I love them!" Tanisi shouted in her adorable accent. "I see what you have done," Tanisi said, laughing. "I was thinking a couple of tea lights and a little boogeyvilla would work fine. Now I see how bad I am at this stuff. I'm really bad, I tell you. I'm really bad."

Since my son and his wife were hosting Thanksgiving, I had the morning free to make the flower arrangements for Friday's events. It took several hours to cut flowers, make ribbons, and clean the vases, but I was ready by Friday morning to meet with Tanisi at the party room of the Temple Beth Shalom.

Arriving with the flowers, we got right to work. We laid out the blue tablecloths Tanisi had borrowed, and we assembled the centerpieces of pine cones and black olive tree branches for Emri's luncheon. They looked bold and masculine, and Tanisi was pleased. We had plenty of extra tree clippings and pine cones to decorate the buffet table as well. Then we unloaded the flower arrangements for Hava's luncheon the next day. As we tucked the arrangements safely away in the kitchen for later use, Tanisi kept thanking me over and over again.

"I couldn't have done this without you, Paula. Thank you from the bottom of my heart."

As Tanisi and I wandered out to the car, she began to talk to me about her mother. "My mother was considered an angel in our hometown in Brazil. She took in many children over the years. She fed them and helped them attend school. She nursed the sick and was tireless in her devotion to the poor. When my mother died, the whole town turned out to honor her." It was obvious that Tanisi was heartbroken that her mother couldn't be at the temple for these holy observances.

Tanisi, my sweet Brazilian neighbor, showed me the yarmulkes the townswomen had made in her mother's honor. "They crocheted dozens of yarmulkes in pink and blue because my mother dedicated her life to charity. She was considered an angel in our small town."

Tanisi showed me the yarmulkes the townswomen had made in her mother's honor. They had crocheted dozens of yarmulkes in pink and blue. I knew, from the internet, that the purpose of the yarmulke was to show someone's reverence and respect toward God by covering their head. So I knew that the gift of this effort from the townspeople was a very special one to Tanisi and her family. She gave me a pink one for my granddaughter and a blue one for my grandson, and I was very touched.

Tanisi's mother, Terezinha Moitinho Santana. Her story is long and beautiful. In addition to her tireless devotion to helping the children of Gravata, Brazil, her goal was to educate all seven of her children, which she did. After her passing, because of her charitable efforts, the mayor inaugurated in the community in her name and honor, a health clinic, a small park, and a community center.

We hugged and, with tears running down her cheeks, Tanisi said, "Before my mother died, I sat by her bedside, holding her hand. I was crying. I told her not to leave me. I needed her there to help me prepare for Emri's bar mitzvah and Hava's special day. 'Please, Mother,' I pleaded, 'I can't do it without you. You know how to do the flowers. You know how to do it all. I know nothing about such things.'

"And you know what my mother told me, Paula?" Tanisi asked, ever so softly. "My mother said, 'Don't worry, little one. An angel will come along and help you do it all.' *You*, Paula, are that angel."

I sobbed like a baby my entire way home. Driving along, I swear that I could feel the presence of this wonderful woman I had never even met. We were bonded, somehow, in life. It seemed that God had sent me to help her "little one," just as Tanisi's mother had helped so many others in Brazil. This turned out to be more than just helping a friend. This was a God thing.

On Saturday, at 3:00 p.m., I arrived at the River House to decorate for the dinner dance gala and final event. The River House is a lovely city-owned facility at the base of the long bridge that separates the Florida mainland from Orchid Island. It has a full kitchen, dance floor, and spacious indoor and outdoor entertaining areas.

Job one for me, on arrival, was setting the tables for dinner. When I saw the draped tablecloths, I almost fell over. They were not the same royal blue tablecloths we had worked with on Friday. No, even better, they were a magnificent turquoise color that shimmered like silk on the tables. They glistened exactly like the peacock feathers in the centerpieces, and made my modest flower arrangements look even more fabulous. I was thrilled. Even the caterer stopped to compliment me on what I had "planned." I wish I had planned that!

A small nucleus of family members and I worked together feverishly for a couple of hours, setting up tables and chairs, filling the bar, and arranging the room. Then I insisted that Tanisi take her sister home to get dressed. The guests would be arriving soon.

Once the gals left, I placed the three large arrangements on the buffet table, which was set against a long white wall. The Peacock feathers and palm fronds looked stunning against that perfectly blank canvas and on the pristine, white-draped buffet. I spruced up the ladies' room with a bouquet and turned on all the tea lights. Exhausted and happy, I made my way to the car and took one last look back.

> *People see God every day, they just don't recognize him.*
>
> —PEARL BAILEY

Yikes! To my horror, I discovered that the main entrance was flanked by two dirty pillars and planters overgrown with scruffy weeds. That would not do. Luckily, I had yard clippers and black trash bags in my trunk from yard work we'd been doing at our apartments. Tired but steadfast, I started trimming, clipping, and pulling weeds. Then, I grabbed the rest of the leftover wide wedding ribbon and wrapped the dirty entrance pillars. I finished each pillar off with a giant elegant bow.

I'm sure Erik, Tanisi's husband, thought I was nuts as he peeked out and asked what I was doing. When I pointed out the less than appealing entrance, he quickly joined me and started sweeping the walkway.

"I didn't notice how bad this looked when we first arrived," Erik stammered. "Honestly, Paula, I can't thank you enough for all you've done. You've made my wife so happy." He accentuated his comments with a grateful hug.

I gathered up my tools and the now weed-filled garbage bags, and slammed down my trunk door just as I heard Erik greet his first guests with "Shalom." As you probably know, the Hebrew word "shalom" is understood

The Stenn family: beginning left, Hava, Emri, Tanise, and Erik, with Abby in front. Shalom indeed.

around the world to mean "peace," but, shalom is more than just peace; it is a complete peace. It is a feeling of deep contentment, completeness, wholeness, wellbeing, and harmony.

Shalom indeed. That's exactly how I was feeling as I drove toward home.

One last thing: I am proud to report that all of the event decorations only cost Tanisi sixty-three dollars. We had come in well under her budget.

Not bad for a gal with ants in her pants and God on her side.

45

Grandkids

Before we had grandchildren, I would get bored hearing my friends tell their stories about how "wonderful it is to be a grandma." Sure, I love kids, but really? More babysitting, cleaning up burps, and changing poopy diapers, that's "wonderful?"

I was at a time in my life when I was feeling totally free, well, to a point. Even fully grown, your children are never out of your life, and, really, I wouldn't want them to be. I was enjoying the freedom of being childless at home; I loved my empty nest, to be honest. Getting up later, no lunch boxes to pack, no school events to attend, no homework to direct, no messy rooms to clean up, and absolutely no back talk, well, except for my husband, whom I have never been able to properly train, but that's another story.

Of course, the day our first grandchild was born, all my concerns turned out to be malarkey. Standing in the hospital, staring through the nursery glass, I was overcome with emotions I just hadn't expected to be there. It

Left: Me with my first grandchild, Thomas Arthur Jones II. Right: You move to Florida, you go to Disneyworld. Peyton and Thomas the year we moved to Vero Beach, Florida. Below: Looking at the photo below, you can certainly understand why Peyton asked, "Grandma, why do you have orange hair?"

was an epiphany. That little baby filled a place in my heart I hadn't realized was empty.

"Oh, my gosh. He's absolutely beautiful," I sobbed to the nurse holding him. "Thank you, God," I whispered into the air.

It was love at first sight and twenty years later, nothing has changed. A text on my phone, "Hi, Grandma. I know what I want for my birthday," feels like a message from God. I know that sounds ridiculous, but talk to any grandparent, and you'll find it's perfectly normal. Thomas Arthur Jones has been, since his birth, the light of my life.

Then, our son married Teri, and with that union, five year old Peyton came into our lives and I was blessed with a second smiling little angel. Adorable, sweet, and so feminine, she came into our lives and instantly put a Cupid's arrow through my heart. Despite her almost breaking my nose, showing me a "funny trick," and asking me out loud, "Grandma, why do you have orange hair?" in front of a crowd, I love that little lady even more, a dozen years later.

Now there is the newest family member: London, Teri and Roger's precious and cuddly two-year old toddler. When they told us they were having a baby, we were worried. Being a late-in-life pregnancy for a diabetic mother, we did a lot of praying for them during those nine long months. But all of our lives were blessed again, and she arrived to be "the best decision we ever made," according to Roger and Teri. Again, I whispered, "Thank you, God."

When our son married Teri, Peyton came into our lives and instantly put a Cupid's arrow through my heart.

Peyton has added so much to our lives. Here I am with her during one of our many family trips.

My grandchildren have been the icing on my cake, sweet and delicious. And little London, the newest grandchild, is the sprinkles on the top. Roger and Teri with Peyton. Natalie and our first grandchild, Thomas Arthur Jones II. London Thomas, aka, Precious.

Why is grandparenting so delightful? I don't know, because it's all the things I dreaded: the burps, the diapers, etc. Maybe it's delightful because you're given a second chance to do it all again, minus the stress and distraction of becoming an adult, building your career(s), and all that sleep deprivation. Maybe it's because you feel like you have an opportunity to right the wrongs. Regardless of the reason, ask any grandma, the second time around is even better.

Unabashedly in love with our grandkids, we laugh about spoiling them rotten and find it funny to hear our grown kids stress-out when their own kids misbehave for them. Oh yes, a little payback can be funny. And, of course, our friends don't mind if we brag about our grandkids' accomplishments and show off the photos and videos on our cell phones, because they know when we're done beaming, it will be their turn to do the same.

Someone said, "Grandmas are moms with lots of frosting," and, that is so true. But for

All the world is made of faith, and trust, and pixie dust.

—J. M. BARRIE, *PETER PAN*

Above left: Baking cookies with London, keeping the tradition alive. Above right: London (age 2½), reminds me of a playful little pixie spreading dust upon us all.

me, an even more accurate description comes from Rudy Giuliani, the former mayor of New York City: "What children need most are the essentials that grandparents provide in abundance. They give unconditional love, kindness, patience, humor, comfort, lessons in life, and, most importantly, cookies."

46

My Advice for Living

In the movie *Parenthood*, the wise old grandmother character tells the children, "Life is a roller coaster." She was right: Life is a roller coaster. There are exhilarating highs and turbulent and frightening lows. Life is a demolition derby of moments, sad, gloriously happy, and downright mediocre. All of the experiences make up life—it's a potluck, and a roller coaster, and a derby. It's a lot of metaphors.

Day-to-day living is a great teacher. After all, you can't really appreciate life until you have approached death. You can't know the thrill of reaching a goal unless you've failed miserably. It's like owning a new car; until you've headed out the door to work a few times only to find a car that won't start, or you've driven precariously down a highway with a hood that won't latch properly, or you've motored around in the snow with a heater that won't work, or come out of the supermarket to tires that have gone flat, you can't *truly* appreciate the sheer joy of owning a fine new automobile.

I remember reading somewhere that life would be so easy if we only knew what to expect. If you got up each day and knew exactly what to say to each person about each problem to create exactly the response you wanted, life would be a snap. But we don't have that luxury. We never know what is going to happen. No matter how hard and carefully we plan and no matter how good a map we have at hand, life can still take a bad hop and we aren't sure what to say and we never know how a single moment is going to turn out. From one second to the next, we stumble blindly through the day. Living life fully is exciting and frightening at the same time. After seventy-four years of living, I have learned much. It may be presumptuous of me to even believe that it's good enough stuff to pass on, but what the heck. Like I said, you never know for sure what the right thing to do or say is. So here goes.

Be yourself—not your idea of what you think somebody else's idea of yourself should be.

—HENRY DAVID
 THOREAU

First, don't take yourself too seriously; learn to laugh at your mistakes and fumbles. You'll get plenty of practice. It's part of the joy of being alive.

Second, be yourself. My favorite American philosopher (actually the only philosopher I ever read), Henry David Thoreau, said, "Be yourself—not your idea of what you think somebody else's idea of yourself should be."

To me that means that it is your life to live, good and bad, up and down, so don't allow people, even those with good intentions, to rob you of the person you want to be. All too often I hear folks say, "I told my son to become an attorney because they make good money." Life is not about money (although it's nice to be financially comfortable; but trust me, I've met miserable millionaires). Life is never about a thing from a store or a catalog. It's not a house, or a car, or a purse. Life's happiness comes from personal fulfillment, and only you will know what will fulfill you. If you're lucky, money will follow you while you are blissfully happy in your own pursuits.

Remember, you are the company you keep. So, keep good company. Yvonne's mother used to say, "Ask yourself, 'Are the people you associate with going somewhere in life or are they simply treading water waiting for life to happen to them?'" Dr. Hoffman said, "Associate with folks you admire." You *are* the company you keep.

Never stop learning. Fill your brain each day with something new. It doesn't mean you have to read a new novel or visit a foreign country or start a new career from scratch. Learn the name of the tree in your yard or discover a different kind of pasta. Just think, at the end of the year, you'll know 365 things you hadn't known before.

Never give up on love. Whether it's the love you share with your children, your family members, your pets, or your spouse, keep working at and feeling love. It's so worth the pain and effort. Don't just fall in love, get it all over you.

Don't go to bed or hang up the phone or drive off to work when you are fighting with someone you care about. Be big enough to say "I'm sorry" or "I screwed up" or "I'm an idiot" or, when all else fails, "Let's just agree to disagree." Life can change forever in an instant, and you might never get the chance again. We are all humans, we are all imperfect. Get over having to win every argument. Who cares? No one on earth is keeping score.

Keep the name and phone number of a gifted psychologist in your contacts. I was blessed to have several in my life, along with the aid and advice of some loving friends and family members. Two minds, or more, are always better than one. Ask a smart person's opinion on a matter, not in an effort to get the person to take your side and agree with you, but rather, ask what he thinks so you can learn. The hardest part of that advice for me was to shut up and listen to the answer. "Say less and listen more," Dr. Hoffman used to say. He had to repeat it to me frequently.

Always own a dog or some other loving creature. I'm convinced pets were put on this earth to comfort humans in need. My dogs have always been there for me. They have offered me love when I was wounded, laughter when I was sad, and companionship when I was lonely. Dogs have been my teachers as well. They taught me patience. A dog will wait by the door for hours until you return and *never* get mad because you were "running late." Dogs have taught me to enjoy the simple things in life, like a quick squirrel chase or a tennis ball throw or the crust of a pizza someone dropped along the road. And dogs have freed my consciousness on many occasions, if only temporarily, from some monotonous task or unpleasant problem I was facing.

Always eat turkey on Thanksgiving and be thankful for all you have. In fact, make a mental list of your daily blessings and any time you invite yourself to a pity party, review that list. Catalog your health, your food, your clothing, the roof over your head, your children, your husband, pets, work, family, friends, peanut butter fudge, hot coffee, a fine new car (or reliable old car!), air conditioning, hot showers, snacks, Starbucks, McDonalds, etc. You get the point. We are so blessed.

Sing when you can. We always sing "Happy Birthday" to strangers in restaurants when the waitress brings out their cupcakes or dessert. Sing Christmas carols, even if you have a hideous voice, like I think I do. Sing loud and strong. Sing the national anthem with gusto. My God, this is the greatest country on earth! Turn up the radio in the car and blast out tunes as you drive. Two of my fondest memories in life involve singing: I loved singing Christmas carols with my family in our neighborhood each Christmas. The songs of the season still bring tears to my eyes when I hear them. The second memory was when my grandson, Thomas, lived with us. It was a crisp fall morning and the sun was coming up on the farm. We sat with the CD player blaring over the beautiful green pasture and we sang the songs of Rodgers and Hammerstein's memorable musical Oklahoma as loudly as we could. Music can transport your soul to another place and time and create moments beyond compare.

Celebrate holidays. Don't ever buy a plastic Christmas tree, unless real trees just get too expensive and it would blow your budget or you get too old to handle all the mess. Remember, also, to keep the dry tree away from the fireplace. Keep life "real" when at all possible. Carve a pumpkin at Halloween and buy enough (too much?) candy for trick-or-treaters. Don't forget what it was like when some nice grownup stood smiling at a door and she was also dressed as a goblin and admired how scary or pretty your costume was. Dye Easter eggs and blow off a firecracker or ignite a sparkler on the Fourth of July.

Remember what holiday means. It is a day of festivity or recreation when no work is done.

Be nice to the neighborhood kids and be a good role model for living. Say "hello" and wish them well when you see them off to school. And, for goodness' sake, buy the stuff they sell door to door. My neighbors in Seal Beach bought one thousand bars of soap from me so I could earn the money for Y-Camp one summer. We buy Girl Scout Cookies by the boatload. It's a debt I owe to others for the kindness and generosity my neighbors afforded me, and I'm hoping I've repaid it double.

Be responsible and take care of yourself. Don't be a burden on society unless you are *truly* in need. Welfare, "the social safety net," was meant to be a temporary hand-up, and I know it has been just that for many good folks during difficult times. But I've seen others sucked into a vortex of poverty, unable to break free. For those folks, welfare doesn't work.

Another area of concern for me, personally, is disability fraud. I don't want you to think I am a cold-hearted person who is unwilling to help those unfortunately disabled. On the contrary, I believe society should look after such folks. However, I have witnessed firsthand people illegally collecting insurance or government funds for disabilities they do not have. I was dismayed by the able-bodied people who would apply to rent one of our apartments and tell me they collected disability, but (with a wink) have additional income because they work on the side. One guy I interviewed received eight hundred dollars a month plus a free phone, food stamps, and medical and dental care from the state because he claimed to have a bad back. He turned around and admitted proudly, "I work for my brother's roofing company on the side and can bring in another couple of thousand a month." These folks aren't just robbing those who work and pay taxes, they are reducing the funds available for those who legitimately need assistance. Also, they are accepting a lesser station in life, wasting their lives going to doctors they don't need, just to cheat the system; to say nothing of the example they set for any children they may have. I am stupefied when they brag about beating the system, seemingly unaware that I am part of that system. It never seems to occur to them that I am one of the people they are cheating! Obviously, not everyone on disability is a cheater. We have witnessed many hard-working folks with serious conditions that prevent working of any kind. And we have a guy who tiles for us who works despite a bad back.

"Oh, I could go on disability, but, I won't. My father would roll over in his grave if one of his sons ever did such a thing," he told me proudly.

Please, learn to cook. It is such a joy and also an unparalleled bonding experience to produce a great meal with or for your friends and family. If you can read, you can cook. Learn to cook your favorite things so you'll always be able to enjoy them when you want them. My mother made peanut butter fudge, which I absolutely loved to devour. Now I make it all the time and have passed the delicious recipe onto my kids. Now, they too can make Grandma's fudge, and a little bit of Grandma Strother still lives. Also, learn to prepare your spouse's favorite meal (and yes, I mean you guys and us gals). My husband would rather eat Grandma Thomas' round steak and country gravy than any gourmet meal on earth. That recipe has also been passed along to our kids, along with the memories of the round steak and gravy Sunday night dinners we've shared. Grandma Thomas must be smiling down from up above.

About daily living: set healthy personal boundaries so your life doesn't get consumed by someone else's drama. Take time out every day to smell the roses and walk your dog. (You remembered to get a dog, right?) The world outside, away from your computer or cell phone, is filled with beautiful clouds and wind and green trees and flowers and birds. A walk can replenish the soul and bring a smile to your face. And, I beg you to not take your phone. Leave it at home; it probably needs a thirty-minute charge anyway. Concentrate on your walk. Live in the present. The rest of your life and texting can wait.

> *Don't waste a minute not being happy. If one window closes, rush to the next one or break down a door.*
>
> —BROOKE SHIELDS

Don't panic when you get lonely. It's normal and happens to everyone periodically. If loneliness becomes a recurring problem in your life, ask for help. When you get ill, go to bed and rest and go to the doctor. It is too important. Seriously, do not procrastinate about your health. A sore tooth does not get permanently better; it may stop hurting, briefly, but it is not getting better.

Start each day by doing the thing you dread most. The rest of your day will be nice once you get that dreaded task behind you. For example, the most heinous task in real estate is to call sellers and tell them their house sale fell out of escrow, especially when they have just boxed up their kitchen and are loading the moving van. It was my wise husband who told me to get the problem off my chest and make that particular call first thing. "After all," he added, "no amount of time is going to change the fact that the call must be made. So, waiting to call will do nothing more than ruin your day." He was right. Another bit of advice he gave me was this: When a big problem arises, ask yourself,

I have learned so many things from my husband during our fifty-plus years together. This book is peppered with events in my life that were impacted by his wise counsel. The other day I overheard him talking to our grandson about love and marriage: "Thomas, life can be tough. Marry a smart woman." When I was reading this passage aloud to Alan he said, "That's not what I said. I said, 'Marry a woman smarter than you.'" I love that guy. I guess we made a good team.

"What's the worst thing that can happen?" The sellers will be furious at me, even though I am blameless, and hate me forever. They will cry. They will sue the buyer. They will threaten to sue *me*. Once you know the answer to that and have decided that you will still survive, you can let it go or even plan for it to happen. That dilemma happened to me on numerous occasions. It's part of being a realtor, and Alan's advice got me through it. Luckily, I shut up and listened when I asked him for his advice. Thanks to you, Dr. Hoffman.

In addition to a talented psychologist, find a really smart CPA, like my gifted husband, Alan Thomas. And, even though they get a bad rap, find yourself a savvy attorney, just in case. Life happens, and when it happens badly, you will want a good, honest attorney.

If you are addicted to anything, food, booze, shopping, shoplifting, sex, or drugs, or if you have a mental disorder, depression, bipolar disorder, etc., don't just be embarrassed, ask for help. You can treat it and beat it, or at least live better *with* it. You deserve happiness and a good life. You do! So get out there and admit you are struggling, whether it's addiction or mental illness, and get the help you need to heal. Trust me, you are not alone. In fact, you are in excellent company. According to Wikipedia, these are just a few of the famous folks who have suffered from some kind of addiction or mental health issue: Abraham Lincoln, Winston Churchill, Thomas Jefferson, Agatha Christie, Truman Capote, Jim Carrey, Drew Barrymore, Carrie Fisher, Elizabeth Taylor, Judy Garland, Marilyn Monroe . . . and the list goes on and on and on. Google it! There's a very good chance someone you admire and look up to has been down this road. There is nothing to be ashamed of: you are not alone and you live in a time where much more is known about these things than when I was a kid.

Don't skimp on the money you spend for books, travel, or education. Make a plan, a budget, and include these important items. You don't have to go to a foreign country to travel. Some of our happiest vacation times were spent camping on the Kern River and enjoying the nearby out of doors. The point is to get out there and go someplace new. Remember, variety is the spice of life.

Be generous with your time, talent, and money. Tip waitresses and others who do a good job. Look for ways to give back. Help those in need. Don't be a cheap person with money or withhold your spirit. Notice the world around you and say something nice to someone who is obviously having a bad day. You can make a difference. I firmly believe that what you put out there comes back at least twofold.

Take your turn at housework and don't be a slob. An organized home is the sign of an organized mind. You don't have to obsess about tidiness, just pick up after yourself, especially if you live with someone else, whether it's a spouse or a roommate. Do remember, if you're a parent, that everything you do is a subliminal lesson for your kids.

Speaking of which, don't ever take your children for granted. They are a gift from God. Tell them you love them every day in person, by phone, by text—find a way. Never strike your children. When you inevitably fall short of doing your best, stop immediately and make it okay. Give your children swimming lessons and Cotillion (if available); it may seem corny, but they will learn how to dance. And for goodness' sake, dance. Dancing is one of life's greatest joys. You don't have to be a pro; make a fool out of yourself. Who cares?

Cannot we let people be themselves, and enjoy life in their own way? You are trying to make that man another you. One's enough.

—RALPH WALDO EMERSON

Encourage your children in their interests, not yours. Just because you wanted to be a tennis pro doesn't mean they do. Introduce your children to a large variety of experiences, but let them decide which of those experiences makes them happy. Guidance is good. Trying to impose an education or an occupation on them is bad. Dr. Hoffman told me that people are happiest when they feel they have control over their own lives, and I believe he was right. It's tricky to find the balance. God knows we tried and were not always successful.

Stay in touch with good friends and good family. Friends and family are an important part of life. They add seasoning to the common everyday moments and make even simple fare delightful and fun.

And lastly, find God or something you can believe in. Life is tough without a higher power. Pray and pray often. And if singing or dancing is your form of prayer, the advice still holds: pray often.

47

I Miss My Children

Some mornings, when the light is just right and I'm sitting at the table with a coffee cup in hand, I miss my children. I miss all the things I took for granted all those years they were growing up, like their sweet little faces slurping up cereal at the breakfast table, or the sound of their voices chatting excitedly about the doings of the day. I miss seeing their warm, cozy bodies wrapped up in blankets laying safely in front of the TV. God, on days like, well, days like this one, I miss my children.

Here I am with my children, Natalie (age 3) and Roger (age 6).

Although I never thought I would, I miss the seemingly endless baseball games, swimming races, and soccer matches where I had to drive. Dear Lord, how many Saturdays were spent on hot dusty fields or at the swimming pool, standing with other parents, sometimes bored, sometimes not? And the parties . . . I miss the pizza parties and the birthday parties and the pool parties. I miss the Valentine's Days and I really miss Halloween—seeing them in bunny suits and monster garb—and dressing up spiffy for special occasions. God, on quiet days like this, I miss the weirdest things.

I miss tubby time, when their slippery little bodies got soaped and rinsed among rubber duckies and plastic buckets. Most of all, I miss tucking them into bed at night, holding my children, looking down into their eyes, feeling the sweet warmth of their bodies and breath. If I could go back in time for just one moment, I'd choose tucking them into bed. Remembering these sad and sweet and silly moments brings tears to my eyes, but at the same time, it's useful pain because it keeps me on my toes and reminds me to take notice that life is always changing and time is forever marching on. When next I see my children, I'll look deep into their older eyes, enjoy their beautiful aging faces, and hear their deeper and wiser voices, and I'll hold on to those sights and sounds, because I know some next morning, when the light is just right and I'm sitting at this table with another coffee cup in hand, I'll miss seeing them all over again.

When life gets you down, just look at your kids and see what life has given you.

—UNKNOWN

I had so many big goals in life, grand things I thought would bring me happiness, like wealth, glory, fame. Some of those things came true and are now in my memory bank. But it turns out it's the littlest things, the private things, the seemingly unimportant daily events of family that I remember most and cherish.

It's these things that have made my life grand.

Food from Family

My book would be incomplete without mentioning what my parents and siblings brought to the potluck. Each had their unique gifts, and my life and table would have been so much less sweet, salty, and savory without their contributions.

Mom and Dad were complete opposites. Their union was not unlike the childhood book *The Country Mouse and the City Mouse*. According to his writings, my dad, Gene, "spent a happy, carefree childhood in the Bluegrass section of Kentucky, a suntanned, barefoot, running boy in overalls and straw hat, playing in the fields with his dog Mutt, and swimming in the creeks." He grew up in a log cabin with as many as ten kids; some were

I remember the day we took this photo. It was unusual because we were dressed up and we were wearing shoes. Most of my life, like my father as a young child, we ran barefoot. Upper left: my mom, Edith, Sharon, Cynthia, and Dad, Gene. Lower left: Kay, Judy, me, Rex, and Alice.

1928
National Champions
Top Row: Kershner mgr., Hemlepp, Fullerton, Allen, Riffe, Anderson, Co
Bottom Row: Strother, Darby, Barney, Phipps, Johnston Capt.

Left: My dad also played minor league baseball in Nebraska with the Lincoln Links. "The Links started the season with Gene Strother from Kentucky at second. He played in a total of thirty-four games in the league in 1933." http://www.nebaseballhistory.com/
Above: My dad, Gene Strother, and his team, the Ashland Tomcats, won the 1928 National Championship and are in the Basketball Hall of Fame.

orphaned cousins and others were just folks who visited and stayed.

On the other hand, my mom, Edith, was the only child of a well-to-do family (Kentuckians love to say that). She grew up in a three-story home across the street from a gorgeous park where she chased and captured lightning bugs each summer. Prim and spotlessly clean, she carried her violin case to school and church in various towns of Indiana and Kentucky, eventually settling in Ashland, Kentucky, a booming steel-mill town on the Ohio River.

Football and basketball crazy, Ashland High paid Gene twenty dollars a week to leave Louisville High and play football and basketball for the Ashland Tomcats. Once in Ashland, Gene met Edith and fell in love. He was the captain of the football team, a young, handsome, and gifted athlete. She was the beautiful cheerleader, refined and elegant. Deeply in love, they eloped years later and remained in love for fifty-plus years.

Edith and Gene Strother. This photo was taken in Ashland, Kentucky at their sixtieth Ashland High School reunion. When they returned from the event Dad said, "Your mom was still the prettiest gal in the room."

Sadly, mom's parents, Oren and Rubye Bell, never accepted Gene for "marrying their beautiful and sophisticated daughter." To them, he was a country bumpkin who lacked a good career and appropriate income to support their daughter "in the life she was accustomed to." (Give the guy a break, it was in the middle of the Great Depression.) I remember my folks saying that Grandmother Bell felt Gene was from the "wrong side of the tracks," and she worried he might have "skeletons in his closet." Seriously, people talked like that.

Rarely visiting us as we grew up, Mom's parents never sent any gifts that I can remember, or even many letters. Only when the Bell Sisters got famous did our family become relatively acceptable to mom's parents. Mom told us many times, "It breaks my heart that my parents never got to know you kids. They missed so much." Makes me sad too. You'd think after all that time and delivering them seven wonderful grandkids, Dad would have proven himself worthy of a little respect.

Dad used to say, "You come from fine stock," a phrase held over from his farming days, I guess. Since we were from fine stock, he expected us to compete at everything, and to win, which we often did. Hard-working and often scary, because of his volatile temper, Dad's contribution to my table was that of a steady and devoted provider. He didn't take a vacation for eleven years, choosing to work instead to earn the extra money.

Few of my siblings had a close connection with Dad. For me, it was like trying to cozy up to a smoldering volcano, distance was safer. A good example of my dad's temper can be seen in how he attempted to teach me to parallel park. With me at the wheel, he got in the car and said, "Ok, pull forward next to the car in front of the parking space. Now, turn the wheel and back up." I was a nervous wreck, knowing full well the lesson would probably turn out poorly. I was so right. When I turned the wheel, I drove too fast and hit the curb hard with the tire. He started screaming and cursing, "Not like that, for Christ's sake. Get out. I'll do it." Let's just say, patience was not one of Dad's virtues.

Dad's short temper and explosive behavior affected me for years. Learning to do new things was difficult for me. Dad's impatience had made me hesitant to *even try* to learn new stuff. More often, when faced with learning something mechanical, I acted like I "already know that," when, in fact, I didn't have a clue. My husband recognized my apprehension at even attempting to learn things when we purchased a video camera one Christmas. He actually had to force me to learn how to use it. I still remember his words to this day, "Paula, you can learn this. Take your time. No one is going to yell at you and get mad. I'll sit here and only help you if you want my guidance." I remember looking at him occasionally as I read the manual, just to verify he wasn't getting mad. Sounds silly now, but Alan's pointing out what he had recognized in my behaviors helped me address my fears and grow. Funny how the tools we develop to survive our childhood often become the obstacles in our way in our adulthood. Despite it all, Dad participated in our lives and attended graduations and school events, always proud of "his beautiful daughters."

When he retired, I began to see Dad more as a human being and less as the person who just came and went to work. I broached the subject one day, telling him how his angry outbursts had frightened me when I was a child. "Really? You were scared?" he asked incredulously. "I had no idea." Looking back, the load he carried financially and the number of hours he worked must have been exhausting and probably contributed to his short fuse. (In a telling side note, my folks held the record in California for the most money ever borrowed and paid back to Pacific Finance Company. "We didn't get out of debt until six years after all you kids left home," Dad told me.)

When he wasn't at work, Dad also fixed the cars when they broke down and did the home repairs. After retirement, Dad helped family members with their apartments and new homes, pitching in on everything from painting to electrical repairs. Generous to a fault, he would willingly share anything he had that someone else needed. And he loved Mom, I never doubted that, and he always told us how beautiful she was. "She could have been a

Paula Strother
Girl Of The Year

Mom was such a talented seamstress. She made all of our dresses for dances and proms. This was one of my favorites. It was knee length and made of emerald green satin and had big puffy sleeves. I remember getting so many compliments when I wore it.

dancer in the Copacabana in New York City," he used to say. Their love for each other was a constant in our lives.

Mom brought herself, in grand abundance, to our family table. She was clever, funny, talented, and hard working. She sewed all our prom dresses, and they were fabulous. She made us costumes at Halloween, helped us write speeches and poems for competitions, and worked tirelessly around the house. Her *Betty Crocker Cookbook* is a testament to her devotion to family. It is filled with notes of family gatherings that, despite a limited budget, she created with amazing flair. Her spunk and determination were admirable, and she rarely complained. An avid reader and life-long student, Mom's creativity was punctuated with educational classes. She reupholstered all of our living room furniture, for goodness' sake.

Later, when the new brood of young ones came along, Mom was a devoted grandmother and racked up hundreds of hours babysitting and cooking for her growing family. She loved my father without reservation, despite their significant differences. Classy and comfortable in most situations, she was fun to travel with and had a great sense of humor. I am the woman I am today mostly because of Mom.

My older sister, Cynthia, as I've said before, was our household conductor and brought music to the table. She introduced us to the great musicals by Rodgers and Hammerstein: *Oklahoma!, Carousel, South Pacific, The King and I*, and *The Sound of Music*. From the record albums she brought home and played incessantly, we learned to enjoy memorable music. To this day, I know the words to practically every Broadway song. Cynthia was also a fashonista, and accessorizing was her forte. Her scarves, purses, and costume jewelry were organized methodically by color, type, and style in her chest of drawers. She graciously allowed us to share her bounty, even knowing full well, because we were young and irresponsible, that there was a chance she'd never see her accessories again. One time, Cynthia bought me a beautiful ring with a pink stone, and presented it to me just before a school concert I was singing in. It must have been my birthday. I thought it was the most beautiful thing I had ever seen. Sixty years have passed and I still remember how special that gift made me feel on that day.

The dancer in the family, not tap and ballet like me, but swing, was Sharon. Fabulous on the floor, Sharon danced with flair and style few could emulate. Sharon, as a teenager, knew how to have fun. All of us envied her adventures to the trendy dance spots she and her handsome boyfriend frequented on the weekends. Sharon taught us all to dance and, thanks to her, my husband and I swing dance whenever we get the chance. Sharon was generous, too. One hot summer day, when she was working as a waitress at the burger joint on the end of the Seal Beach pier, she treated me and a friend to a hamburger, French fries, and a chocolate malt from her hard-earned tips. For the record, we were starved, having been swimming all day. That is still the best burger of my life. On my twelfth birthday, Sharon drove me and a boy to Belmont Shore so I could reach one of my goals in life, to try Chinese food. Those are just a couple of Sharon's little acts of kindness that I still remember half a century later.

The professor in the family was Kay. She was an exceptional student and a terrific role model. Once she spied a spelling test that had fallen from my backpack onto the kitchen table and noted I had gotten a C grade.

"Didn't your teacher give you the spelling words to study in advance?" she asked sternly. When I said, "Yes," she added matter-of-factly, "Then you should have gotten an A."

Looking back, I can honestly say that until she told me that, it had never even occurred to me to properly study.

During summer vacations, Kay would be our teacher and give us school lessons in our rickety wooden garage, before it blew away. She, too, was a fashion expert and on many occasions helped me put together an outfit that was "simply divine." Like my other sisters, generous and loving to me while I was growing up and underfoot, Kay was a kind and valued friend. As kids in college and later in life, we shared many traveling adventures. In fact, I was with Kay on my eighteenth birthday when I met my future husband in Avalon. It was from modeling Kay's behavior that I eventually learned how to properly research and plan a trip.

The athlete amongst us was Judy. She could out catch,

out throw and out hit everybody on my brother's baseball team, much to the obvious chagrin of Dad, who wanted *Rex*, his only son, to follow in his footsteps and become a sporting champion. I'll never forget the baseball coach who discovered Judy playing short stop at Zoeter Elementary School and asked her to join the team. Poor guy, he was devastated when one of her braids flopped out of her ball cap, exposing that she was a mere girl. Girls just didn't play organized sports back in the early 1950s. Her gifts to my potluck were football, baseball, and kick-the-can, which our gang played until dark almost every night, all summer long. Unlike me, Judy was extremely smart in math and other subjects that evaded me completely. I was amazed when she easily got an A in chemistry.

Chronologically, I was the next in line after Judy, and the joker of the family. Making people laugh was what I did best. Acting out stories and making silly faces, I learned to use laughter to heal the pain and turn embarrassing or scary events into something funny we could laugh about later. It was my defense mechanism as well. I was the only one in the family who could distract dad when he was volcanic and prevent one of his angry outbursts. When I failed in these efforts, I felt that I had let the family down. I probably could have

Only the family, society's smallest unit, can change and yet maintain enough continuity to rear children who will not be "strangers in a strange land," who will be rooted firmly enough to grow and adapt.

—SALVADOR MINUCHIN, *FAMILIES AND FAMILY THERAPY*

been a comedian, the likes of Phyllis Diller, without her cackling laugh. Do you remember Diller? She was a stand-up comedian and actress with an eccentric stage persona, self-deprecating humor, and wild hair and clothes. At parties, I would "hold court" and have people in stitches with stories about my ridiculous adventures, all of them quite true, if lightly exaggerated. Being funny was fun; my stories cracked me up as well.

My only brother, Rex, also brought humor to the table, with his hilarious stories and wit. Handsome and bright, he endured quite a challenge living with six sisters and a father who hammered at him relentlessly to become a great athlete. Dad wanted Rex to vicariously complete his career in sports, which had been cut short by the Great Depression and also the fact that Dad "never could hit the curve ball." I felt sorry for my brother. Dad had him in a vise as far his future was concerned. My dad wanted Rex to finish a career in baseball, that career that had eluded my father in his youth. In preparation for the "big leagues," Dad insisted Rex work out daily, following the Charles Atlas Body Building Program. But you can't force a kid to have the same drive and desire you have. So Rex would fake it. Many a morning, I would find my brother standing outside, below my parent's bedroom window, dipping toast in hot chocolate. In between dunks, he'd make the exaggerated sounds of deep breathing, swooshing in and out loudly. Later, at breakfast, Dad would remark, "I heard you working out this morning. Good job, son." Dad never seemed to notice that Rex, despite these morning "workouts," wasn't becoming "the world's most perfectly developed man." Mom told me she felt guilty that she hadn't spent more time with Rex, but Dad was adamant: "You raise the girls. I'll raise Rex."

Last, but not least, in our family was Alice, little Tinker Bell. Being the last in line can't have been easy. Always getting hand-me-downs and being "too little to do that," Alice lived in a perpetual state of "been there, done that." Anything Alice experienced in *her* life had already been talked to exhaustion around the dinner table or done six times before. Despite this, Alice was as bright as a penny, enthusiastic, gentle, patient, generous, and loving. She and I have always been particularly close. We both had kids born just months apart, and we lived in close proximity. Stay-at-home moms, we spent many a day together washing and folding clothes, talking about life, kids, men, and marriage. From Alice, I learned to be kinder, more forgiving, and less critical of others. I can't imagine how empty my table would have been without Alice at my side.

Another important person who graced my table was Betty Boultinghouse, a single woman

The Bell Sisters had just been discovered when we attended the annual Richfield Oil Refinery company picnic, held in Irvine Park, California. It was an old-fashioned, day-long event with games like tug of war, baseball, three-legged races, and egg toss. Also, it was a contest between families to see which family could win the most prizes. We came in second only because Dad forgot he had slipped one of the prizes we won, a harmonica, into his breast pocket. We were such a competitive bunch. Sixty-five years after this event, the first thing my sister Judy says when she looks at the photo is, "That other family didn't win. Dad forgot we won the harmonica."

who lived next door and was our neighbor for over fifty years. The grandmother figure in my life, Betty's tiny beach cottage was a safe and friendly haven in the evenings after school. Her house was always open to us Strother kids, and she never seemed to run out of Oreo cookies or milk for all us perpetually hungry kids. She was our tutor for school projects and an amateur oceanographer. She was always taking classes about sea life and sharing what she had learned. It was Betty who taught me to love the ocean and respect the miraculous creatures that make the sea their home.

The grandmother figure in my life was our next-door neighbor, Betty Boultinghouse. A kind and gentle spinster, Betty became our teacher, friend, and confident. "I remember the day your family drove up and parked next to my wooden fence. You startled me. Suddenly, seven little kids piled out of the car, popped their heads over the fence, and started talking to me."

Betty took us swimming in the evenings after work and on "Grunion runs" late at night. Betty taught us "not to catch the scout Grunion, which come in first to lay their eggs, and to see if the beach is safe." On a good run, the beach would be awash with thousands of shiny, silver, flapping, sardine-like fishes. We'd catch them by the bucketsful, and take them home to deep fry and eat, soft bones and all. Generosity was another thing I learned from Betty. Her front yard vegetable garden, which she tended religiously, generated a constant bounty of corn, tomatoes, carrots, onions, lettuce, and potatoes, which she shared with Mom to supplement our family's table. Kind and caring, she left a box of groceries on our back stoop every Friday, for years.

One of Betty's greatest gifts to me was that of listening. You could tell her anything and she never corrected you or suggested that what you were telling her could not possibly be true. After attending my first track and field event in grade school, I remember telling Betty excitedly, "The winner ran a mile in one minute!" My sister Judy, who was eating cookies next to me at the table, said loudly, "No they didn't. That's impossible!"

Betty just smiled and said, "What else happened today, Paula?"

Growing up in a big family was such a gift, and also a curse. It was a gift because someone was always around to fix your hair or help you with one of the endless school projects a teacher assigned. A large family offered life coaching about how to behave on a grand scale. When one of my siblings suffered a setback because of a poor decision or choice, if I were paying attention, I learned not to make that mistake myself. Likewise, if I saw something one of them did that really worked well, I tried to put that in my memory bank for future use. I reveled in my siblings' joy and their accomplishments, and I was proud to call them "family."

Growing up in a big family was also difficult. Even though watching my siblings mature taught me much, it also caused me pain. Sensitive as I was, I experienced some of my siblings' disasters as if they were my own. I felt their pain and disappointment and genuinely hurt along with them when they were crying or in distress. The sheer number of people I lived with created a bumper crop of emotional stress that I felt powerless to control as I experienced all the drama in their lives, vicariously. Witnessing so much emotion, for a little kid, was sometimes overwhelming.

"Why is it, Dr. Hoffman, that I see things my husband doesn't even notice?" I asked my wonderful therapist during one session. For example, when we would go out for the evening, I'd say to Alan afterward, "Wasn't that sweet the way that couple was acting?" or "Did you notice that couple arguing in the corner?" His answer was always the same: "I didn't notice."

Dr. Hoffman went on to explain that much of the empathy I have for others and being cognizant of their behavior was partly due to my upbringing. "You are intensely aware of people and their emotions." That too is a gift and a curse, he explained. "It is a gift because you are capable of feeling wonderful things very intensely and deeply. It's a curse because, when the experience you witness is something negative, you have the capacity to also feel that deeply and intensely." The man was a genius.

Looking back on my life, I really wouldn't change a thing; definitely not the blessings, and not even the curses. I have been lucky to have more health and happiness that I ever dreamed I might as a kid growing up in a small town in California. No one's life is perfect, and certainly mine was not. Like everyone, I've known sadness, pain, success, and failure. But my blessings of family have been abundant, and my table has been full.

I wonder what they'll write about me in the newspaper when I pass. Will I get a headline? Probably not, as I'm hoping not to die in a fiery crash or gruesome accident (natural causes just ain't headline material).

I think I'll write one just in case it's needed or wanted: "Local Woman Makes Good, Writes Book, and Proves High School Counselor Was an Idiot!"

That should cover it.

CPSIA information can be obtained
at www.ICGtesting.com
Printed in the USA
LVOW13s1206050618
579636LV00004B/9/P

9 780999 473009